# MANAGE ACCOUN

C000095259

## Brian Murphy

BA, MSc, ACMA, FCCA, DMA
*Head of Department of Accountancy and Finance,*
*Huddersfield Polytechnic*

**TEACH YOURSELF BOOKS**
Hodder and Stoughton

TO VIVIENNE, PAUL AND ALISON

*First printed 1970*
*Second edition 1978*
*Third edition 1985*

British Library Cataloguing in Publication Data

Murphy, Brian, *1940–*
Management accounting.—3rd ed.—(Teach
yourself books)
1. Managerial accounting
I. Title
658.1'511        HF5635

ISBN 0–340–38482–4

*Printed and bound in Great Britain for*
*Hodder and Stoughton Educational,*
*a division of Hodder and Stoughton Ltd,*
*Mill Road, Dunton Green, Sevenoaks, Kent*
*by Richard Clay (The Chaucer Press) Ltd,*
*Bungay, Suffolk.*

*Typeset by Macmillan India Ltd, Bangalore-25*

# Contents

**Preface**                                                                          v

**1**   Introduction                                                                 1
**2**   The Fundamentals of Accounting                                               8
**3**   Financing the Business                                                      20
**4**   Funds Flow Analysis                                                         35
**5**   Historical Costing                                                          52
**6**   Standard Costing                                                            65
**7**   Budgeting and Budgetary Control                                             82
**8**   Marginal Costing and Cost-Profit-Volume
          Relationships                                                            111
**9**   Accounting Ratios                                                           136
**10**  Uniform Costing and Interfirm Comparisons                                   149
**11**  Capital Investment Appraisal                                                166
**12**  Accounting for Price Level Changes                                          188

**Suggested Answers**                                                               205

**Glossary of Terms**                                                               240

**Bibliography**                                                                     244

**Index**                                                                            247

# Acknowledgments

I should like to express my thanks to the Institute of Cost and Management Accountants for granting permission to quote from their publications, and also to the Centre for Interfirm Comparison which provided me with a wealth of information.

I must also thank Sidney Goodwin for his valuable assistance once again with the revision of this book.

My thanks are also due to Helen Tarbatt for typing up all the revisions and amendments and to my wife, Vivienne, for the help and encouragement which she has given me in its preparation.

# Preface

Since the publication of the first edition of this book in 1970, there have been substantial developments within the accountancy field. Perhaps the most important from the point of view of the advancement of accounting knowledge and techniques was the establishment in 1970 of the Accounting Standards Committee in the UK together with the increased interest shown in establishing international standards which would become applicable in a world-wide context. The ASC has been very active since its inception and statements of standard accounting practice have been issued covering a wide variety of topics.

The other main influence on accountancy thought during this period has been inflation. The problems of presenting meaningful financial statements when annual inflation is as high as 25% has meant a substantial re-thinking of many of the accounting conventions which have been in use for many years. Both the professional accountancy bodies and the Government have been concerned to try and find some method of accounting for inflation. Although the high rates of the 1970s no longer apply in the UK the search for an acceptable method of adjustment for inflation continues. This third edition has therefore been amended to take account of the above developments.

The text should provide a sound introduction to management accounting for students who are studying the subject for professional examinations of the Institute of Chartered Accountants, the Institute of Cost and Management Accountants and the Association of Certified Accountants. In addition it should prove useful to management students studying for a number of examinations, for example the Diploma in Management Studies, Certificate in Industrial Management, and the Certified Diploma in Accounting and Finance.

It is also suggested that the format and content of the book will be ideal for the general reader who wishes to obtain an introduction to the management accounting function.

# 1 Introduction

## What is management accounting?

The term is defined by the Institute of Cost and Management Accountants as '. . . the presentation of accountancy information in such a way as to assist management in the formulation of policies and in the planning and control of the operations of the undertaking'. From this definition it will be appreciated that there is a distinction to be drawn between the management accounting function and the role of the financial accountant, whose prime aim is to analyse, clarify and record financial transactions in order to illustrate the effects of such transactions on the performance and financial position of the business. It is important, however, to ensure that this apparent difference in function between financial and management accountancy does not lead to two separate and distinct fields of accounting theory and practice with no inter-relationships.

In no type of organisation is it possible for the accountant to work in isolation. He must have a working knowledge of the many other areas which impinge on the organisation and his activities. Such knowledge should encompass the fields of economics, law, management, statistics and behavioural studies. He should be able to relate his knowledge of these subjects to his own particular area of accountancy. Economics, for example, will help to explain to the accountant what determines prices and what is likely to be the optimum output for his particular organisation, why interest rates change, etc. He must also remember that *people* are responsible for making decisions and incurring costs; and a knowledge of psychology will help him to understand why certain actions are followed, particularly in cases where the most economical policies are not always pursued. For instance, an owner may be prepared to forfeit maximising profits in order to be able to locate his business in an area which gives him personal satisfaction. The accountant's role as information manager will also bring him into constant contact with *people*, either seeking information from him or depending on him to interpret it for them, and it is essential that in this role he contributes to the efficient operation of the organisation and avoids creating conflicts. He should appreciate, however, that his training is primarily as an accountant and if he requires advice on economics, law, etc., he should take his problem to the specialist in these fields.

In his capacity as information manager he will collect and produce information for three broad purposes:

1   For use by management within the organisation to plan and control current operations and future short-term operations.

2   To enable management to make special decisions and formulate long-term plans, for example capital investment decisions.

3   To report historical information for subsequent transmission to interested outside bodies, such as shareholders and the Inland Revenue.

This last aspect is generally known as financial accounting, and its main aim is to present a true and fair view of the financial affairs of the organisation. This aim will apply just as much to the non-profit-making organisations such as local authorities and charities as to the business enterprise. The main records used to show this information will be the Trading and Profit and Loss Account and the Balance Sheet, together with the Directors' and Auditors' reports. The preparation and presentation of these final accounts will follow established principles, some of which have been embodied in such major Acts as the Companies Acts 1948 to 1985 in the United Kingdom. The majority of these principles are, however, based on the recommendations of the various accountancy bodies such as the American Accounting Association and the Accounting Standards Committee, comprising representatives of all the major accountancy bodies in the UK. The ASC prepares exposure drafts on individual topics of interest and after considering comments, a statement of standard accounting practice is issued which should normally be adopted and implemented by all members of the participating bodies. Standards have been established for a wide variety of items, for example treatment of stocks and work in progress, accounting for the results of associated companies and calculation of earnings per share. Such bodies are constantly developing improved ways of presenting financial information and to follow the accepted principles will usually mean that the best available procedures are being adopted. However, individual cases call for individual action and a certain amount of flexibility in applying these principles may be necessary.

The presentation of this *historical* information is a very necessary task. It must be remembered that the shareholders of a company are the owners of that company and the directors are managing the company on their behalf. It is essential that periodical reports of the directors' stewardship should be given to the owners. This information is conventionally given in full once a year, with interim reports being made during the course of that year. This enables the shareholders to judge whether the performance of the company in the past twelve months has been satisfactory. From their standpoint this usually means that sufficient profits have been made to give them an adequate return on their investment. It also allows some assessment to be formed of the future prospects of the company. The Inland Revenue will be equally concerned with the performance of the concern for the past twelve months in order to ensure that a correct assessment is made of the tax liability of the concern on its trading activities for the period.

The whole outlook of the financial accountant will be seen to be concerned with historical information and is based on the static concept of yearly accounting. In a going concern the normal state is dynamic, not static. This is best illustrated by the balance sheet which presents a picture of the concern on one particular day, for example the 31st October each year. It will be apparent that the whole picture presented by this statement may well have been changed the following day. New assets may have been purchased, creditors may have been paid, debtors may have been raised and stock reduced, to give but a few examples of the normal day-to-day activities which will affect figures shown on the balance sheet. Another point is that the compilation of these statements takes time and it may take months until the Final Accounts, as they are called, are presented for external inspection. Attempts may be made to overcome this time-lag by presenting accounts more frequently, say once a month, but this involves many problems of valuation of assets and liabilities and apportionment of expenses. Although they are a step in the right direction, even these monthly statements usually take a week or more to prepare, which means again that the facts are out of date by the time they are considered.

Another limiting factor of financial accounting is that the accounts show the overall trading picture of the concern for a particular period. It is not possible to ascertain from such accounts whether the concern is pursuing its most profitable lines of business or what the cost of operating a department is, or whether the most effective use is being made of the organisation's resources, that is materials, labour and machines. Accounts usually cover a period of twelve months (the period used also for taxation calculations), but the trade cycle of the business may be more or less than twelve months. Some cycles may be quite long, for example if the firm is involved in large scale contracts such as shipbuilding, or they may be very seasonal as in the textile industries, or outdoor leisure industry. Management accounting techniques are designed to give a more detailed analysis of financial information which may be utilised by management for control purposes. Consider the following illustration:

**Trading and Profit and Loss Account for the Year Ending. . . .**

|  | £ ('000) |  | £ ('000) |
|---|---|---|---|
| Materials used | 15 000 | Sales | 50 000 |
| Wages | 25 000 | | |
| Gross profit on trading (20 %) c/d | £10 000 | | |
| | £ 50 000 | | £ 50 000 |
| Administration expenses | 3 000 | Gross profit b/d | 10 000 |
| Selling expenses | 1 500 | | |
| Distribution expenses | 500 | | |
| Net profit (10 %) | 5 000 | | |
| | £ 10 000 | | £ 10 000 |

It will be seen that the company appears to have made a satisfactory profit for the year of £ 5m. which represents 10 % of the turnover (i.e. sales). However, if the figures are analysed into the products which are made, the contribution which each makes to this 10 % can be established. Let us assume that the company deals with three products, A, B and C.

An analysis of the costs and income reveals the following:

|  | | Products | | |
|---|---|---|---|---|
|  | Total | A | B | C |
|  | £ ('000) | £ ('000) | £ ('000) | £ ('000) |
| Materials used | 15 000 | 6 000 | 4 000 | 5 000 |
| Wages | 25 000 | 10 000 | 8 000 | 7 000 |
| | 40 000 | 16 000 | 12 000 | 12 000 |
| Administration expenses | 3 000 | 1 300 | 800 | 900 |
| Selling expenses | 1 500 | 800 | 300 | 400 |
| Distribution expenses | 500 | 300 | 100 | 100 |
| Total expenses | 45 000 | 18 400 | 13 200 | 13 400 |
| Sales | 50 000 | 23 000 | 11 000 | 16 000 |
| Profit | 5 000 | 4 600 | — | 2 600 |
| Loss | — | — | 2 200 | — |
| Percentage of sales | 10 % | 20 % | — | 16·25 % |

These detailed allocation accounts reveal that Product A is earning 20 % on turnover and product B is incurring a £ 2·2m. loss during the period. Obviously it should be possible to improve the overall profitability of the concern by directing attention to product B. It may be that product B is a by-product which helps maintain the labour force and is therefore a necessary expense. Whatever the reason for this loss it should be investigated and the facts placed before the management to enable them to take a decision on the future of the product.

This type of statement will be prepared by the cost accountant, but if he is producing his information in accordance with purpose (2) outlined earlier (page 2), that is to enable management to plan and control current operations, action should have been taken at an early stage to correct the position revealed above.

The management accountant deals with the present and the future rather than the past. His role is to help management to fulfil the objectives of the business. These objectives, incidentally, are not covered by the general statement that a concern is in business to make a profit. Obviously unless it is able to make an adequate return on its endeavours it will not stay in that particular business; but the objectives of a business also include the reason for the business existing, whether to make motor-cars or electric kettles or pot plants. The management accountant presents management (the decision-makers) with the best possible financial information upon which they can base their decisions, and he also establishes control systems to ensure that the best use is being made of the concern's resources of men, machines, materials and money.

The main systems and techniques which are at present available to the management accountant to enable him to achieve these aims will be considered in subsequent chapters. The main framework consists of:

**Financial planning**   This will cover the various methods available to finance the business, and the importance of working capital. The source and application of funds will also be considered together with the value of accounting ratios and interfirm comparisons.

**Historical costing**   This is concerned with actual costs which have been incurred. Although these are of limited value (see above), they are essential in order to operate a standard costing system.

**Standard costing**   This involves setting up predetermined standards for costs, actual costs then being compared with the standards and the differences, or variances, analysed and reasons sought for them.

**Budgetary control**   Plans are prepared for a future period in financial terms. This ensures that responsibilities for expenditure and revenue are established and a continuous comparison may then be made of the actual with the budgeted figures, to enable the differences to be analysed into the 'controllable' and the 'uncontrollable'. Suitable corrective action can then be taken as soon as necessary.

**Marginal costing**   This involves first the division of costs into 'fixed' and 'variable,' and second, the effect on profit of changes in the volume or type of output. Only costs which vary with production are charged to the operations, fixed costs being written off to profits in the period in which they arise.

**Decision information**   The accountant should be in a position to present management with the financial implications of alternative schemes, for example whether to make a product or buy it from outside suppliers. Capital investment decisions may similarly be subject to the scrutiny of the accountant using such techniques as 'discounted cash flow' in order to assess the real value of alternative proposals and to ensure that an adequate return is being obtained on the capital employed in the business. Problems of maintaining the capital of the concern in periods of continuing inflation will also be of concern to the accountant, although as outlined later in Chapter 12 these problems have only recently concerned the majority of accountants and few companies have yet formulated a satisfactory policy to help solve such problems.

The progression of the book is from a brief look at the fundamentals of accounting to a consideration of the external constraints placed upon a firm by the need to obtain finance in its various forms. The way in which external and internally generated funds flow through the business is followed by a detailed consideration of costing procedures needed to control the day-to-day operations efficiently. The need for sound planning particularly in the short term is followed by a consideration of pricing policies and cost-profit-volume relationships. The next section considers the need and methods of performance evaluation both within the organisation and by comparative studies with similar organisations. The longer term planning decisions are then discussed with a final chapter on the problems and possible solutions of accounting for Price Level Changes.

## Questions

**1** What is management accounting?

**2** What are the three broad purposes for which the accountant produces information?

**3** Which three statements does the financial accountant use to present his historical information?

**4** Explain the limitations of the balance sheet.

**5** Is it possible to ascertain from the financial accounts whether business is pursuing its most profitable line of business?

**6** Who will usually be responsible for preparing a detailed breakdown of costs and sales, over products?

**7** What is the role of the management accountant in the organisation?

**8** Name the four resources of a business which management should make sure are being fully used.

**9** Outline the purpose of budgetary control.

**10** What type of decision will be subject to the technique of discounting cash flows?

# 2 Fundamentals of Accounting

In order to appreciate fully the role of management accounting in the business organisation it is necessary to have some knowledge of the basic concepts of accounting, and this chapter will be devoted to a discussion of these concepts.

Let us consider how an individual might show his financial position at a particular date. He would probably first consider what his assets are and then offset these against his liabilities: this would leave him with a sum which might be said to represent his net worth.

Consider the following figures which might represent the position of Mr Average:

| Assets | Owned 31st December |
|---|---|
| | £ |
| House | 65 000 |
| Car | 5 000 |
| Furniture | 8 000 |
| Caravan | 3 500 |
| Building society deposit | 8 000 |
| Investment in unit trusts | 2 000 |
| | £91 500 |

Some of these assets are not fully owned by Mr Average and the amount outstanding must be shown as a liability.

| Liabilities and Claims | 31st December |
|---|---|
| | £ |
| Mortgage on house | 25 000 |
| Bank loan on car—outstanding | 2 000 |
| Hire purchase on furniture | 1 500 |
| Bank overdraft | 500 |
| Total Liabilities | 29 000 |
| Net worth or owner's capital | 62 500 |
| | £91 500 |

Not all Mr Average's assets and liabilities are listed here.

He may, for example, be married with two children and he may have some difficulty in deciding which side of his balance sheet these should appear – whether as assets or as liabilities. The major difficulty would, however, be to put a money value on such items; and for this reason items requiring a subjective assessment of worth are usually not included.

These two statements show the assets which Mr Average owns and the way in which they have been or are being financed. It will be seen that the total of the assets agrees with the total of the liabilities and claims, but this does not mean that the figures in the statements must be correct just because they 'balance'. We have in fact balanced the liabilities statement by showing the difference between the liabilities and the assets as the owner's capital. If the asset values were to remain unchanged and were fully owned by Mr Average the balance sheet would look like this:

|  | Assets £ |  | Claims £ |
|---|---|---|---|
| House | 65 000 | Owner's capital | 91 500 |
| Car | 5 000 |  |  |
| Furniture | 8 000 |  |  |
| Caravan | 3 500 |  |  |
| Building society deposit | 8 000 |  |  |
| Unit trusts | 2 000 |  |  |
|  | 91 500 |  | 91 500 |

The balance sheet still 'balances' at £91 500, but now all the assets are fully paid for and the owner's capital is increased from the previous figure of £62 500 to £91 500.

The balance sheet of a business will contain the same basic information as the balance sheet of Mr Average, but because of the more complex nature of a business undertaking the list of assets and liabilities is likely to be longer and more detailed. The main items which appear in a business balance sheet are shown below:

**Assets**

| *Fixed* | *Current* |
|---|---|
| Land and buildings | Stocks of raw materials |
| Plant and machinery | Work in progress |
| Fixtures and fittings | Debtors |
| Motor vehicles | Cash at bank |
|  | Cash in hand |

The claims or sources of capital which relate to these assets are usually classified on a time basis, i.e. long-term (5 years or more), medium-term (1 to 5 years) and short-term (up to 1 year).

### Claims and Liabilities

| | |
|---|---|
| *Permanent or Long-Term* | *Medium-Term* |
| Share capital | Loan capital |
|   Ordinary shares | Debentures (Mortgages) |
|   Preference shares | |
| Retained profits | |

*Short-Term*
Bank overdraft
Creditors

Once again the totals of these two statements will 'balance'.

We are now in a position to consider the accountancy equation and the meaning of double-entry accounting. It is interesting to note that the double-entry system, which results in a balance sheet 'balancing', was in use as long ago as the thirteenth century and was developed by the merchants of Italy of that period. A perfect set of books on the double-entry principle is in existence which dates from 1340 and records the affairs of Marsan of Genoa.

The basic equation is:

$$\text{Assets} = \text{Liabilities} + \text{Shareholders' equity}$$
$$\quad\text{(A)}\qquad\quad\text{(L)}\qquad\qquad\qquad\text{(SE)}$$

Shareholder's equity is made up of the original capital which has been subscribed by the shareholders, plus profits which have been retained in the business for future activities but which could have been paid out to the shareholders as dividends.

The equation could therefore be written as:

$$A = L + \text{Shareholders' capital} + \text{Retained profits}$$

A profit arises when the total revenue during the period exceeds the total expenses incurred in that period. If we say that none of the profit was paid out as a dividend, in other words that all the profit was retained in the business, then the equation may be written:

$$A = L + \text{Shareholders' capital} + \text{Total revenue} - \text{Total expenses}$$

Transposing gives us:

$$A + \text{Total expenses} = L + \text{Shareholders' capital} + \text{Revenue}$$

The left-hand side of the equation = the right-hand side.

If the left-hand side is represented by **debit** and right-hand side by **credit**, then **debit = credit**.

The recording of total revenue and total expenses takes place in individual accounts which at the end of the accounting period are brought together in the Trading and Profit and Loss Account. If there has been a satisfactory trading period, then the subsequent profit will increase the shareholders' equity by increasing the retained earnings figure. If, on the other hand, a loss has been made then this will reduce the shareholders' equity.

It is important to realise that the retained earnings do not represent a 'pot' of cash which the shareholders might claim at any time. It would be very wasteful if this were the case as cash in itself earns nothing, and the business must use any available cash to purchase revenue-earning assets or reduce its liabilities. If it was likely to be needed at short notice it might be retained in liquid form by, for example, being placed on deposit at the bank.

To illustrate the point in the previous paragraph let us see what happens to the original cash which the owner of a business initially puts up. The figures have deliberately been kept small in order that the principles involved are more clearly seen. The opening balance sheet would look like this:

| *Assets* | | *Claims and Liabilities* | |
|---|---|---|---|
| | £ | | £ |
| Cash | 1000 | Owner's capital | 1000 |

He now purchases certain equipment which costs £400. After this transaction the balance sheet would be:

| | £ | | £ |
|---|---|---|---|
| Cash | 600 | Owner's capital | 1000 |
| Equipment | 400 | | |
| | 1000 | | 1000 |

The cash has been reduced by the £400 paid for the equipment and this equipment is now shown in the balance sheet as an asset.

Let us assume that the rest of the cash is spent on stock. The balance sheet would now look like this:

|  | £ |  | £ |
|---|---|---|---|
| Cash | Nil | Owner's capital | 1000 |
| Equipment | 400 |  |  |
| Stock | 600 |  |  |
|  | 1000 |  | 1000 |

If the stock is sold, say for £800, then this will mean a reduction of the stock figure to nil, an increase in the cash figure to £800, and the difference between the cost of the stock and the revenue from selling it, in other words £200 represents the profit earned on the transaction and in balance sheet terms will be shown as retained earnings:

|  | £ |  | £ |
|---|---|---|---|
| Cash | 800 | Owner's capital | 1000 |
| Equipment | 400 | Retained earnings | 200 |
| Stock | Nil | (profit) |  |
|  | 1200 |  | 1200 |

The owner may now decide to buy the same amount of stock and to use the other £200 of cash to buy some new equipment. After these transactions have taken place the balance sheet would be:

|  | £ |  | £ |
|---|---|---|---|
| Cash | Nil | Owner's capital | 1000 |
| Equipment | 600 | Retained earnings | 200 |
| Stock | 600 |  |  |
|  | 1200 |  | 1200 |

It will be seen that the retained earnings are now represented by assets other than cash, either by equipment or stock. It would not be possible for the owner suddenly to decide to take out of the business the retained earnings, as they are represented by assets which are not easily divisible, or realisable.

The double-entry system requires that for each debit entry in an account there must be a corresponding credit entry in some other account. For each item in the balance sheet there will be a separate account. In addition there will be numerous accounts recording revenues received and expenses incurred during the period. At the end of the period these are totalled and any balance on the account is taken to the Trading or Profit and Loss Account, which itself forms part of the double-entry system.

We will work through a simple practical example to illustrate these points.

The opening balance sheet of J. Bloggs at 1st January is shown in the first column on page 14. During the year the following transactions took place.

1   £300 of stock was purchased for cash. (This will increase the stock figure by £300 and reduce the cash by £300.)

2   New equipment costing £400 was purchased, the seller agreeing to a sale on 'credit terms'. (This will increase the equipment account by £400 and increase the liabilities under the heading 'creditors' by £400.)

3   Stock was sold for £200 cash, the original cost being £150. (This will decrease the stock by £150, increase the cash by £200, and increase the retained earnings or profits by £50.)

4   A debtor pays his account, which is for £200. (The cash will be increased by £200 and debtors reduced by £200.)

5   Payments totalling £250 were made to creditors. (This will reduce cash by £250 and reduce creditors by £250.)

6   Stock was sold for £300, on credit terms, the original cost being £200. An invoice was sent to the buyer. (Stock is reduced by £200, debtors are increased by £300 and retained earnings are increased by £100.)

Consider the account of J. Bloggs shown on page 14.

It will be seen that after the dual aspect of each transaction has been recorded, the left-hand side (the debit side) still equals the right-hand side (the credit side). The balance is either nil as in the case of items 1 and 4, or a sum which shows a change in balance on at least two accounts.

It should be mentioned that a balance sheet when used in its proper function is not part of the double-entry system but just shows the balances which are standing on those accounts which have not been closed off for the period and carried to the Trading and Profit and Loss Account. A published balance sheet is usually presented in tabular form showing the net assets employed in the business and how these have been financed. The figures for J. Bloggs would be presented as follows:

# J. BLOGGS

## Assets

| | 1st Jan. £ | 1 | 2 | 3 | 4 | 5 | 6 | £ |
|---|---|---|---|---|---|---|---|---|
| **Fixed Assets** | | | | | | | | |
| Land and building | 2000 | | | | | | | 2000 |
| Furniture and equipment | 1500 | | +400 | | | | | 1900 |
| **Current Assets** | | | | | | | | |
| Stock | 400 | +300 | | −150 | | | −200 | 350 |
| Debtors | 250 | | | +200 | −200 | | +300 | 350 |
| Cash | 350 | −300 | | | +200 | −250 | | 200 |
| | £4500 | Nil | +400 | +50 | Nil | −250 | +100 | £4800 |

## Claims and Liabilities

| | 1st Jan. £ | 1 | 2 | 3 | 4 | 5 | 6 | £ |
|---|---|---|---|---|---|---|---|---|
| Owner's capital | 4000 | | | | | | | 4000 |
| Retained earnings | 200 | | | +50 | | | +100 | 350 |
| **Current Liabilities** | | | | | | | | |
| Creditors | 300 | | +400 | | | −250 | | 450 |
| | £4500 | Nil | +400 | +50 | Nil | −250 | +100 | £4800 |

J. BLOGGS

**Balance Sheet as at 31st December 19—**

| | £ | £ | £ |
|---|---|---|---|
| Fixed assets | | | |
| Land and buildings | | 2000 | |
| Furniture and equipment | | 1900 | 3900 |
| | | | |
| Current assets | | | |
| Stock | 350 | | |
| Debtors | 350 | | |
| Cash | 200 | | |
| | | 900 | |
| Less current liabilities | | | |
| Creditors | | 450 | |
| Net current assets | | | 450 |
| | | | |
| Net assets | | | 4350 |
| | | | |
| | £ | £ | £ |
| *Financed by* | | | |
| Owner's capital | | 4000 | |
| Retained earnings | | 350 | 4350 |

Accounting is an art rather than an exact science and in order to ensure some uniformity in the system of accounting it is necessary to have certain generally accepted guidelines which are capable of formulating a basic framework in which the system can work. Without such guidelines the whole art of accounting would flounder and no party, either internal or external, would be able to place any reliance on the results shown by the accountant. However, it must be noted that there is much academic debate surrounding the guidelines and this is an ongoing process.

Statement of Standard Accounting Practice No 2 deals with fundamental accounting concepts, accounting bases and accounting policies. One of the main purposes of the Standard is to require a company to disclose in its financial accounts clear explanations of accounting policies which have been followed. This is to try to ensure some uniformity in the presentation of published accounts which should lead to a clear understanding of them by all potential users.

The Statement recognises four fundamental concepts which are regarded as having general acceptability. These are as follows:

1 *The going concern concept.* This concept presumes that the business is treated as a continuing entity, so that valuations of assets, etc. are based on the assumption that they will be used to help produce further goods or will be sold in the normal course of trading. Otherwise the accountant would have to try to value assets on the basis of the business closing down tomorrow, which under normal circumstances would be unrealistic, and would require many subjective decisions. Machinery, for example, which might be in good condition but only capable of producing a certain product manufactured by the business would have no value, if account had to be taken of what the position would be if the business was closed down the next day. If, however, the business is viewed as a going concern, the machine is a valuable asset capable of earning revenue for the business in future years, and a monetary value should be placed on it.

2 *Expenses are matched with revenues.* Costs should be matched with the revenue which they earn. Once the accounting period has been settled (e.g. twelve months), all costs incurred in earning the revenue received during that period should be shown. These costs may have occurred in past years (e.g. the purchase of plant and equipment), or the present year (e.g. wages), or will incur cash in a future year (e.g. rent which is paid in arrears).

Items which have not been fully used in earning the revenue of the period will be shown in the balance sheet as assets. In this respect they represent stored-up costs which will be used to produce future revenues and will be set against such revenues when they are used.

3 *Consistency.* The statements prepared by the accountant must be consistent from period to period. The same methods of valuation must be employed from year to year for the results to be meaningful; and the accounts should not be manipulated to provide a desired result which would be inconsistent with previous procedures adopted. This does not, of course, mean that no changes should ever take place, but changes should be infrequent and should be clearly noted on the relevant statements.

4 *Prudence concept.* Revenues should not be recorded until they are realised, but losses should be recorded even though they may not yet have occurred. This is the conservative approach which has an important influence on the accountant when he is recording transactions. In connection with the sale of some commodity the accountant would only take account of the sale when the goods were delivered to the buyer. No income would be shown throughout the stages

necessary to get the goods into a saleable state, despite the fact that money had been spent on the processes.

The main exception to this is in the case of long-term contracts such as shipbuilding, where it is prudent to show a proportion of the revenue each year to avoid violent fluctuations from year to year. Again, however, the recorded income would be conservatively estimated, and might be three-quarters of what had actually been earned during the period from the work done.

In addition to the above there a number of other concepts which are relevant, for example:

1 *The entity concept.* Each business, whether it is run by one man or by a partnership or as a limited company, is regarded as a separate entity and accounts are kept for each entity. This means that in the one-man business it is necessary to distinguish between the individual as an individual and the individual as owner of the business. We can illustrate this point by considering the man who owns a grocery store. Let us assume that his business balance sheet shows his equity (i.e. his original capital plus retained profits) to be standing at £1000 and that his stock figure is shown at £200. Now consider that he wishes to use some of his stock for his own family. Say this stock has a value of £20. From our previous discussion of double-entry accounting we know that two accounts must be affected by this transaction. The stock figure is going to be reduced by £20, but where is the other entry to be made? There are two solutions, both of which show how the business transactions must be kept separate from the owner's private transactions.

The first solution would be for the owner to treat the stock as being sold to him just as it might have been sold to a customer. He will then, as the customer would, pay for the stock in cash, out of his own pocket into the till. The second and more usual solution would be to reduce the owner's equity by the cost of the stock, so that the equity would now be £980 and the stock £180. In the case of a limited company, the company has a separate legal entity from the shareholders who own it and it is fairly easy to distinguish between the transactions of each.

2 *Measurement is in money terms.* Only factors which can be expressed in money terms are shown. The balance sheet shows in monetary terms certain facts relating to assets of the business and the various claims, again in monetary terms, against these assets. It will not reveal facts which may have a very important bearing on the

future of the business but which are not capable of being reduced to the common denominator of money, for instance, that relations with the unions are strained, or that a large quantity of plant is likely to become obsolete in the next six months because of a new invention.

3   *Stable monetary unit.* It is generally accepted that objective evidence should be the accounting basis for recording transactions. This involves valuing the resources of a business at cost or market price, whichever is the lower. It does mean that the balance sheet of a business cannot be used as a measure of the current worth of that business, particularly when there is an unstable currency which, because of inflation, is constantly being devalued in real terms. The main reason against making up-to-date assessments of current values is, once again, the subjective nature of such assessments and the lack of reliable information about price changes on which assessments could be made. As a compromise, when it is obvious that an asset has increased in value (e.g. land), a number of companies have undertaken a revaluation of the asset and made the appropriate adjustments in the balance sheet.

In recent years the accountancy profession has addressed itself to these issues and their problems are outlined in Chapter 12.

## Questions

**1**   If assets are £10 000 what is the total of claims and liabilities?
**2**   If assets are £10 000 and liabilities £4000 what are the owner's claims?
**3**   Write out the accountancy equation.
**4**   What is meant by the entity concept?
**5**   What is meant by the going concern concept?
**6**   Explain what you understand by the expression 'dual aspect' of each transaction.
**7**   The Accountant deals only in facts which can be reduced to monetary terms. What other facts might have an effect on the future of the business?
**8**   Explain the matching concept.
**9**   What is meant by the realisation concept?
**10**   Joe Piper on the 1st July 19–8 wins £20 000 on the football pools and decides to enter the grocery trade. He pays £20 000 on 1st July 19–8 into a business bank account. He calls the business 'Piper Enterprises'.

(*i*)   Prepare a balance sheet using this information and each of the following stages.

(*ii*)   On the 2nd July 19–8 he purchases a freehold shop for £10 000, paying by cheque.

(*iii*)   On the 5th July the following transactions took place:
Purchased groceries on credit from J. Brown for £800
Purchased Fixtures and Fittings paying by cheque £200
He pays a joiner £20 by cheque for installing Fixtures and Fittings.

(*iv*)   On the 8th July 19–8 further transactions took place as follows: sold
groceries on credit to L. Crowther for £300; the goods cost Piper £200;
purchased a van for delivery purposes paying by cheque £500.

# 3 Financing the Business

Whatever the type of business organisation, whether sole trader, partnership or limited company, it will require initial capital to enable it to commence its operations and no doubt additional capital as its activities expand. There are a number of ways in which this capital can be raised, and with ever increasing interest rates it is essential that all possible means should be considered before the final source or sources are chosen.

The initial capital requirements will be based on a funds forecast. The purpose of this is to estimate the expenditure which is likely to be incurred in establishing the business, including the initial asset requirements such as land, buildings, plant and machinery, preliminary expenses such as legal fees, issuing house fees, and also the amount needed to finance the actual production until income from initial sales is received (i.e. working capital). The forecast may be a complicated document if we are considering a medium-size company, or just a simple statement if the needs of the sole trader are being considered.

## Financing the sole trader and partnership

The initial capital requirements of a sole trader or of a partnership are usually met by the introduction of cash or other assets by the owner or partners. This may be supplemented by loans from friends or members of the family, perhaps even on interest-free terms. (This, of course, is by far the best method of financing, if such generous relatives can be found.) Once the business has become established and achieved a good 'credit rating', it will be able to meet short-term cash requirements from the bank either on overdraft or by a loan; and to some extent it will be able to finance its trading transactions on credit, perhaps by paying for last month's purchases from this month's sales.

## Financing of companies

The management accountant is most likely to be concerned with the financing of a business which operates as a limited company. The importance of limited liability is that the shareholders are liable only for any unpaid amounts on their shares and once these are fully paid, as the majority are, their liability ceases, regardless of the extent of the liabilities of the company in which they hold shares.

We will consider the financing of a company under the same three broad classifications used in Chapter 2: permanent or long-term, medium-term and short-term capital.

## Permanent capital

The principal method of obtaining permanent capital is by the issue of shares. The Companies Acts, 1948 to 1981 do not specify the type of shares which a company must issue and such matters are covered in the Articles of Association (i.e. the internal rules of the individual company). The investors who will subscribe for the shares are mainly interested in the risk, the expected yield, and the voting powers of the shares, while the company issuing them will be attempting to obtain finance at the lowest cost.

The two main classes of shares are ordinary shares and preference shares.

### *Ordinary shares*
The majority of shares issued are ordinary shares. They have a nominal value, and they may be issued at a discount or at a premium. If issued at a discount they are subject to strict control. The ordinary shareholder provides the main risk-bearing capital of the business and as such he is entitled to a share of the surplus profits after the debenture holders and preference shareholders have been paid. As the ordinary shareholder receives only a share of the profits after the rights of the preference shareholder and debenture holder have been satisfied, it is only natural for him to expect to receive a bigger percentage of the profits than they receive. He is, after all, bearing the risks, and is the first to suffer if the level of profit drops. Because of the risk element ordinary shareholders may rightly expect to have some say in the way in which the business is run. This is achieved by attaching voting rights to the ordinary shares which allow the holders to vote at company meetings. In certain circumstances non-voting shares are issued, where it is wished to retain control in the hands of the original shareholders but where it is also necessary to otain new capital. Such shares have been subject to a great deal of criticism because of their non-voting element over the past few years, and a number of companies have converted non-voting shares into voting shares as the opportunities arose.

## Preference shares

Preference shareholders are entitled to receive a fixed rate of dividend before any profits are divided among the other classes of shareholder. The shares are usually cumulative: if there are insufficient funds to pay the full rate of dividend in any particular year, that sum must be added to the dividend payment for the next year and the full payment must be made before other shareholders can participate in profits. If shareholders are given the right to a second dividend (e.g. 1 % for every 5 % paid to ordinary shareholders in excess of 10 %) the shares are known as 'participating preference shares'. A company may be authorised by its Articles to issue redeemable preference shares. These allow the company to obtain initial capital and later, when earnings increase, to redeem these shares and so enable a larger distribution to be made to the remaining shareholders. However, if the shares are redeemed out of profits there must be an equivalent amount transferred to a Capital Redemption Reserve Fund, in order to maintain the capital at its original figure and so protect the shareholders' interests. It should be noted that preference shares are rarely issued in a modern capitalisation because of the changes embodied in the corporation tax system introduced in 1966. However, the practice of issuing Convertible Preference Shares allowing conversion into equity shares at a fixed price in the future is now becoming more popular.

## Business Expansion Scheme

This scheme was introduced in 1981 to encourage investment in the equity capital of unquoted companies. These investments carry risks, but also the chance of considerable rewards. The Business Expansion Scheme provides a generous tax incentive to the investor which can substantially reduce the cost of the investment and therefore increase the potential return on it. The investor gets relief at his highest marginal rate of tax (up to 60 %) so long as he is purchasing newly issued ordinary shares in an unquoted company. A 60 % taxpayer could thus increase his net investment by 250 % simply by recovering his original subscription. By providing this incentive the scheme should dramatically improve the flow of equity capital into small businesses. The company receiving the investment must be unquoted and carry on a trade wholly or mainly in the UK.

The scheme covers virtually the whole range of manufacturing, construction and service industries, including tourism, retail and wholesale trades. The main exclusions are companies concerned with banking, leasing and hiring, dealing in stocks and shares or items amounting to finance investment (i.e. in commodities), farming and the provision of legal or accountancy services. The investor may lose his relief if the company obtains a listing on the Stock Exchange or on the Unlisted Securities Market within a three year period from the date of the investment.

The investor must subscribe for newly issued ordinary shares in the business to qualify and must be resident in the UK for tax purposes. He must not own more than 30 % of the company's share capital or be otherwise closely associated with it (for example, he must not be a director receiving directors fees or an employee or partner of the company; nor can he invest in a company controlled by his parents, grandparents, spouse, children, grandchildren or business partners). The maximum qualifying investment is £ 40 000 per person in a given tax year although the whole amount can be spread between several qualifying companies subject to a minimum investment of £ 500 per company in a tax year. The investment must be held for five years to retain the full tax relief.

*Share Buy Back Scheme*
Under the provisions of the 1981 Companies Act, it is now possible to issue redeemable ordinary shares. These shares may be redeemed at the option of either the company or the shareholder. What simply happens is that the company pays the cash back to the shareholder, cancels the shares and the remaining shareholders have a larger slice of a smaller cake.

**Loan capital –long-term**

Loan capital does not form part of the share capital and usually takes the form of a debenture. The debenture is the document which acknowledges the loan and also stipulates the terms and conditions upon which the loan is based, for example the rate of interest payable and the charge, if any, on the company's assets. If there is such a charge, the debenture holder is placed in the position of being a 'secured creditor'; if there is no charge he will be an 'ordinary unsecured creditor'. These latter debentures are known as 'simple' or 'naked' debentures and because of the lack of security they can usually be issued only by firms with a high financial standing. They may carry the right to convert the nominal value of the debenture into ordinary shares at a future date and this can often prove an attractive proposition to an investor.

The more usual type of debenture is the mortgage debenture which gives a charge over the company's assets. The charge may be specific, as on a building or plot of land, or – more usually – a floating charge may be given on the whole of the concern's assets. The main disadvantage with a fixed charge is that the concern is restricted in the way in which it can handle the charge; it cannot sell it. With a floating charge, however, assets may be dealt within the normal way until such time as the concern defaults on a conditon of the debenture, when all the assets as they then exist become the subject of a fixed charge. Any charge created by the concern must be registered with the Registrar of Companies within twenty-one days. The company may redeem debentures by buying them on the stock market before the actual date for redemption, otherwise the whole debenture issue becomes redeemable on the due date. There is frequently a period for redemption to take place. For example, a debenture dated 1985/90 means that redemption may take place any time between 1985 and 1990, usually at the option of the company, but redemption must be made by the 1990 date.

*The Loan Guarantee Scheme*
Following the Wilson Committee Report this scheme was established in 1981 by the government to encourage bankers to lend money to small businesses which had exhausted all the normal channels for obtaining finance, and when the banker might have been prepared to lend but for the lack of security and/or track record.

Under this scheme, the government guarantees the banker that, in the event of the customer being unable to repay the loan, the government will pay the banker 70% of the money outstanding. For his part, the banker may not take any personal security from the borrower. However, the borrower is expected to pledge all the business assets as security for the loan.

Loans may be from two to seven years with the possibility of up to a two year capital repayment holiday. Interest rates are arranged by the lending banker and the Government makes a small charge for the guarantee, being a percentage of the amount of the loan outstanding. The maximum amount which may be borrowed under this scheme is £75 000.

Almost all businesses qualify, as long as the bank manager indicates that he wishes to make the loan, but could not do so without the benefit of the government guarantee. The main activities excluded are: agriculture, banking, education, forestry, house and estate agents, insurance, recreational or cultural services, tied public houses and travel agents.

## Medium-term capital

The main sources of medium-term finance are bank loans, mortgages, sale and lease back property, hire purchase and equipment leasing, European Investment Bank and the European Coal and Steel Community.

### *Bank loans*

The medium-term loan schemes offered by the principal clearing banks are usually secured. A bank's standard fixed and floating debenture will be usual. These loans are quite wide ranging and are becoming increasingly flexible. Borrowers may opt between fixed and floating interest rates and terms range up to 20 years. The popular schemes are the main business loans – the Lloyds Business Loan, The Nat West Business Development Loan, the Barclays Business Expansion Loan and the Williams and Glyn's Business Borrowing Plan.

The main benefit of these 'term loans', as they are called, is that there is no danger of the loan being prematurely recalled. This is always the problem facing the businessman who uses overdraft facilities, and such recalls are often made when he can ill afford to make the repayments.

### *Mortgages*

Mortgages, which may be available to the business from such institutions as insurance companies, investment companies and trust funds, are similar to debentures, which have already been discussed. The money borrowed forms a charge upon the assets of the company and if the business defaults on the mortgage interest repayments, the insurance company etc. may take possession of the asset. The period of the mortgage will vary from approximately five to twenty years. This method of finance is usually an expensive one; high rates of interest have to be paid, and heavy conditions may be stipulated.

### *Sale and lease back of property*

If the business needs additional finance it may sell any valuable property which it owns to a property investment company under an agreement allowing the business to lease back the property from the investment company at an agreed rate, for a specified period with the option of renewal at the end of the original lease. This is a valuable method of obtaining a permanent increase in working capital, but it should be remembered that fixed rental charges will have to be met over a period of years when profits may fluctuate widely. There is also a reduction in the value of the fixed assets, shown on the balance sheet.

*Hire purchase*

The main advantage of buying assets on hire purchase is that the business is able to use the earnings from employing the asset to pay the hire purchase charges as they fall due. The asset must normally have a longer expected life than the length of the hire purchase agreement, and the value should also be in excess of the amount outstanding on the agreement. This will mean that no extra security for the asset will be required.

The main disadvantage of hire purchase financing is that the interest rates are usually fairly high,around 15 % p.a. As this rate is applied to the full amount of the purchase price the *effective* rate of interest is nearly double the actual rate (in this instance 30 % p.a.) which makes this method of financing very expensive. If an asset is purchased outright, then in addition to saving the hire purchase charges all the earnings of that asset can be used for furthering the business's activities. Also the risk of obsolescence, although it exists in the same way no matter how the asset was financed, will be reduced to a greater degree since outright purchase means that payments will not still have to be made on an asset which has ceased to earn revenue for the business.

The main types of business using hire purchase as a means of finance are those whose work necessitates their expenses and profits being spread over a lengthy period, such as the building construction industry. Once the payments have been completed the ownership of the asset normally passes to the hirer.

*Credit sale*

Another form of purchase similar to hire purchase is known as credit sale. It is not subject to quite so many legal formalities as hire purchase and the ownership of the goods passes at the time of the agreement rather than remaining with the owner until the end of the agreement, as in hire purchase.

*Equipment leasing*

This is very similar to leasing of property, already considered. Although equipment leasing is a relatively new concept in Britain it has operated in America for many years. A finance company buys the equipment required by the business and then leases it to them on a contractual basis for a set period. This should not be confused with hire purchase financing as there is never any question of the ownership passing to the business under a lease. Leasing is an obvious way for a business with limited capital resources to be able to expand its activities in the hope that the revenue earned from the leased equipment will more than repay the fairly high leasing charges. Leases on equipment will usually be for about five years with the possibility of an extension at a reduced rental, but much will depend on the type of equipment to be leased. An everyday example of equipment leasing is the renting of television sets by individuals from firms specialising in this activity.

*European Investment Bank*
The European Investment Bank can provide medium-term fixed rate finance for businesses which promote the interests of the community, regional development or are in industries with structural problems. The loans are for up to 50 % of the cost of capital expenditure with a fixed rate of interest over eight years. The government operates an exchange risk guarantee scheme to protect borrowers against losses arising from adverse exchange rate movements. The borrower, therefore, takes on only a sterling liability with the government carrying the exchange risk in return for a fee based on the outstanding balance of the loan. EIB loans (including exchange risk cover), are about 2 % cheaper than comparable borrowing from UK sources of finance.

Companies employing up to 500 people in manufacturing industry, or industry related services through the UK are eligible for EIB loans for between £15 000 and £25 000. Businesses in Assisted Areas, undertaking larger projects, (up to £4·25 m) also qualify for EIB loans. Services firms with a wider than local market will normally be eligible, but local consumer services are excluded.

*European Coal and Steel Community*
The European Coal and Steel Community can also provide medium-term finance which, in addition, carries a subsidy in the form of up to 5 % interest rebate for the first five years of the life of the loan. ECSC loans are available to companies employing less than 500 people and creating jobs for ex-coal or steel workers within 15 miles of a coal or steel closure.

*Venture capital facilities*
Over the past few years there has been an upsurge in institutions offering venture capital. Some are backed by central government, for

example the Council for Small Industries in Rural Areas (COSIRA) or the British Technology Group, and others by local government. Most of the lending banks have their own vehicle for venture capital provision – Growth Options Ltd by the National Westminster Bank, or Hambros Advanced Technology Trust sponsored by Hambros Bank, and so on. The financial institutions such as pension funds and insurance funds also support a number of different types of venture capital organisations. In total, at the time of writing, it was possible to name over 100 venture capital providers.

Perhaps the best known of these fund providers is the Industrial and Commercial Finance Corporation. Its current portfolio contains over 4000 companies and it is backed by the nine clearing banks and the Bank of England. It usually provides fixed interest loans of medium and long-term length up to £2m. It assists small and medium-sized companies, both public and private, and under normal circumstances does not require a seat on the board or a share stake.

*Industrial holding companies*
A further method by which a company, particularly a small one, can obtain capital is to align itself with one of the industrial holding companies such as Hanson Trust PLC. What usually happens is that the takeover arrangements by the holding company provide for the existing management to stay on and run the company. The small company therefore acquires the facilities and resources of a large financial group without the need to sacrifice its independence completely. The holding company acts rather like an investment company spreading its business over a wide field and providing little interference with the management of the group members, but the small concern is no longer the same independent entity it was and may have to account for its actions to the holding company.

## Short-term capital

The main sources of short-term capital are bank overdraft, acceptance credits, delay in paying creditors and retained funds.

*Bank overdraft*
This is probably the most commonly used method of obtaining short-term finance. The rate of interest is usually between 1 and 3 % above the clearing banks Base Lending Rate. A business would normally operate on an overdraft limit agreed with the local bank manager. This would mean that the business could go into overdraft at any time

provided the limit was not exceeded. Interest is paid only on the outstanding daily balance, which makes it cheaper than obtaining a loan at a fixed rate of interest. The main drawback of overdrafts is that the borrower may be required by the bank to repay the amount outstanding at any time. Such demands are usually made during a period when credit is in short supply, which is the very time when the business needs to use its overdraft to the full.

### Acceptance credits

This method of finance is normally cheaper than bank borrowing, but the difference is usually only significant when dealing in large sums. The system operates as follows. The business will open an account with a merchant bank which specialises in acceptance credits. The bank will issue a letter of credit to the business, once it has established its financial standing, and the business may now draw bills of exchange which will be accepted by the accepting house, thereby making them 'prime bank bills'. These may be discounted, in other words sold to a discounting house (the House paying a sum less than the full value of the bill, which represents an interest payment). When the bill becomes payable, usually ninety days after it was drawn, the business will provide the accepting house with the necessary funds to meet it. It will however have had the use of that money, less a small amount paid to the discounting house as interest, for the period of the bill.

Once this type of arrangement is in operation, it is generally possible to renew it for, say, another period of ninety days on the expiry of the current credit.

### Delay in paying creditors

Although not an obvious source of capital it will be apparent that if the business is able to arrange with certain of its larger creditors to delay settlement of their accounts for a specific period it will be able to use the cash which would otherwise have been paid over to them. However, such arrangements are likely to be of a very temporary nature, and persistent requests for such facilities may result in the good credit rating of the business being downgraded.

### Retained funds

A major source of capital consists of funds which are retained in the business either in the form of profits not distributed to shareholders, or provisions and reserves set up for specific or for general purposes (e.g. a general reserve fund).

Internal finance is not necessarily the cheapest form of financing expansion but obviously any business must attempt to provide funds for investment from its current operations. It will be limited by the total amount of profit earned and the dividend policy which is followed by the individual business. It is now usual practice for the rate of dividend to be stabilised over a period so that a company pays approximately the same rate of return each year on the capital contributed. If the capital increases, the same rate of dividend requires a higher proportion of existing profits to pay for it; therefore, increased earnings from the new capital must be at least equal to previous percentage rate of earnings in order to finance the dividend without increasing the percentage taken from profits.

Consider the following simplified example (ignoring taxation):

### Balance Sheet at End of Year 1

| | £ | | £ |
|---|---|---|---|
| Capital (8000 £1 shares) | 8 000 | Assets | 10 000 |
| Profit | 2 000 | | |
| | £10 000 | | £10 000 |

If the company's policy is to pay as a dividend 50% of its profits then each shareholder will receive $12\frac{1}{2}$p for every share he owns:

$$\frac{\text{Profit available for distribution}}{\text{Capital}} \quad \frac{£2000}{£8000} \times 50\% = 12\frac{1}{2}\text{p}$$

If during Year 2 the share capital is increased to £10 000 and the profit remains the same, then the shareholders will now only receive 10p per share:

$$\frac{\text{Profit available for distribution}}{\text{Capital}} \quad \frac{£2000}{£10\,000} \times 50\% = 10\text{p}$$

For $12\frac{1}{2}$p per share to be paid the distributed profit percentage must be increased to approximately 63%, leaving only 37% of the profit available for internal use within the company.

For the original percentages to apply and still result in all the shareholders receiving $12\frac{1}{2}$p per share as a dividend the profit for the second year must be £2500. Thus:

$$\frac{\text{Profit available for distribution}}{\text{Capital}} \quad \frac{£2500}{£10\,000} \times 50\% = 12\frac{1}{2}\text{p}$$

The rate of increase in the capital is exactly the same as the rate of increase on earnings: capital increase from £8000 to £10 000 represents 25 % increase as does the increase in profit available, from £2000 to £2500.

## Gearing

The amount which an ordinary shareholder is likely to receive by way of dividend is also governed by the gearing of the particular company. The term 'gearing' is used to describe the ratio between the ordinary share capital section of the capital structure and the fixed interest capital. A highly geared capital structure is one in which the fixed interest part forms a large part of the total and the ordinary shareholder is in a minority. A low-geared company is therefore one in which there is little fixed interest capital.

As you will remember, the ordinary shareholder receives a dividend only after all the fixed interest capital has been paid, and obviously the more of this capital which has prior claim on profits the less chance the ordinary shareholder has of receiving anything, as he is last in the queue.

Let us consider two examples showing extreme high and low gearing.

Each company has a total capitalisation of £500 000. It is made up as follows:

|  | | *Company A*<br>£ | *Company B*<br>£ |
|---|---|---|---|
| | Ordinary shares | 400 000 | 100 000 |
| Fixed | Preference shares (8 %) | 50 000 | 250 000 |
| | Debentures (10 %) | 50 000 | 150 000 |
| | | £500 000 | £500 000 |

Gearing ratio $= 4:1 \dfrac{£400\,000}{£100\,000} \quad \dfrac{£100\,000}{£400\,000} \quad 0{\cdot}25:1$

Company A is low geared (i.e. it has a high ratio) while Company B is highly geared (i.e. one with a low ratio).

It will be seen that the cost each year to Company A to enable it to finance its fixed capital is £9000. This is made up of preference dividend £4000 plus debenture interest £5000.

The cost to Company B is £35 000 made up of £20 000 on the preference shares and £15 000 on the debentures.

It should be noted that debenture interest is a charge against profits, before taxation, while dividends are an appropriation of profits after taxation.

It is clear from the above figures that profits available to ordinary shareholders are subject to a much greater degree of fluctuation in a highly geared company than in a company with a low gearing.

Let us assume that the two companies had identical profits for two successive years before charging debenture interest, these being £105 000 in the first year and £85 000 in the second. Taxation is assumed to be 50 % and all the available profit is distributed.

### Year 1

|  | Company A £ | Company B £ |
|---|---|---|
| Profit before charging debenture interest | 105 000 | 105 000 |
| Debenture interest | 5 000 | 15 000 |
|  | 100 000 | 90 000 |
| Taxation – 50 % | 50 000 | 45 000 |
| Profit available for distribution | 50 000 | 45 000 |
| Preference dividend | 4 000 | 20 000 |
| Profits distributed to ordinary shareholders | £46 000 (11·5 %) | £25 000 (25 %) |

### Year 2

|  | Company A £ | Company B £ |
|---|---|---|
| Profit before charging debenture interest | 85 000 | 85 000 |
| Debenture interest | 5 000 | 15 000 |
|  | 80 000 | 70 000 |
| Taxation – 50 % | 40 000 | 35 000 |
| Profit available for distribution | 40 000 | 35 000 |
| Preference dividend | 4 000 | 20 000 |
| Profits distributed to ordinary shareholders | £36 000 (9 %) | £15 000 (15 %) |

The figures in parentheses represent the rate percentage on the ordinary share capital.

It will be seen that a reduction in profit of 19 % from Year 1 to Year 2 has caused a fall of dividend rate in the case of Company A of 22 %, from 11·5 to 9 %; but in the case of Company B, because of the high proportion of the second year profit ($£35\,000$) which has to be paid out to the fixed interest section of the capitalisation, the dividend rate falls by 40 % from 25 to 15 %. This type of fluctuation is very disturbing for the ordinary shareholder in such a company.

Buying shares in a highly geared company can therefore be a hazardous experience, but, of course, just as a fall in profits produces a substantial reduction in the ordinary share dividend percentage, a rise in profits will cause a more than proportional rise in this dividend. Consider in our two companies that profits for Year 3 were $£135\,000$. The position now would be:

**Year 3**

|  | Company A £ | Company B £ |
|---|---|---|
| Profit before charging debenture interest | 135 000 | 135 000 |
| Debenture interest | 5 000 | 15 000 |
|  | 130 000 | 120 000 |
| Taxation – 50 % | 65 000 | 60 000 |
| Profit available for distribution | 65 000 | 60 000 |
| Preference dividend | 4 000 | 20 000 |
| Profits distributed to ordinary shareholders | £61 000 (15·3 %) | £40 000 (40 %) |

If the dividend percentages for Years 2 and 3 are compared it will be seen that the increase in profit has resulted in a much more than proportionate rise in the rate of dividend available to Company B's ordinary shareholders.

The relative importance of gearing to the company and to the investor is likely to vary somewhat. The company will want to ensure as little interference as possible either now or in the future from preference shareholders and debenture holders, so the larger the proportion of ordinary shareholders the better.

There are two basic types of investor. One who is looking for a steady and regular income with prospects of long-term growth and the other who is willing to bear high risks in return for high dividends. In general the first type of investor will prefer a low-geared company and the second type a high-geared one. One further point to be considered is that a company which is already highly geared, particularly if the fixed interest capital takes the form of debentures, is likely to find difficulties in increasing its capital in the future, whereas the low-geared company can always have recourse to debentures if its expansion programme requires an influx of additional permanent capital.

## Questions

1  What is meant by *gearing*?
2  Discuss the effect of high gearing on the earnings per share.
3  The following are two alternative capital structures proposed by the management of the Uno Co. Ltd:

|  | Structure (1) | Structure (2) |
|---|---|---|
|  | £ | £ |
| Ordinary shares of £1 each | 90 000 | 20 000 |
| 6% debentures of £10 each | 10 000 | 50 000 |
| 8% preference shares of £1 each | — | 30 000 |
| Total capital | £100 000 | £100 000 |

You are required:

  (i)  to compute the gearing ratio for each capital structure and state which structure is relatively high geared and which structure is relatively low geared.
 (ii)  to compute the earnings per ordinary share when:
        (a) earnings before interest and tax are likely to be £50 000,
        (b) earnings before interest and tax are likely to be £10 000,
        (c) to compute the rate of return on a £1 ordinary share for each level of earnings and structure.

Assume Corporation Tax is at the rate of 52%.
4  Discuss the constraints to higher gearing.

# 4 Funds Flow Analysis

It has already been pointed out that a business is a continuing entity and during the course of business operations many changes take place in assets, equities, income and expenses. The funds which are used in a business must be constantly on the move. There must be an even flow through the cycle of operations with no bottlenecks or dead ends. One of the best ways to illustrate the use of funds in the business is to liken them to the domestic hot-water system. The usual arrangement in the home is to have a cold-water storage tank into which the main injection of water flows. Once the system is established, in other words when the storage tank is full, a continuous process is brought into operation. If you draw hot water from, say, the bathroom tap, as the level in the storage tank falls it is replaced from the mains until it is full once again. If for any reason the mains water is not available it will still be possible at first to draw water from the bathroom tap; but eventually the storage tank will be empty and the whole system will break down.

Let us now see how this continuous flow process operates in a business. Consider the diagram overleaf.

It will be seen that the initial injection of funds comes from the shareholders and from loan capital. Further injections may be made from time to time by short-term loans, for example bank overdraft. This initial injection of funds will be used to buy the necessary assets to enable the concern to begin operations; and in addition there must be sufficient funds to finance production until the results of such production are sold and the cash is received by the business.

Once the cash from sales is received (immediately in the case of cash sales, but perhaps not for a month or more when goods are invoiced to the customer) the continuous cycle begins. The receipts may be used to finance further production which in turn will result in new sales. The sales should exceed the cost of producing the goods, the difference being profit, which is of course available for distribution to the shareholders but a proportion of which would be retained in the flow to allow for further expansion and development of products and to pay taxes.

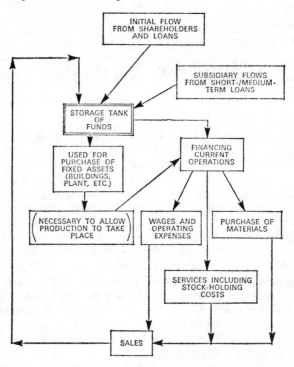

**Fig. 4.1**   The inflows from sales should exceed the outflows representing expenses. This excess (i.e. profit) will then result in further outflows covering taxation, dividend payments and the purchase of new assets, etc.

It will be seen that sales are vital if the process is to be a continuous one. As with the domestic hot-water system, if the main supply, in this case sales, is reduced or stops altogether there is likely to be little immediate effect on production, but unless action is taken to remedy the situation there will soon be a breakdown in the system. There will be no funds available for paying labour and for purchasing materials. This will mean redundancies and perhaps even liquidation of the company. You can now see the importance of maintaining the flow of funds through all the stages of operations.

It is usual to prepare three basic flow statements from available financial data. These are:

(*a*)   the income statement, or profit and loss account;
(*b*)   the statement of sources and application of funds;
(*c*)   the statement of cash receipts and disbursements.

## The income statement

This measures in total for a given period the earnings and expenses resulting from trading activities or from providing a service. An excess of earnings is known as net income or profit, while a deficiency is known as a loss. Such a statement is prepared as part of the final published accounts of the business.

## Sources and application of funds

It is often perplexing to try to establish what has happened to the profits which have been earned during the accounting period, and the position may be made much clearer if a statement is prepared showing the sources of funds and how they have been applied.

*Sources of funds:*

(*a*)   profits, before charging depreciation;
(*b*)   new capital introduced during the period;
(*c*)   new long- or short-term loans;
(*d*)   reductions in short- or long-term assets, e.g. investments sold;
(*e*)   proceeds from the sale of fixed assets, e.g. sale of factory.

*Application of funds:*

(*a*)   payment of dividends to shareholders;
(*b*)   reduction in long- or short-term liabilities;
(*c*)   increase in short- or long-term financial assets;
(*d*)   payments for the purchase of new fixed assets.

Item (*a*) in the sources statement perhaps deserves some explanation. Depreciation is a correct charge against the profits for the year as it is an attempt to place a monetary value on the extent to which an asset has been reduced in value during the accounting period. (More will be said about the problems of such valuations in a later chapter.) However, the charge for depreciation involves no actual outflow of funds; it is merely a book entry and it must therefore be added back to the net profit figure. The total sources of funds in any accounting period must equal the total application of these funds. An initial difference between the two sides of the statement will represent an increase or decrease in net working capital.

*Net working capital*

Before examining a practical problem involving source and application of funds let us consider what is meant by net working capital and why it is of such importance. Working capital is generally defined as the excess of current assets over current liabilities. This will include the following items under Current Assets:

Stocks
Work in progress
Debtors
Payments in advance
Cash at bank
Cash in hand

and under Current Liabilities:

Creditors (including current taxation)
Bank overdraft

It is from these items that the real 'flow' of funds is generated. Stocks of raw materials are needed to enable continuous production to take place and stocks of finished goods to enable orders from customers to be met without delays. Debtors arise as a result of sales, and creditors as a result of purchases, both on credit terms. The bank and cash balances are needed to meet the delay in payment which occurs between the incurring of the expenses of production and the receipt of the revenue from sales. It is essential to try to convert both debtors and stock into cash as soon as possible, as only after such conversion can profits be realised. On the other hand, when the cash is received it should not be simply left in the bank but put to work either by increasing current operations, if there is sufficient demand for the concern's products, or by investing in fixed assets with an eye on future expansion, or in equities outside the business to earn income.

Working capital is therefore essentially circulating capital; but the desirable ratio between fixed and circulating capital will vary greatly, depending on the type of business. A ship-building firm, for instance, will require a large amount of fixed capital such as the shipyard and ancillary equipment; while the racecourse bookmaker will require very little fixed capital but a fairly large sum for working capital.

Management is concerned with two very important problems in which working capital plays a part. These are maintaining profitable operations and maintaining a solvent financial position. Profits are very important, but a firm must also be able to pay its debts when they fall due. It is possible for a firm to expand so rapidly that its whole financial solvency is brought into question because there is insufficient current circulating capital to pay for the expansion. This is known as 'over-trading', and has been the downfall of many apparently successful companies.

Each of the individual items which constitute working capital is capable of being controlled with a view to ensuring that the maximum amount of working capital is always available.

**Stocks** Attention should be paid to stock levels, and minimum/maximum stock levels should be established. The cost of stock-holding is the loss which is incurred because the capital tied up in the stock cannot be used for financing other activities or even invested in equities etc. The aim should be to keep stocks as low as possible consistent with being able to supply the demands of production. One of the best examples of raw material stock control is found in the car industry, where the materials have hardly arrived as stocks before they are required for production. The time interval is frequently less than a week.

**Debtors** A constant check should be maintained to ensure that debtors pay their accounts by the due date. Incentives might be offered to encourage them to pay early, such as a $2\frac{1}{2}\%$ cash discount if paid within seven days. Too much pressure to pay may, however, have the effect of making the customer take his trade elsewhere.

**Creditors** Accounts should not be paid before the due date but where discounts for prompt payment are offered they should usually be accepted because they represent a good return on the money paid.

**Cash** This has already been considered, but the dangers of financing expansion by bank overdraft should be noted. As already mentioned overdrafts may be called in by the bank manager at very short notice and this could have serious consequences for a concern which is already short of liquid resources.

Let us now consider a practical example.

**EXPANDO PRODUCTS LTD.**
**Balance Sheet as at 31st December**

| | Year 1 £ | Year 2 £ | | Year 1 £ | Year 2 £ |
|---|---|---|---|---|---|
| Issued share capital | 80 000 | 80 000 | *Fixed Assets at net* | | |
| General reserve | 5 000 | 10 000 | *book values* | | |
| Profit and Loss A/c. | 10 500 | 14 000 | Land and buildings | 64 000 | 70 000 |
| Debentures 9% | 12 000 | 10 000 | Plant and machinery | 20 000 | 23 000 |
| | | | Furniture and fittings | 12 000 | 7 000 |

|  | Year 1 £ | Year 2 £ |  | Year 1 £ | Year 2 £ |
|---|---|---|---|---|---|
| *Current Liabilities* |  |  | *Current Assets* |  |  |
| Creditors | 6 000 | 8 000 | Stock | 8 500 | 8 000 |
| Current taxation | 4 500 | 6 000 | Debtors | 14 000 | 17 000 |
| Bank overdraft | 500 | — | Cash | — | 3 000 |
|  | £118 500 | £128 000 |  | £118 500 | £128 000 |

Depreciation in Year 2 was as follows:

Plant and machinery, £2000
Furniture and fittings, £3000

From the balance sheet we establish the movement in working capital and the statement of sources and application of funds for Year 2 as follows:

## Working Capital Calculation

|  | Year 1 £ | Year 2 £ | ± £ |
|---|---|---|---|
| *Current Assets* |  |  |  |
| Stock | 8 500 | 8 000 | − 500 |
| Debtors | 14 000 | 17 000 | +3 000 |
| Cash | — | 3 000 | +3 000 |
|  | 22 500 | 28 000 | +5 500 |
| *Less:* |  |  |  |
| *Current Liabilities* |  |  |  |
| Creditors | 6 000 | 8 000 | +2 000 |
| Current taxation | 4 500 | 6 000 | +1 500 |
| Bank overdraft | 500 | — | − 500 |
|  | 11 000 | 14 000 | +3 000 |
| Net working capital | 11 500 | 14 000 |  |
| Increase in working capital |  |  | +2500 |

Note that the increase in current liabilities, that is +3 000, reduces the overall working capital position because it is taken away from the current assets figure.

## Sources and Application of Funds

|  | £ |
|---|---|
| *Sources* |  |
| Increase in general reserve | 5 000 |
| Increase in profit and loss account | 3 500 |

|  | £ | £ | £ |
|---|---|---|---|
| Depreciation: |  |  |  |
| Plant and machinery | 2 000 |  |  |
| Furniture and fittings | 3 000 |  |  |
|  |  | 5 000 |  |
|  |  | 13 500 |  |
| Sale of furniture and fittings (*a*) |  | 2 000 |  |
|  |  | £15 500 |  |

| *Applications* | £ |
|---|---|
| Purchase of land and buildings | 6 000 |
| Purchase of plant and machinery (*b*) | 5 000 |
| Redemption of debentures | 2 000 |
|  | 13 000 |
| Net increase in sources, i.e. addition to working capital | £2 500 |
|  | £15 500 |

*Notes*

(*a*)   Furniture and fittings for Year 1 stood at £12 000. The figure for Year 2 is £7000 which has been reduced by £3000 depreciation. Without this depreciation the figure would have been £10 000 which is £2000 less than Year 1. This means that £2000 of furniture and equipment must have been sold during Year 2, which is a source of funds and is shown in the statement.
(*b*)   The £5000 is calculated in a like manner. If there had been no depreciation in Year 2 the figure for plant and machinery would have been £25 000. This represents an increase of £5000 over the Year 1 figure and this is the amount spent on new plant during Year 2.

Sources and Application of Funds Statements have now become an accepted part of published accounts. This is because of the requirements of SSAP 10 which applies to all companies with a turnover in excess of £25 000 per annum. In order to familiarise the reader with the usual format of such statements the example in the Standard is produced overleaf.

## Working capital forecasts

The statement of sources and application of funds is useful to management in an historical context, in other words after the events have happened. However, it is perhaps more important that management should be aware of the amount of working capital needed either

## COMPANY WITHOUT SUBSIDIARIES LTD
### Statement of Source and Application of Funds

|  | *This Year* | | | *Last Year* | | |
| --- | ---: | ---: | ---: | ---: | ---: | ---: |
|  | £ | £ | £ | £ | £ | £ |
| *Source of funds* | | | | | | |
| Profit before tax | | | 1 430 | | | 440 |
| Adjustments for items not involving the movement of funds: | | | | | | |
| Depreciation | | | 380 | | | 325 |
| *Total generated from operations* | | | 1 810 | | | 765 |
| *Funds from other sources* | | | | | | |
| Issue of shares for cash | | | 100 | | | 80 |
| | | | 1 910 | | | 845 |
| *Application of funds* | | | | | | |
| Dividends paid | | (400) | | | (400) | |
| Tax paid | | (690) | | | (230) | |
| Purchase of fixed assets | | (460) | | | (236) | |
| | | —— | (1 550) | | —— | (866) |
| | | | 360 | | | (21) |
| *Increase/decrease in working capital* | | | | | | |
| Increase in stocks | | 80 | | | 114 | |
| Increase in debtors | | 120 | | | 22 | |
| (Increase) decrease in creditors – excluding taxation and proposed dividends | | 115 | | | (107) | |
| Movement in net liquid funds: Increase (decrease) in: | | | | | | |
| Cash balances | (5) | | | 35 | | |
| Short-term investments | 50 | | | (85) | | |
| | —— | 45 | | —— | (50) | |
| | | —— | 360 | | —— | (21) |

to maintain existing operations, to cover expansion or a new contract or to commence operations.

It is a fact that many new businesses do not survive because of the failure to appreciate how much working capital can be needed before the cycle of cash flows is established. In establishing a working capital forecast there are many factors to be taken into account. Many of these will depend on the type of business and different practices within the industry but most businesses will have to qualify the following matters:

(*a*)  The cost of materials, wages and overheads.
(*b*)  The stock holding period – in other words how much stock must be held in order to ensure that production can be supplied with raw materials as and when required. This will obviously depend on the rate of production and the length of time it takes to receive deliveries from suppliers. The question of bulk discounts for large purchases must also be evaluated.
(*c*)  The time during which the product is processed by the business.
(*d*)  The time that finished goods are in stock before being sold to customers.
(*e*)  The lag in payment of debtors, creditors, wages and overhead expenses.

The following example illustrates the above points and demonstrates the need to prepare a working capital forecast:

The Board of Muffit Engineering require you to submit a statement showing the working capital needed to finance a level of activity of 4800 units per year. You are given the following information:

| Element of Cost | Amount per Unit (£) |
|---|---|
| Raw materials | 7 |
| Direct labour | 3 |
| Overheads | 5 |
| Total cost | 15 |
| Profit | 5 |
| Selling price | 20 |

Raw materials are in stock on average for two months. Materials are in process on average for one month. Finished goods are in stock on average for 5 weeks. Credit allowed by customers is one month. Credit allowed to debtors is two months. Lag in payment of wages is $1\frac{1}{2}$ weeks.

You are informed that production is carried on evenly during the year (48 weeks), and wages and overheads accrue similarly.

## MUFFIT ENGINEERING
### Working Capital Forecast Level of Activity 4800 units per annum

| Stem | Period (in weeks) | Raw materials (£) | WIP (£) | Finished goods (£) | Debtors (£) | Creditors (£) | Total (£) |
|---|---|---|---|---|---|---|---|
| *Materials* | | | | | | | |
| In stock | 8 | 5600 | | | | | |
| In process | 4 | | 2800 | | | | |
| In finished stock | 5 | | | 3500 | | | |
| In debtors | 8 | | | | 5600 | | |
| | 25 | | | | | | 14 700 |
| *Less creditors* | 4 | | | | | 2800 | |
| | 21 | | | | | | |
| *Wages* | | | | | | | |
| In process | 4 | | 1200 | | | | |
| In finished stock | 5 | | | 1500 | | | |
| In debtors | 8 | | | | 2400 | | |
| | 17 | | | | | | |
| Less lag in payment | 1·5 | | | | | 450 | |
| | 15·5 | | | | | | 4650 |
| *Overheads* | | | | | | | |
| In process | 4 | | 2000 | | | | |
| In finished stock | 5 | | | 2500 | | | |
| In debtors | 8 | | | | 4000 | | |
| | 17 | | | | | | 8500 |
| *Profit* | | | | | | | |
| In debtors | 8 | | | | 4000 | | 4000 |
| | | 5600 | 6000 | 7500 | 16 000 | (3250) | 31 850 |

*Notes*

1   If the level of activity is to be 4800 units per year and production is for 48 weeks on an even basis then it may be assumed that 100 units are produced per week.

2   The average costs per week will therefore be:

| | |
|---|---|
| Raw materials | £ 700 |
| Direct labour | £ 300 |
| Overheads | £ 500 |
| Total cost | £1500 |
| Profit | £ 500 |

3   The period column recognises the length of time for each cost heading before any cash flow can be expected for the outlay. Therefore materials starting life as raw materials and costing £700 in Week 1 will not result in generating any income until 25 weeks later. However, because the material does not itself have to be paid for until four weeks after purchase this is credited in the period calculation.

It will be seen therefore that in order to cover the costs of production Muffit Engineering will require to have working capital of £31 850.

## Statement of cash receipts and disbursements

This statement is narrower in concept than the sources and application of funds statement, as the latter is concerned with transactions which affect the net working capital while the former is only concerned with transactions that have a direct impact on cash.

Management needs to know how much cash will be available to pay creditors, interest on loans, taxation, dividends, etc. In some months there may be insufficient cash to meet these commitments, and it will then be necessary to arrange for a short-term loan, usually on overdraft from the bank. In months when the cash receipts exceed the cash payments, proper use should be made of the extra cash, either by paying off a short-term loan or by investing it for a suitable period. With careful planning it should be possible to ensure that there is always sufficient cash available to meet obligations, with the cash balance kept to a minimum.

Many businesses are of a seasonal nature, for example tent manufacturing, fruit farming and deck-chair hiring. It is essential for such trades to prepare an operating cash budget for the full trade cycle so that plans can be made for additional finance which may be needed in the off-peak months. Bank managers usually insist on seeing such budgets before they agree to grant overdraft facilities to cover the lean months, as they want to know the earliest time at which the overdraft can be repaid, and also wish to make sure that there will be sufficient cash available during the cycle to pay off the sum borrowed.

It is usual to prepare such budgets for a period of twelve months to give an overall picture of the cash position, but more frequent statements will be required for control purposes. These may even be daily as, for example, in the case of a local authority, where it is extremely difficult to assess the amount of cash which will be received on any one day.

An outline of a cash budget is shown below:

**Cash Budget Covering the Period January to December 19—**

| | Jan. | Feb. | Mar. | ... | Dec. |
|---|---|---|---|---|---|
| *Receipts* | | | | | |
| Opening cash balance | | | | | |
| Cash sales | | | | | |
| Cash received from debtors | | | | | |
| Any other income | | | | | |
| | —— | —— | —— | ... | —— |
| *Payments* | | | | | |
| Cash purchases | | | | | |
| Payments to creditors | | | | | |
| Wages payments | | | | | |
| Payments relating to selling expenses | | | | | |
| Payments relating to distribution expenses | | | | | |
| Payments relating to administration expenses | | | | | |
| Payments in respect of capital transactions | | | | | |
| Other ... detail | —— | —— | —— | ... | —— |

**Cash surplus/deficiency**

Let us consider how a cash budget might be prepared for a new company for the first six months of its operations.

The Newcomers Co. Ltd. was established on the 1st January with a subscribed capital of £50 000. It purchased in that month buildings for £20 000, plant and machinery for £8000, furniture and fittings for £6000, stock for £7000.

The estimated sales for the six months were January £2000, February £10 000, March £12 000 and £15 000 for April, May and June, and debtors were expected to settle their accounts at the end of the second month after the sale.

Purchases of merchandise for the period were estimated to be January £1000, February £6000, March £8000, April £10 000 and £12 000 for May and June.

Creditors accounts were to be paid the month following the purchase.

Wages paid each month were estimated to be £1000 and other expenses estimated to be £800 per month.

The cash budget would be as follows:

|  | Jan. £ | Feb. £ | March £ | April £ | May £ | June £ |
|---|---|---|---|---|---|---|
| *Receipts and Balances* | | | | | | |
| Shares | 50 000 | | | | | |
| Sales | | | 2 000 | 10 000 | 12 000 | 15 000 |
| Balance b/f | | 7 200 | 4 400 | | | |
| Balance overdrawn c/f | | | 1 400 | 1 200 | 1 000 | |
| | £50 000 | £7 200 | £7 800 | £11 200 | £13 000 | £15 000 |

|  | Jan. £ | Feb. £ | March £ | April £ | May £ | June £ |
|---|---|---|---|---|---|---|
| *Payments and Balances* | | | | | | |
| Buildings | 20 000 | | | | | |
| Plant and Machinery | 8 000 | | | | | |
| Furniture and fittings | 6 000 | | | | | |
| Stock | 7 000 | | | | | |
| Purchases | | 1 000 | 6 000 | 8 000 | 10 000 | 12 000 |
| Wages | 1 000 | 1 000 | 1 000 | 1 000 | 1 000 | 1 000 |
| General expenses | 800 | 800 | 800 | 800 | 800 | 800 |
| Balance in hand c/f | 7 200 | 4 400 | | | | 200 |
| Balance b/f | | | | 1 400 | 1 200 | 1 000 |
| | £50 000 | £7 200 | £7 800 | £11 200 | £13 000 | £15 000 |

The actual cash balance position revealed from this budget is:

|          | *In hand* | *Overdrawn* |
|----------|-----------|-------------|
|          | £         | £           |
| January  | 7200      |             |
| February | 4400      |             |
| March    |           | 1400        |
| April    |           | 1200        |
| May      |           | 1000        |
| June     | 200       |             |

*Balance*

It will be seen that after the first two months the company will be short of cash, March producing the largest deficit of £1400. It is therefore possible from the outset for the company to make arrangements to cover this cash shortage, and if this statement is submitted to the bank manager with a request for overdraft facilities for the three-month period, March, April and May, of around £1500, the liquidity problems of the first six months of trading should be overcome. Only by planning in this manner is it possible for the overall cash position to be established. Once the initial budget has been prepared it can be amended if necessary; and suitable action can be taken as alterations to forecasts become necessary.

The preparation of plans and budgets is not restricted to the cash position of a company. It is possible, and necessary, to plan and budget for the whole operation of the business, both financial and non-financial.

The subject of budgeting and budgetary control will be considered in Chapter 7.

## Questions

1  Illustrate by using a diagram how funds flow through a business.

2  State which three basic flow statements are usually prepared from available financial data.

3  Outline the main sources and applications of funds.

4  Define working capital and explain its importance.

5  Explain the controls which management should institute over the various elements of working capital, i.e. stock, debtors, cash and creditors.

6  Why is depreciation added back to the net profit figure?

7  What do you understand by the term 'over-trading'.

8  Explain the importance of preparing cash budgets.

9  How frequently should cash forecasts be prepared?

**10**

|  | 19–7 | | 19–6 | |
|---|---|---|---|---|
|  | £ | £ | £ | £ |
| *Fixed assets* | | | | |
| Premises at cost | | 59 000 | | 30 000 |
| Plant at cost | 20 000 | | 20 000 | |
| *Less* depreciation | 14 000 | 6 000 | 12 000 | 8 000 |
| | | 65 000 | | 38 000 |
| *Current assets* | | | | |
| Stock | 20 000 | | 10 000 | |
| Debtors | 22 000 | | 30 000 | |
| Cash | 3 000 | 45 000 | 25 000 | 65 000 |
| | | £110 00 | | £103 000 |
| *Issued share capital* | | | | |
| Ordinary shares of £1 each | | 36 000 | | 30 000 |
| *Revenue reserves* | | | | |
| Retained profits | | 34 000 | | 23 000 |
| *Current liabilities* | | | | |
| Trade creditors | 17 000 | | 18 000 | |
| Tax liability | 23 000 | 40 000 | 32 000 | 50 000 |
| | | £110 000 | | £103 000 |

| *Additional information* | £ | £ |
|---|---|---|
| Sales | 110 000 | 182 500 |
| Purchases | 80 000 | 100 000 |
| Net profit before tax | 40 000 | 60 000 |
| Net profit after tax | 20 000 | 30 000 |
| Dividends paid | 25 % | 25 % |
| Opening stock | 10 000 | 15 000 |
| Closing stock | 20 000 | 10 000 |

You are required to prepare a Sources and Application of Funds statement showing how the cash position has been reduced from £25 000 in 19–6 to £3000 in 19–7. No plant has been sold during the periods under review.

**11** Draw up a cash budget for T. Goody from the following infomation for the six months from 1st July 19–9 to 31st December 19–9.

(*a*) Opening cash (including bank) balance 1st July 19–9. £3000.
(*b*) Sales at £40 per unit.

*Sales in units*

| Apr. | May | June | July | Aug. | Sept. | Oct. | Nov. | Dec. |
|------|-----|------|------|------|-------|------|------|------|
| 220  | 240 | 280  | 320  | 360  | 380   | 260  | 160  | 140  |

Debtors will pay two months after they have bought the goods.
( *c* )  Production in units:

| Apr. | May | June | July | Aug. | Sept. | Oct. | Nov. | Dec. | Jan. |
|------|-----|------|------|------|-------|------|------|------|------|
| 300  | 340 | 360  | 400  | 260  | 220   | 220  | 180  | 140  | 120  |

( *d* )  Direct labour of £10 per unit is payable in the same month as production.

( *e* )  Raw materials cost £12 per unit and are paid for 3 months after the goods are used in production.

( *f* )  Other miscellaneous variable expenses are £6 per unit. Two-thirds of the cost is paid for in the same month as production and one-third in the month following production.

( *g* )  A machine is to be bought and paid for in October for £6000.

( *h* )  Fixed expenses amounting to £300 per month are paid one month in arrears – and were the same last year.


**12**  From the following information relating to a departmental store you are required, for the three months ending 31st August, 19–4, to prepare:

( *a* )  by months, a cash budget, on a receipts and payments basis and
( *b* )  for the three months period, a budgeted source and disposal of funds statement.

It is anticipated that the working capital at 1st June, 19–4, will be as follows:

|                          | £000s |
|--------------------------|-------|
| Cash in hand and at bank | 545   |
| Short term investments   | 300   |
| Debtors                  | 2570  |
| Stock                    | 1300  |
| Trade creditors          | 2110  |
| Other creditors          | 200   |
| Dividends due            | 845   |
| Tax due                  | 320   |

**Budget profit statement**

|  | *June* | *Months* *July* | *August* |
|---|---|---|---|
|  | *£000s* | *£000s* | *£000s* |
| Sales | 2100 | 1800 | 1700 |
| Cost of Sales | 1635 | 1405 | 1330 |
| Gross profit | 465 | 395 | 370 |
| Administrative, selling and distribution expenses and interest | 315 | 270 | 255 |
| Net profit prior to tax | 150 | 125 | 115 |

**Budgeted balances at the end of each month**

|  | *30th June* | *31st July* | *31st August* |
|---|---|---|---|
|  | *£000s* | *£000s* | *£000s* |
| Short-term investments | 700 | — | 200 |
| Debtors | 2600 | 2500 | 2350 |
| Stock | 1200 | 1100 | 1000 |
| Trade creditors | 2000 | 1950 | 1900 |
| Other creditors | 200 | 200 | 200 |
| Dividends due | 485 | — | — |
| Tax due | 320 | 320 | 320 |

Depreciation amounting to £60 000 is included in the budgeted expenditure for each month.

Capital expenditure amounting to £800 000 is expected to be incurred during July and proceeds from the sale of plant and equipment of £50 000 is expected in August.

# 5 Historical Costing

In financial accounting, transactions are classified according to type and then summarised, to enable the annual financial statements and reports for shareholders to be prepared. The limitations of financial accounting as an aid to management were shown in the example in Chapter 1, pages 3 and 4.

Management requires much more detail than is available from the financial accounts if it is to run the business effectively. It will need to know how much it costs to operate a particular section of the business, or how much it costs to produce and sell a specific product or group of products. This detailed information is produced by the cost accountant, but it must not be assumed that cost accountancy is an entirely different accounting system. It is really only an extension of the general accounting system, a different interpretation being placed on costs by the cost accountant.

In financial accounting the costs are reported in aggregate, while in cost accounting the costs are broken down into certain categories and charged to a cost centre on a unit basis. This recording of the actual costs is known as 'historical costing', and as such, forms an essential part of any costing system. However, these costs do relate to past events and as such are no real aid to measuring efficiency. This can best be achieved by first establishing standards by which the actual costs can be compared, and then calculating variances and finding explanations for them. This is known as 'standard costing' and will be dealt with in the next chapter.

## Elements of cost

The prime cost of a product consists of three basic elements:

(*a*)   direct materials;
(*b*)   direct labour;
(*c*)   direct expenses.

These together form what is known as 'prime cost' and all expenses over and above prime cost are known as 'overhead expenses'.

Let us take a closer look at these three basic elements. They represent the only costs which can easily be directly allocated to a specific manufacturing cost centre. Overhead expenses are usually apportioned on some equitable basis to the individual cost centres, as they cannot be directly allocated.

**Direct material** This includes all materials relating to the specific job or batch whether drawn from stores or specially (separately) purchased. The information will be obtained from the stores requisitions and material invoices, priced at the appropriate rate for the amount of material used.

**Direct labour** This is the cost of labour which is directly traceable to the creation of the product. The labour may be skilled or unskilled; and the information is obtained from employees' time sheets or job cards, which have been completed by them and then processed by the wages department to reveal the cost in wages of each job appearing on a time sheet.

**Direct expenses** This represents any other direct costs which are incurred specifically for the particular job – royalties on production, carriage inwards, costs of special tests, and hire of special equipment. This information will be obtained from receipted accounts and invoices.

**Overhead expenses** The same material, labour and expense classification is used for overhead expenses, but they are now called:

(*a*)   indirect material;
(*b*)   indirect labour;
(*c*)   indirect expenses.

In general terms, 'overhead' represents all the expenses which are not direct expenses, and are incurred in connection with the general organisation of the whole business. These expenses are subdivided into four main categories, namely:

(*a*)   production expenses;
(*b*)   selling expenses;
(*c*)   distribution expenses;
(*d*)   administration expenses.

The build-up of costs can be illustrated by the diagram overleaf:

Production overhead includes all indirect expenditure incurred by the works from the receipt of the production order until the finished product is ready for despatch. Examples of expenses coming within this category are indirect materials (grease, cotton waste) indirect wages (foremen, cleaners) and general departmental expenses such as

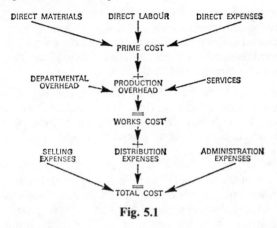

Fig. 5.1

rent, lighting and heating of the factory. Services which are included in the production overhead will cover such sections as repair and maintenance, production control etc.

Selling expenses include the cost of obtaining the orders for the goods; for example salaries and expenses of salesmen, advertising and sales showroom costs.

Distribution expenses cover all expenditure incurred in handling the finished product from the time of its despatch until it reaches its final destination. Examples are the upkeep and maintenance of delivery vehicles, warehouse costs and packing expenses.

Administration expenses are those which are incurred in controlling and directing the business, including offices, salaries and upkeep, depreciation of office machinery and directors' expenses.

These overhead expenses are often referred to as 'period costs' indicating that they are more related to time than to volume of production.

It will be appreciated that these overhead expenses form a large proportion of the overall expenditure of the concern; and it is a major problem to allocate these expenses to the individual products or jobs. It is usual to charge each job with a share of each works department through which it passes; and then to this total works cost an appropriate charge in respect of the other major overhead expenses (i.e. selling, distribution and administration) is added.

### Allocation of production overhead

The methods commonly adopted for allocation of production overhead are:

(a) percentage on direct materials;
(b) percentage on direct wages;
(c) percentage on prime cost;
(d) direct labour – hour rate;
(e) machine hour rate.

Generally speaking (a) and (c) are unsatisfactory since it is rare for production overheads to vary in proportion to the material or prime cost content of a job; (b) will give reasonable results where wage rates are uniform throughout a department.

Typical production overheads are Depreciation of Plant and Machinery, Rates, Indirect Labour, Heating and Lighting, Production Engineers' Salaries and Production Supervision etc. A common characteristic of most of these costs is that they will tend to vary in relation to time, and therefore each product should be charged with a due proportion of production overhead based on the time it takes to produce it.

For example, suppose there are two products being assembled in the assembly department. The two products are known as 'X' and 'Y'. X takes one hour to assemble and Y two hours. The production overheads for the assembly department are budgeted at £20 000 for the year and the budgeted operating hours for the department for the same period are 10 000 labour hours. The direct materials which are bought from an outside supplier cost £10 for X and £15 for Y, direct labour costs being X-£12, and Y-£20.

The production cost for X and Y will be as follows:

|  | X £ |  | Y £ |
|---|---|---|---|
| Direct materials | 10 |  | 15 |
| Direct labour | 12 |  | 20 |
| *Prime cost* | 22 |  | 35 |
| * Production overheads: assembly: |  |  |  |
| 1 hour @ £2 per hour | 2 | 2 hours @ £2 per hour | 4 |
| *Production cost* | £24 |  | £39 |

$$\frac{*\text{Budgeted assembly overheads for year}}{\text{Direct labour hours for year}} = \frac{£20\,000}{10\,000} = \frac{£2}{\text{per hr.}}$$

In the above example, the overheads have been allocated to the product on the basis of a rate per direct labour hour. This will usually give an equitable distribution of production overhead when the rate of production is largely controlled by manual labour, and the amount of machinery used is small. On the other hand, in the case of a machine shop where there are large amounts of capital expenditure in plant and machinery and the pace of production is largely controlled by the machine, a rate per machine hour should be used so as to give an equitable distribution of production overhead over different products using the department's facilities.

It should be remembered that whichever method is adopted the resultant charge is only an estimate. There will rarely be complete agreement between the total charges made during a period based on budgeted estimates and the actual overhead expenditure incurred during the same period. This is because it is necessary to estimate the overheads for the coming period and base the recharges on the budgeted figures. It would not be possible to decide upon a recharge figure for each job as it was completed if this were not done.

If the job has to go through a number of different cost centres then overhead cost rates (i.e. production overhead absorption rates) will be calculated for each cost centre.

Where such separate cost centres are in operation the estimation of the overheads applicable to each cost centre must first be decided.

The object is to ensure that allocation of expenses reflects the facts as accurately as is possible where an arbitrary apportionment has to be used. An actual basis is the ideal to be used wherever possible; depreciation of each machine can then be allocated directly to the relevant centre. Where it is necessary to make some form of equitable allocation, attention should still be directed to relevant activities; for example, rent and rates can be allocated on the floor space occupied by the cost centre, and canteen and welfare facilities in accordance with the number of employees working in each centre.

Recovery rates should be frequently reviewed as over- or under-recovery will tend to mean that selling prices, if based on total costs, are too low or too high.

## Allocation of selling and distribution expenses

There is frequently no relationship whatsoever between the amount of selling effort and the actual sale achieved. A telephone call may bring in a large order while a number of personal visits to a customer may result in a small order or even no order at all. However, if more than one product is sold it is essential, in the interests of accuracy, for some agreed basis to be adopted for allocation of selling expenses. This may take the form of a percentage on selling price or a rate per article sold. Special expenses incurred on one particualr product should be charged to that product; extensive advertising to launch a new item should not be recharged over all the products generally, but to the new item. In this way it is possible to establish the real cost of each product. If the business produces only one type of product, selling and distribution expenses may be conveniently recharged as a percentage of works cost. Distribution expenses are often peculiar to a particular job or product and it should therefore be possible to calculate a fairly accurate rate per article distributed or rates per job to recover these expenses.

## Allocation of administration expenses

These expenses are usually much smaller in amount than works expenses and are not closely related to production. However, as more sophisticated control techniques are brought into operation, including computers, this expense is becoming more important year by year. The usual basis has been to allocate as a percentage on works cost, but more direct allocations may be necessary where it is possible to tie costs down to individual jobs. For example, computer time may be recharged on an hourly basis to cost centres within the overall administration expenses and to specific jobs if possible.

The following example shows the build-up of a cost for two specific products known as Alpha and Delpha. The Company, Enterprise Products Ltd., manufactures a wide range of goods and has prepared the following budget for the year 19—:

|  | £ | £ |
|---|---|---|
| Direct materials |  | 60 000 |
| Direct wages: |  |  |
| Machine shop (100,000 machine hours) | 40 000 |  |
| Assembly (50 000 labour hours) | 30 000 | 70 000 |
| *Budgeted prime costs of production* |  | 130 000 |

| *Production overheads:* | £ | £ |
|---|---|---|
| Machine shop | 50 000 | |
| Assembly | 20 000 | 70 000 |
| | | |
| *Budgeted production costs* | | 200 000 |
| Administration overheads | | 20 000 |
| Selling and distribution overheads | | 30 000 |
| | | |
| Budgeted total costs | | 250 000 |
| Budgeted profit | | 50 000 |
| | | |
| *Budgeted sales* | | £300 000 |

Both products pass through the machine shop and assembly departments. Other details are:

| *Per Unit* | **Alpha** | | **Delpha** | |
|---|---|---|---|---|
| Direct materials | £14 | | | £15 |
| Direct labour: | | | | |
| Machine shop | | | | |
| 4 hrs @ £3/hr | 12 | 6 hrs @ £3/hr | | 18 |
| Assembly | | | | |
| 5 hrs @ £2/hr | 10 | 10 hrs @ £2/hr | | 20 |
| Selling prices | £60 | | | £90 |

Administration overheads are recovered as a percentage of production cost and selling and distribution overheads as a percentage of £'s sales.

| *Cost of Product* | **Alpha** | | **Delpha** | |
|---|---|---|---|---|
| | £ | | £ | |
| Direct materials | 14 | | 15 | |
| Direct labour: | | | | |
| Machine shop: | | | | |
| 4 hrs × £3 per hr. | 12 | 6 hrs × £3 per hr. | 18 | |
| Assembly: | | | | |
| 5 hrs × £2 per hr. | 10 | 10 hrs × £2 per hr. | 20 | |
| | — | | — | |
| *Prime cost per unit* | 36 | | 53 | |

| *Production overheads:* | £ | | | £ |
|---|---|---|---|---|
| *Machine shop:* | | | | |
| 4 hrs × £0·50 per hr. | 2 | 6 hrs × £0·50 per hr. | 3 | |
| Assembly shop: | | | | |
| 5 hrs × £0·40 per hr. | 2 | 10 hrs × £0·40 per hr. | 4 | |
| | — 4 | | — | 7 |
| *Production cost* | 40 | | | 60 |
| Administration overheads 10% on production cost | 4 | | | 6 |
| | — | | | — |
| Selling and distribution overheads 10% on selling price | 44 | | | 66 |
| | 6 | | | 9 |
| | — | | | — |
| *Total cost per unit* | 50 | | | 75 |
| Selling price | 60 | | | 90 |
| | — | | | — |
| *Profit per product* | 10 | | | 15 |

* Overhead rates have been computed as follows:

*Production overheads rates*
*Machine shop:*

$$\frac{\text{Budgeted overheads}}{\text{Budgeted machine hours}} = \frac{£50\,000}{100\,000 \text{ (hrs.)}} = £0·50 \text{ per hour}$$

*Assembly:*

$$\frac{\text{Budgeted overheads}}{\text{Budgeted assembly hours}} = \frac{£20\,000}{50\,000 \text{ labour hours}} = £0·40 \text{ per hour}$$

*Administration:*

$$\frac{\text{Budgeted administration overheads}}{\text{Budgeted production costs}} = \frac{£20\,000}{£200\,000} \times 100$$
$$= 10\% \text{ on production cost}$$

*Selling and distribution:*

$$\frac{\text{Budgeted selling and distribution costs}}{\text{Budgeted sales}}$$
$$= \frac{£30\,000}{300\,000} \times 100 = 10\% \text{ on selling price}$$

## Reliability of costing

Objections are often raised, particularly by the small concern, to the introduction of a costing system on the grounds of expense and this point should always be borne in mind. It is pointless for a business which previously made a £100 profit to introduce a costing system only to find that because of the extra expense incurred it now suffers a £100 loss. It is little satisfaction to the owners to be able to see how the loss arose.

Once established it is possible to place too much reliance on the costing system. A works manager might be asked to state the components of Job 123 by his managing director and he would be able to reply quite accurately. But if the question was how much Job 123 costs, his reply would of necessity be based on a number of estimates which would prevent absolute accuracy. It is essential that the person asking the questions should not expect as much accuracy in the answer to the second question as he might be able to in the first.

It is equally important to realise that just because a profit is made on each job in terms of the cost accounts it does not mean that the financial profit and loss account will reveal a similar healthy state. Certain items are omitted from cost accounts, such as loan interest, taxation and exceptional costs caused by, say, a fire. As these first two are originally management decisions, management should be aware of them when determining profit margins; but a more difficult problem is the over- or under-recovery of overheads. It has already been pointed out that the recovery rate is based on estimated expenses and if the estimates vary from the actual then there will be over- or under-recovery. Both these states can give rise to inaccurate costing statements. Under-recovery of overheads will mean that the costed profit is too great, for example:

| | |
|---|---|
| Estimated overhead | £5000 |
| Estimated machine hours | 1000 |
| Overhead recovery rate | £5 per machine hour |
| Actual overhead | £4000 |
| Actual machine hours | 700 |

The total amount recovered will be $700 \times £5 = £3500$, but the actual overhead amounted to £4000. This means that the costing profit is overstated by £500.

Over-recovery is equally dangerous, since the pricing policy of the concern may be needlessly high and uncompetitive because too high a charge is being made for overheads.

It is essential that reconciliation statements should be prepared at frequent intervals to ensure that after making the appropriate adjustments, the financial and cost accounts are in unison. The ideal situation is to have a fully integrated financial and costing system as part of the overall planning strategy using standard costing and budgetary control.

## Costing methods

Although the basic elements of costing apply to all concerns including non-profit-making bodies such as local authorities and hospitals, the needs of various types of concern are different, and costing systems have been designed to suit particular types of organisation.

The three main types of costing systems are:

(*a*)  job, contract or batch costing;
(*b*)  process costing or unit costing;
(*c*)  operating costing.

The first grouping is used where definite contracts or jobs are undertaken. Each job or contract is given a distinct reference number to which all the direct costs are charged. Indirect costs will form only a small proportion of the total cost of the job, particularly in contract costing. Batch costing is an extension of job costing where there are a number of similar items to be manufactured, but it is still possible to identify the particular batch and reference it accordingly.

Concerns likely to use contract costing are public works contractors and shipbuilders. Heavy engineering works might use job costing for, say, the production of individual electric alternators; and this system would also be used by the jobbing builder, plumber, electrician etc. Batch costing might be used to control the production of gear units or electric motors where perhaps a few thousand of each design are required.

A specimen job cost sheet is shown overleaf.

Process costing is applicable to concerns in which the product passes through a number of processes during its manufacture and it is required to ascertain the cost of each stage of the processing.

Industries such as soap-making, paper-making and distillation processes are all suitable for using this system.

The normal requirements for the system to operate effectively are that the end-product of one process should form the raw material of the next process, with any by-products of each process being accounted for in the process in which they occur. Examples of by-

**Job cost sheet**

Works Order No............................

Particulars: ......................................

......................................

DATE

CUSTOMER/DEPARTMENT: ...........................................................

Commenced .....................Completed.........................

| DATE REF. *Material* | | DETAILS *Labour* | | DIRECT COSTS *Expense* | | WORKS *Overhead* | |
|---|---|---|---|---|---|---|---|
| £ | p | £ | p | £ | p | £ | p |
| | | | | | | | |

Summary

Direct material
    „    wages
    „    expenses
Works overhead    ————
ADD
Administration
    overhead
Selling and
    distribution
    overhead    ————
Total cost
Profit            % on total cost .................

Selling price    Sales invoice
    ————    reference ......................

products are coke and tar in gas production, or cattle food in oil refining from copra.

A separate cost account is kept for each process, the allocation of costs being according to the normal method already outlined. At the end of each period a cost sheet will be prepared to show the total and unit costs of each process, and for the finished product.

Unit costing or output costing is used where only one commodity is produced and it is not normally necessary to require an extensive analysis of costs. This system may be used by a brickworks, ascertaining the cost per 1000 bricks, or a cement works ascertaining the cost per ton of cement produced. The cost sheet would show the costs incurred at each stage of manufacture under appropriate expense headings and the cost per unit of output during the period.

An example of a process cost sheet is shown on the following page.

**Operating costing**

This system is applicable to undertakings which perform a service rather than manufacture articles. The system is designed to show the cost of the service together with a cost per unit. Such services as hospitals (unit per patient/week) and police service (unit cost per 1000 population served or per police officer) are examples. In many cases it is not necessary to keep a separate set of cost accounts as the financial accounts can be designed to produce the necessary figures for the unit calculations.

Of necessity this chapter gives only the briefest outline of historical costing, and it is intended to act primarily as an introduction to cost terminology which will be met in later chapters.

## Process cost sheet

*Accounting Period:* ............................

| Item | Process No. 1 Description ................ Units Produced............ | | | Process No. 2 Description ................ Units Produced............ | | |
|---|---|---|---|---|---|---|
| | Quantity | Value | Cost per Unit | Quantity | Value | Cost per Unit |
| Material in process 1/-/-- Raw material | | | | | | |
| Less material in process 31/-/-- | | | | | | |
| Process expenses (from cost accounts) | | | | | | |
| Less value of residuals | | | | | | |
| Loss in weight (a) | | Nil | Nil | | Nil | Nil |
| | | | | | | |
| Net works cost | | | | | | |
| Corresponding figures last period | | | | | | |

(a) Loss in weight occurs in many processes and affects the quantity but not of course the cost i.e. there is no value attributed to the loss.

Historical costs may be useful for analysing past results and revealing weaknesses, but mistakes are not discovered or remedied until after the event. There is also no yardstick by which the actual results can be measured, and it is insufficient to be satisfied merely with the fact that a profit has been made. Management also needs to know whether profits are being maximised and assured that inefficiencies and wastage have been eliminated.

In order that management can control costs much more effectively and have something to measure results against it is necessary to operate a standard costing system.

The management accountant will be primarily concerned with the operation and results of such a system, and the next chapter will therefore outline the setting up and operation of a standard costing system.

## Questions

**1** What are the various elements of cost?

**2** Distinguish between a cost which is considered to be a direct cost and a cost which is deemed to be an indirect cost.

**3** Discuss the various methods of allocating costs to products.

**4** 'It is never possible in a multi-product industry to obtain the true cost of a specific product. At best it is a good estimate.' Discuss.

**5** The 'TUXO' Company produces two products X and Y. Management has decided that production overheads be allocated to the products on a percentage of direct materials basis. The following data applies:

|  | **X** $£$ |  | **Y** $£$ |
|---|---|---|---|
| Direct Materials: |  |  |  |
| 4 kg @ $£$1/kg | 4 | 10 kg @ $£$2/kg | 20 |
| Direct wages: |  |  |  |
| 2 hrs. @ $£$2·50/hr. | 5 | 2 hrs. @ $£$2·50/hr. | 5 |
| *Prime cost* | 9 |  | 25 |

Budgeted production overheads for the period are $£$40 000.
Budgeted direct materials cost for the period are $£$80 000.

You are required to compute the production cost for products X and Y and to state whether you agree with management on the method of allocating production overheads.

# 6 Standard Costing

The setting of standards as a basis of measurement and comparison applies to many different fields of activity. A school, for example, will establish standards by which academic achievements may be measured and compared, or an inspection department in a manufacturing plant will set standards against which actual production can be measured and either be passed or rejected.

A standard may therefore be said to be a basis for the measurement of the adequacy or inadequacy of the results of a particular activity. When applied to cost accounting, standard costing involves the establishment of predetermined costs usually on a unit basis, in other words a standard quantity of materials, a standard labour rate, a standard time and a standard overhead rate, necessary to produce a given unit of output. The standards will remain unchanged as long as the method of operation and basic prices used to set the standards remain the same.

The differences between the actual costs and the standard costs are known as 'variances', and the breakdown of the total variances into different components is known as 'variance analysis'.

The main advantages of standard costing are:

1   The setting of standards involves establishing the most efficient methods of producing the unit which in itself may lead to economies.

2   Actual performance may be compared with a predetermined standard revealing favourable or adverse variances and also allowing the principle of 'management by exception' to operate when everything is going according to plan.

3   Cost-consciousness is stimulated throughout the organisation.

4   It is possible to establish which variances are due to external influences (for instance, a price increase over which management have little control) and which are caused by internal influences.

5   By the establishment of cost centres it is possible to define responsibilities. (A cost centre may be a location, a person or an item of equipment to which costs can be allocated and used for control purposes.)

Budgetary control and standard costing are closely linked, since they both involve the forecasting of expenses and the comparison of the actual results with the forecast. Although it is possible to operate one without the other it is usually much more satisfactory if they are operated together. For example, once standard costs are established it is easy to prepare the production and sales budgets, and the setting of the standard costs is made easier if a budget is already in existence which shows expected levels of output.

The word 'standard' is meaningless unless it is qualified by a description of the type of standard being contemplated. Standards fall into three broad categories:

(a)   strict or ideal;
(b)   attainable or expected actual;
(c)   loose (this would obviously never be knowingly set by management).

### Strict standards

These represent the maximum of efficiency of all the cost elements and may be said to be the standard of perfection, which is obviously unrealistic and would only be experienced for very short periods of time. The setting of such standards may motivate employees to increase their output to the maximum, but if the standards are still not attained, their morale may be seriously affected.

### Attainable standards

These are the standards which are expected to be achieved in the period, with reasonable effort. The variations which do arise are more likely to be measures of superior or inferior performance than variances due to poor original standards. But it still may be that the standards are too low for the better type of employee and too high for the less skilled worker.

### Loose standards

If standards are easily achieved, actual results may be better than standard, allowing management to indulge in self-congratulation. However, such achievements may result in employees' reducing their output to conform with the standards and there is certainly no inducement to increase performance.

It is most beneficial if both an ideal and an expected actual standard are calculated. This ensures that actual results can be compared with two standards and prevents the expected standard from becoming a loose standard.

If standards are set which are expected to be in operation for some considerable time, they are called 'basic standards', and when revisions become necessary they are made using index numbers. This is the same principle as that used to record the changes in the cost of living: a base period is fixed (say, 1st January 19-- = 100) and subsequent increases or decreases in the cost of living are represented by additions or subtractions to the basic 100 figure.

It is necessary to establish standards for each type of cost – labour, materials, overheads – and this will normally be the responsibility of management. The cost accountant must, however, work in close co-operation with other departments, and particularly with the time-and-motion study engineers whose work will have a great influence on the times set for the particular tasks.

## Variances

One of the most valuable uses of standard costing as an aid to control by management is in the presentation of variances. Where actual results are better than the standard a favourable variance will be shown. When the results are worse than estimated an adverse variance arises.

Basically there are two types of variances: one results from a change in price and the other from a change in quantity or volume.

Several different variances are used to reflect particular reasons for differences which may occur, but they all depend on these two basic functions, price and quantity. The importance of variance analysis is as a controlling device, enabling management to ascertain the reason for variances from the people responsible for incurring them, and to take corrective action whenever necessary. It must be appreciated that every adverse variance has the effect of reducing the budgeted profit and the sooner action is taken to remedy such trends the less will be the effect on the final profit target. The principal variances which we will consider are:

(*a*)  total cost variance;
(*b*)  direct materials cost variance;
(*c*)  direct wage variance;
(*d*)  overhead variance.

Different variances will be used by different industries but these four will be common to all. It will probably be appreciated that the variance (*a*) is made up of variances (*b*) + (*c*) + (*d*). Each of these latter three variances is subject to further analysis to enable the effect of our two basic functions to be ascertained – price and quantity.

The diagram on page 71 shows the relationships between the different types of variances.

It is important to remember that the difference between the actual cost and the standard cost of a particular activity is the total cost variance and each of the other variances must add up to this figure. Similarly the direct wages variance is a combination of the direct wages rate variance and the direct labour efficiency variance. It follows that if you have two out of three of these variances the other can be found either by subtraction or addition:

Direct wages rate variance + Direct labour efficiency
  variance
  = Direct wage variance

or

Direct wages variance – Direct wages rate variance
  = Direct labour efficiency variance

However, it is as well to calculate all the variances to ensure that no errors have been made. It should be noted that the formula used to calculate the variances in this chapter are so framed that a positive result will mean a favourable variance and a negative result an adverse variance. This procedure differs from that of a number of textbooks, but it is felt that by adopting this system a better understanding of the concept of variance analysis is possible.

## Material cost variance

This is the difference between the standard cost of materials specified for a particular operation and the actual cost of the materials used. The formula is:

$$SC - AC$$
(Standard cost – Actual cost)

**Material price variance**    This is the difference between the standard price of the material specified and the actual price paid. The formula is:

$$AQ(SP - AP)$$
(Actual quantity (Standard price – Actual price))

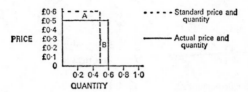

**Material usage variance** This is the difference between the standard quantity which should have been consumed and the actual quantity used, calculated at the standard price. The formula is:

$$SP(SQ - AQ)$$
(Standard price (Standard quantity − Actual quantity))

Let us consider a practical example:

It is estimated that 1 kg of material will produce 10 articles. The standard price of material is £0·50 per kg. During a specified period 100 kg of material were issued which cost £45 and the actual production was 1100 articles.

The calculation of the variances is as follows:

*Materials cost variance:*

$$SC - AC$$

Standard cost

= Actual production (1100) × Standard cost/unit

$$\left( \text{i.e.} \quad \frac{\text{Standard cost per kg} \text{£}0·50}{\text{Standard output per kg } 10} = \text{£}0·05 \right)$$

$$= 1100 \times \text{£}0·05 = \text{£}55$$

$$SC - AC$$

£55 − £45 = £10 favourable

*Price variance*:

$$AQ(SP - AP)$$

100 kg(£0·50 − £0·45)

100 × £0·05 = £5 favourable

*Usage variance:*

$$SP(SQ - AQ)$$

$$\text{Standard quantity} = \frac{\text{Actual quantity}}{\text{Standard output}} = \frac{1100}{10} = 110$$

£0·50(110 − 100) = £5 favourable

*Check*:

|  | £ |
|---|---|
| *Price variance* | 5 favourable |
| *Usage variance* | 5 favourable |
| *Total material variance* | £ 10 favourable |

It is possible to illustrate the principles of variance analysis diagrammatically and this is illustrated on page 69.

Assume that the standard price of material is £0·60 per kg and that each unit uses 0·5 kg of material. The actual price of the material was £0·50 per kg and the actual usage was 0·6 kg per unit.

The price variance is represented by the quadrant **A**:

$$£0·10 × 0·5 = £0·05 \text{ favourable}$$

The usage variance is represented by quadrant **B**:

$$£0·50 × 0·1 = £0·05 \text{ unfavourable}$$

The net result is:

|  | £ |
|---|---|
| *Price variance* | 0·05 favourable |
| *Usage variance* | 0·05 unfavourable |
| *Total variance* | NIL |

This result can be checked from the information contained in the example:

|  |  | £ |
|---|---|---|
| *Standard cost* | £0·60 × 0·5 = | 0·30 per unit |
| *Actual cost* | £0·50 × 0·6 = | 0·30 per unit |
| *Variance* | | NIL |

This example does illustrate the value of breaking down a total variance, in this case the material variance, into its component parts. The total variance is nil but the breakdown reveals an unfavourable usage variance for which management will require an explanation.

This diagrammatic presentation reveals its limitations when both variances are favourable, and it is better to master the formula approach to variance analysis to avoid these limitations.

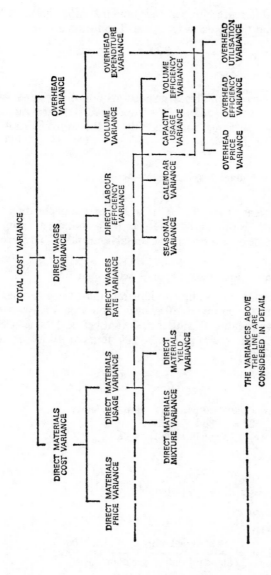

**Fig. 6.1** Cost variance analysis chart

TOTAL COST VARIANCE

DIRECT MATERIALS COST VARIANCE

DIRECT MATERIALS PRICE VARIANCE

DIRECT MATERIALS USAGE VARIANCE

DIRECT MATERIALS MIXTURE VARIANCE

DIRECT MATERIALS YIELD VARIANCE

DIRECT WAGES VARIANCE

DIRECT WAGES RATE VARIANCE

DIRECT LABOUR EFFICIENCY VARIANCE

SEASONAL VARIANCE

CALENDAR VARIANCE

OVERHEAD VARIANCE

VOLUME VARIANCE

OVERHEAD EXPENDITURE VARIANCE

CAPACITY USAGE VARIANCE

VOLUME EFFICIENCY VARIANCE

OVERHEAD PRICE VARIANCE

OVERHEAD EFFICIENCY VARIANCE

OVERHEAD UTILISATION VARIANCE

THE VARIANCES ABOVE THE LINE ARE CONSIDERED IN DETAIL

**Direct wages variance**

This is the difference between the standard wages specified for the operation and the actual wages paid. The formula is:

$$SC - AC$$
(Standard cost – Actual cost)

**Wages rate variance**   This is the portion of the direct wages variance which is due to the difference between the standard rate of pay specified and the actual rate paid (this is the equivalent of a price variance). The formula is:

$$AH(SR - AR)$$
(Actual hours (Standard rate – Actual rate))

**Labour efficiency variance**   This is the portion of the direct wages variance which is due to the difference in the standard labour hours specified for the operation and the actual hours taken. The formula is:

$$SR(SH - AH)$$
(Standard rate (Standard hours – Actual hours))

Let us consider an example to illustrate these wage variances. The standard time for producing 10 units is 2 hours and the standard rate of pay is £4 per hour. During the relevant period 1100 articles were produced and the wages paid were 200 hours at £3·75 per hour.

*Wages variance:*

$SC - AC$

Standard cost = actual output at standard rate/units
  = 1100 × £0·80 = £880
  £880 − £750 = £130 favourable variance

*Rate variance:*

$AH(SR - AR)$
200 (£4·00 − £3·75) = £50 favourable

*Efficiency variance*

$SR(SH - AH)$

$$\text{Standard hour} = \frac{\text{Actual output}}{\text{Standard output per hour}} = \frac{1100}{5}$$

  = 220
£4·00 (220 − 200) = £80 favourable

*Check:*

| | £ |
|---|---|
| *Rate variance* | 50 favourable |
| *Efficiency variance* | 80 favourable |
| | |
| *Total wage variance* | 130 favourable |

One point which must be considered when calculating wages variance is idle time. Although an allowance will have been made for this when the standard hour was calculated it would not cover such abnormal happenings as prolonged machine breakdowns. If separate account is not taken for these periods employees may be blamed for an adverse efficiency variance which was in fact nothing to do with them. If in the above example the 200 actual hours included 10 hours idle time, then an adverse idle variance would arise calculated as follows:

Idle hours × Standard rate
$$10 \times £4{\cdot}00 = £40 \text{ adverse}$$

This would increase the efficiency variance by a similar amount, that is from £80 favourable to £120 favourable.

## Overhead variances

We have already made a distinction between fixed overheads and variable overheads and variances are calculated for both types of overhead expense. The variable overhead is fairly straightforward as it will vary more or less directly with output.

**Variable overhead variance** The formula is:

$$SC - AC$$
(Standard cost − Actual cost)

Example: the standard variable overhead is £0·40 per unit. During the period the actual variable overhead expenses incurred were £500, and the actual production was 1100 units.

$$SC - AC$$
$$£440 - £500 = £60 \text{ adverse}$$

**Fixed overhead variances** These variances are probably the most difficult ones to appreciate and they have the largest number of any of the variances. Fixed overheads imply that the expenses do not vary with changes in the level of production unless there is a deliberate change of policy by management. They include such items as depreciation, rent, rates, salaries, etc., and they will not vary whether the output is 70% of capacity or 95%. The amount of overhead recovered will depend on the output, however, and the difference between the amount of overhead charged to output and the actual overhead expenses incurred results in over- or under-recovery of fixed overhead.

**Cost variance**   This is the difference between the overhead recovered at standard rates and the actual overhead incurred. The formula is:

$$SC - AC$$
(Standard cost − Actual cost)

**Volume variance**   This is the portion which is due to the differences between the budgeted and actual output at standard overhead rates. The formula is:

$$SR(AQ - BQ)$$
(Standard rate (Actual quantity − Budgeted quantity))

**Expenditure variance**   This is the portion of the cost variance which is due to differences between the budgeted overhead for the period and the actual overhead incurred. The formula is:

$$BC - AC$$
(Budgeted cost − Actual cost)

**Efficiency variance**   This is the difference between the actual quantity of units produced and the standard quantity which should have been produced multiplied by the standard overhead rate. The formula is:

$$SR (AQ - SQ)$$
(Standard rate (Actual quantity − Standard quantity))

**Capacity variance**   This is the difference between the budgeted quantity and the standard quantity multiplied by the standard rate. (Such a difference will usually be due to fewer hours being worked than expected, e.g. if the budgeted output for a 40-hour week is 1000 units and the standard output per hour is 25 units, then, if through idle time only 38 hours are worked in a particular week, the number of units which should be produced in the time available is $38 \times 25$, i.e.

950 units.) The formula is:

$$SR\ (SQ - BQ)$$
(Standard rate (Standard quantity − Budgeted quantity))

Both the efficiency and the capacity variance are sub-variances of the volume variance. The relationships are illustrated in the diagram below which forms part of the total cost variance diagram appearing on page 71.

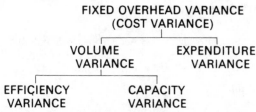

Let us now see how these variances work out in a practical problem.

Example: During a period the budgeted output was 1000 units, 20 000 units being the budgeted output for the year at a budgeted fixed overhead of £50 000. Standard performance is 5 units per hour and the actual fixed overheads were £3300. The actual hours worked were 200 and the actual output was 1100 units.

*Fixed overhead variance* (*cost variance*):

SC − AC
Standard cost = Actual output × Standard rate
$$= 1100 \times £2 \cdot 50$$
$$= £2750$$
£2750 − £3300 = £550 adverse
$$\left( \text{Standard rate is found by} \frac{\text{Budgeted fixed overhead}}{\text{Budgeted output}} \right)$$

*Volume variance*:

$$SR\ (AQ - BQ)$$
$$£2 \cdot 50\ (1100 - 1000) = £250 \text{ favourable}$$

*Expenditure variance:*

$$BC - AC$$
$$£2500 - £3300 = £800 \text{ adverse}$$

$$\left( \text{Budget cost} = \frac{\text{Budgeted output for period}}{\text{Budgeted output for year}} \times \text{Total fixed budget} \right)$$

$$\left( \frac{1000}{20000} \times £50\,000 = £2500 \right)$$

*Check*:

| | £ |
|---|---|
| *Volume variance* | 250 favourable |
| *Expenditure variance* | 800 adverse |
| *Fixed overhead variance* | 550 adverse |

*Sub-volume variances: Efficiency variance*

$$SR (AQ - SQ)$$
Standard quantity = Actual hours × Standard
quantity per hour
$$£2{\cdot}50 (1100 - 1000) = £250 \text{ favourable}$$

*Capacity variance:*

$$SR (SQ - BQ)$$
$$£2{\cdot}50 (1000 - 1000) = 0$$

*Check:*

| | £ |
|---|---|
| *Efficiency variance* | 250 favourable |
| *Capacity variance* | 0 |
| *Volume variance* | 250 favourable |

You will no doubt have noticed that the examples used to illustrate each of the main variances (i.e. materials, labour and overhead) are related and we can now consider the complete problem.

*Summarised problem*
During a particular period the following standards and estimates were in operation:

1 kg of material will produce 10 articles
Standard price of material is £0·50
Standard time for producing 10 articles is 2 hours
Standard rate of pay is £4·00 per hour
Budgeted output is 1000 units
Budgeted variable overhead is £0·40 per unit
Budgeted fixed overhead is £2500

The following actual costs, etc., were incurred during this period:

100 kg of material was issued at a cost of £0·45 per kg
Actual production was 1100 articles

200 hours were worked at a cost of £3·75 per hour
Variable overhead expenses were £500
Fixed overhead expenses were £3300

The basic variances may be summarised by the following tables.
These are the figures which have been calculated earlier in this chapter
using the relevant formulae.

| *Variance* | *Adverse* | *Fav.* | *Net ±* |
|---|---|---|---|
| | £ | £ | £ |
| Direct materials: | | | |
| Price | | 5 | |
| Usage | | 5 | 10 + |
| | | — | |
| Direct wages: | | | |
| Rate | | 50 | |
| Efficiency | | 80 | 130 + |
| | | — | |
| Variable overhead: | 60 | | 60 − |
| Fixed overhead: | | | |
| Volume | | 250 | |
| Expenditure | 800 | | 550 − |
| | | | ——— |
| *Total cost variance* | | *adverse* | £470 |

This total cost variance can also be checked by comparing the
actual costs with the standards for the actual output.

| *Cost Element* | *Standard* | | *Actual* | *Variance* | |
|---|---|---|---|---|---|
| | *Per article* | *Per output 1100 articles* | | *Fav.* | *Adv.* |
| | £ | £ | £ | £ | £ |
| Materials | 0·05 | 55 | 45 | 10 | |
| Labour | 0·80 | 880 | 750 | 130 | |
| Variable overhead | 0·40 | 440 | 500 | | 60 |
| Fixed overhead | 2·50 | 2750 | 3300 | | 550 |
| | ——— | ——— | ——— | ——— | ——— |
| | 3·75 | £4125 | £4595 | £140 | £610 |
| Net | | | | | £470 |

Management must be presented with the results produced by the standard costing system as quickly as possible if the full benefits of utilising such a system are to be obtained and the necessary action to correct variances must be taken immediately.

The statement presented to management would be as follows for our example, assuming that sales are £5000:

**Profit and Loss Statement for the Period Ending 31/12/––**

|  | £ | £ |
|---|---|---|
| Sales (actual) |  | 5000 |
| *Less* Standard cost of sales |  |  |
| Materials | 55 |  |
| Labour | 880 |  |
| Overhead | 3190 | 4125 |
| *Standard net profit* |  | £875 |

*Variances:* (The table on the previous page would be produced here)

Total cost variance £470 adverse

Actual net profit   £405

From this statement management is able to see that profit for the period was £470 less than anticipated, mainly owing to the actual variable and fixed overhead expenses being more than the estimated amounts.

Explanations for these variances should be obtained from the buyer etc. and appropriate action taken to remedy the situation. It may be that the standards for these variances require amending.

## Sales variances

Many companies that have installed a standard cost system restrict it to showing the effects on profits of adverse or favourable variances of labour, materials and overhead costs. However, a complete system should also produce sales variances.

There are two methods for calculating sales variances and their results are not compatible. One method shows the effect of a change in sales on turnover and the basic variance is found by taking the actual sales from the budgeted sales, in other words BS – AS. This basic variance is composed of two sub-variances, in other words volume variance represented by (*a*) *Budgeted sales – Standard sales* and (*b*) a price variance represented by *Standard selling price – Actual selling price*.

The other method shows the effect of a change in sales on profits rather than turnover. The basic variance is calculated by the formula, *Budgeted profit − Actual profit*, and again the two components of this basic variance are volume, represented by *Budgeted profit − Standard profit*, and price, represented by *Standard profit − Actual profit*.

It is not proposed to show a detailed example, as the calculations using the above formula are quite straightforward. The only items which perhaps require an explanation are standard sales and standard profit. Standard sales are calculated by multiplying the actual sales in units by the standard or budgeted price per unit and standard profit is found by multiplying the actual quantity by the standard or budgeted profit per unit.

The variances not considered in detail in this chapter, such as material mix and yield, overhead calender etc., are rather complicated and beyond the scope of this book. If further information on these variances is required, suitable texts will be found in the bibliography at the end of this book.

## Questions

**1** Discuss the main advantages of standard costing.
**2** What are the three broad categories of the word 'standard' as applied to standard costing?
**3** Draw a chart to show the main variances and sub-variances as applied to standard costing.
**4** Design a suitable statement for presenting variances to management.
**5** 'Standards provide an incentive for improvement, thereby producing new and better standards.' Discuss.
**6** The following data applies to the production of a standard product known as product X: Standard quantity 500 kg of material P, standard price per kg £1·20. During a certain month 600 kg of P was actually used and the actual price paid for material P was £0·80 per kg.

You are required to compute:

(*i*)   the total direct material cost variance
(*ii*)  analyse the total variance in (*i*) by computing

    (*a*)   the material price variance;
    (*b*)   the material usage variance.

**7** The standard time allowed for producing one unit of a standard product is 45 minutes. The standard rate of pay is £3·20 per hour. During a certain month 2000 units of the product were produced at a labour cost of £5100. The time actually taken to produce 2000 units was 1500 hours.

From the above data:

(*i*)   Compute the total variance and analyse this variance into
(*ii*)  Wage rate variance
(*iii*) Labour efficiency variance.

**8**   The standard variable overhead for a particular production department
has been budgeted as follows:

Budgeted variable overhead for the period: £50 000.
Budgeted volume of production for the period: 100 000 units.

During the period under review the actual variable overheads incurred
amounted to £70 000, the actual production was 120 000 units.
Compute the variable overhead variance.

**9**   At a certain factory the budgeted quantity of units to be produced was
5000 units for a 20 working day month. The budgeted fixed overhead for the
period was £10 000.

During the month the actual quantity produced was 3750 units. Actual
fixed overhead incurred amounted to £12 000. The standard rate of
production has been set at 250 units per working day. Only 18 days were
actually worked during the month.

You are required to compute the following variances:

(*i*)   Volume variance
(*ii*)  Expenditure variance
(*iii*) Capacity variance
(*iv*)  Efficiency variance.

**10**   The following data applies to the Denby Cheese Shop.

### Budgeted Sales for Week

*Budgeted*

| Cheese Type | Qty. kg | Selling Price per kg | Std. Cost per kg | Profit per kg |
|---|---|---|---|---|
| 'Glendale' | 160 | £1·50 | £1·00 | £0·50 |
| 'Ireshire' | 60 | £1·00 | £0·70 | £0·30 |

*Actual Sales for Week*
*Actual*

| | AQ | Act. SP | Std. cost per kg | Act. std. profit per kg |
|---|---|---|---|---|
| | 120 | £1·60 | £1·00 | £0·60 |
| | 40 | £0·80 | £0·70 | £0·10 |

*Actual cost of sales:*

£0·90 per kg ('Glendale')
£0·80 per kg ('Ireshire')

 (*i*)   Compute the total sales margin variance and analyse into:

     (*a*)   Sales volume variance

     (*b*)   Sales price variance.

 (*ii*)  Compute the purchase price variance.

(*iii*)  Draw up a Profit and Loss Account showing the variances and actual profit.

(*iv*)  Reconcile the actual net profit in (*iii*) with a conventional profit and loss account.

# 7 Budgeting and Budgetary Control

In any business or even in any non-profit making organisation the need to plan ahead is imperative. The very discipline of planning is in itself a vital component for success, since in formulating a plan or strategy it is necessary to bring to bear a critical appraisal of existing conditions and this may result in economies at the outset.

To plan is to formulate a strategy, and this in turn gives the business a sense of direction. Once the business has set its goals, the tactical plans will enable it to navigate towards its objectives. Where, after the plan has been put into operation, conditions prevail which tend to cause deviations from the plan, corrective action can take place to steer the business back on course.

The main functions of management are to plan, co-ordinate, motivate and control, and the application of these functions is vital if the firm is to achieve its objectives. Since the very survival of a business depends ultimately upon its financial function the technique of Budgeting and Budgetary Control makes a vital contribution to the management function.

A firm does not operate in a closed system but is like a ship at sea exposed to the external environment, which, as will be appreciated, can be unpredictable and volatile. It might be said by some that if the external environment is so unpredictable, why bother planning for the future? Surely, however, it is far better to have a plan than no plan at all. Indeed, if one was embarking on a voyage or flight one would surely plan the route and a prerequisite for such a plan would be to know the ultimate destination or goal.

Of course, during the voyage one may be forced off course but every effort will be made to correct such deviations from the navigational plan in order to reach the goal. Perhaps this very correction factor exercised by means of control may be needed for ultimate survival. Therefore it must be conceded that it is better to have a plan rather than no plan at all.

The Institute of Cost and Management Accountants define budgets as 'Financial and/or quantitative statements prepared and approved prior to a defined period of time of the policy to be pursued during that period for the purpose of attaining a given objective. They may include income, expenditure and the employment of capital.' This definition is very much concerned with planning, and planning as such must form an important function of management, covering all aspects of business activity. Both long-term projects and day-to-day operations need planning in accordance with future expectations. The plan which is prepared to show how resources will be required and used over a period is known as a budget, the act of preparing the plan is known as budgeting and the use of the plan to control activities is known as budgetary control.

In Chapter 2 we showed that it was possible for a balance sheet to be prepared for an ordinary individual in the same way as for sole traders, partnerships and companies. Similarly everyone prepares and uses a budget of one sort or another. An individual will estimate what he is likely to earn in the coming months and plan his expenditure on food, rent, car expenses and so on. In order to be able to control his expenditure it is normally necessary for him to set limits on how much he will spend on individual items. The housewife will budget for an even shorter period, usually a week. As actual expenditure is incurred, a comparison can be made with the budgeted estimate and revisions undertaken, depending upon whether actual expenditure exceeds or is less than the estimate.

A business will prepare a budget for similar purposes; but it will need to be more detailed so that control can be exercised over all aspects of the enterprise.

## Advantages of budgets

Despite the obvious advantages there are still many businesses which never use budgets. They claim that budgeting is possible in some concerns but not in their own, because they maintain that there are too many complications and uncertainties to make it worth while. However, once a concern is persuaded to adopt budgeting it rapidly becomes convinced of its benefits and is surprised that it was ever able to succeed before introducing the system. Certainly it will usually be found that the leading concerns in any industry are those that use budgeting, together with other relevant techniques such as standard costing and variance analysis, to the full. The preparation of a budget is itself extremely beneficial, as it forces the person responsible for incurring expenses or for generating income to plan for the future, and to anticipate changes and make suitable adjustments. Too frequently a business is run on a day-to-day basis without any thought being given to the future. The proprietor is likely to finish up by fulfilling Mr Micawber's second, gloomy, prediction – 'Annual income twenty pounds, annual expenditure nineteen and six, result happiness. Annual income twenty pounds, annual expenditure twenty pounds nought and six, result misery.' The objectives and goals of the business are then lost, or take a back seat to current pressures; but unless these goals are prominent the whole organisation lacks direction, and results are difficult to predict.

To prepare the overall or master budget it is necessary for all sections of the business to co-operate and to be aware of other section's limitations as well as their own. To prepare the actual figures it is necessary to have a sound system of recording information; this in itself facilitates better control, as the information obtained from such records can be used to compare performances with the budget and as a guide for future budgets.

The preparation and use of budgets also ensures that all members of the organisation are aware of the need to conserve business resources, and are aware that they may be called to account for expenses which they incur.

It is possible for inefficiencies to be revealed either during the budget preparation period or when comparisons of actual performances with estimates are made.

Control becomes centralised while individual managers become responsible for their particular activity. This planning and control should result in maximum profitability being achieved because the planned use of resources yields better results than haphazard use.

## Requirements for budgeting

For a budgeting system to be effective it is necessary to have a sound organisation structure. It is then possible to create budget centres within such a structure with clearly defined responsibilities. Departments may be budget centres or, if such departments are large, sub-groupings may be arranged, for example a number of similar machines or a particular process. Each centre will have a manager or centre head who will be responsible not only for the preparation of the budget information for his centre but also for the actual results as compared with the original estimates.

It is helpful to prepare a budget manual which sets out the responsibilities of all persons connected with the budgeting system and the procedure to be followed. Each person should know what the system is and what are its objectives. He should know the procedure to be followed when submitting relevant information, including deadline dates and the various codes which may be in use. Such a manual will often be in loose-leaf form so that amendments are easily made. Network analysis can be a valuable tool in budget preparation. This technique involves scheduling the various stages involved in budgeting and then preparing a logical sequence diagram which enables control to be exercised over the time element in the preparation of each stage.

It is necessary to have someone responsible for budget preparation. In a small concern this may be the job of the accountant but in a large concern a budget committee is frequently established which exercises overall control over the budgeting procedures. Such a committee will usually be chaired by the chief executive officer and may well consist of all heads of the various departments.

The accountant may act as budget officer, co-ordinating the committee's work in addition to preparing his own budgets such as the cash, capital expenditure and administration budgets.

The budgeting system can be shown diagrammatically as set out on the following page.

The time-span for budgeting will vary depending upon the uncertainties involved and the type of business. Long-range budgets are usually concerned with capital expenditure and may span five or more years. Short-term budgets, such as the cash budget, may only cover a week. Master budgets which consolidate an organisation's overall goals are usually prepared on an annual basis, mainly to fall in line with taxation/accounting requirements. For control purposes it is usual to subdivide the annual budget into a monthly or four-weekly period budget. This does create problems of allocation, since many expenses do not occur evenly throughout the year, but variances are spotted sooner and action may be taken to remedy deficiencies as soon as the monthly comparisons have been made.

It is important that the individual carrying out a particular task should be consulted when the budget for that task is being prepared. It is probably a good idea to allow the individual to prepare his own budget, which can then be incorporated in the general budget for the particular cost centre. The advantages of involving the individual in budget preparation are as follows:

1   The person doing the job is in the best position to make reliable estimates.
2   He will realise that his work matters and that he is a member of a team working towards a common objective. He will also be able to appreciate how his section of work fits into the overall pattern.
3   If he makes his own estimate he is likely to try to see that it is carried out.

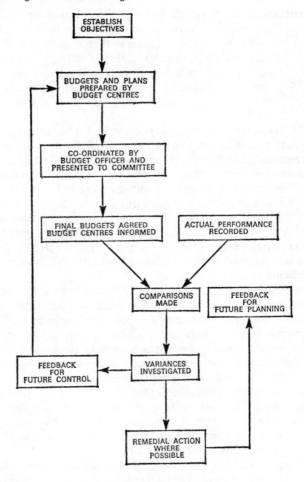

**Fig. 7.1**   The budget procedure

4   It is difficult for him to blame anyone but himself if the estimate proves to be wrong.

It is important that these individual estimates are subject to scrutiny by a senior member of the cost centre to ensure that the estimates are realistic, and that they have not been inflated to produce an apparently favourable variance when comparisons between actual results and estimates are made.

## The limiting factor

The 'limiting factor', or 'principal budget factor' as it is often called, is of vital importance when the budget is being prepared. It may not be the same factor for each budget period, but the extent of its influence must be fully assessed in order to ensure that the functional budgets are realistic.

Some examples of limiting factors which may have to be considered are:

( *a* )  production capacity;
( *b* )  shortage of space;
( *c* )  shortage of key personnel;
( *d* )  shortage of material;
( *e* )  low market demand;
( *f* )  limited amount of capital available;
( *g* )  poor management of resources.

Generally the two most important factors are demand for the products, and production capacity. It is a waste of time producing 10 000 items if only 5000 can be sold; alternatively, the business is not maximising its profits if 10 000 could be sold profitably but only 5000 are produced. It is important therefore to establish what the normal volume of activity is before the functional budgets are begun. This ensures that all sections are aware of the restrictions to which the business is subject, and that money is not wasted on excessive material purchases, or excessive labour costs, or 'pie-in-the-sky' budgeting.

## Types of budget

The Master Budget will comprise a number of Functional Budgets, in other words those which relate to a particular function of the business, together with the Financial Budgets such as the Cash Budget, the Statement of Sources and Application of Funds and the Budgeted Final Accounts. The main functional budgets are:

( *a* )  Sales;
( *b* )  Production;
( *c* )  Plant utilisation;
( *d* )  Manpower;
( *e* )  Direct materials;
( *f* )  Direct labour;
( *g* )  Manufacturing overheads;
( *h* )  Selling and distribution expenses;
( *i* )  Administrative expenses;
( *j* )  Cash;
( *k* )  Capital;
( *l* )  Financial.

All these budgets are, of course, interrelated: for example, it is not possible to draw up the materials purchase budget without knowing the type and quantity of product to be manufactured. A cash budget cannot be prepared until all the sales and expenses have been estimated.

It is usual, unless there are special circumstances, for a business to begin its budgeting by preparing the sales forecast for the budget period. This can then be used as a basis for the production budget, selling expenses budget, materials budget, cash budget and so on.

The relationship between the various budgets is shown diagrammatically below.

As already mentioned the sales budget is usually of vital importance, but unfortunately it is also one of the most difficult to prepare. The sales budget will be based upon a sales forecast, which in itself is subject to many factors, such as the pricing policy of the business, the general economic outlook and the outlook for the products of the

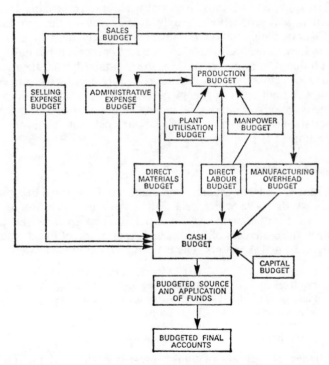

**Fig. 7.2** Budget relationships

particular business. For example, in times of austerity one might expect the sales of luxury goods to be reduced and the opposite to be the case in times of prosperity.

## Sales forecast

Much progress in this field has been made in recent years, but there is still a long way to go before the process is anywhere near perfect. The two main methods involved are dealt with below.

1 *Opinion of salesmen and sales managers*
As these are the people most directly concerned with sales their opinions can be a valuable guide to future sales. Each area sales manager and each salesman is issued with a forecast sheet for the coming period. Each individual prepares his own forecast, and these can then be compared and an overall sales estimate prepared. Only products which have been selling for some time should be included on the forecast sheet as it would be unfair to expect a salesman to estimate the demand for an entirely new product.

The usual information contained in such a forecast would be, for each product, the sales for the previous year, the average over a number of years, the trend over say three years, and a column for the estimate.

This is illustrated as follows:

### THE EXPANDO CO. LTD
**Sales Forecast for the Year Ending 31st December 19--**

Sales Area  ...........................

Salesman ............................

| Product Average | Average Sales for Last Five Years | Trend for Past Three Years % ± | Sales last Year | *Units* Estimate |
|---|---|---|---|---|
| A | | | | |
| B | | | | |
| C | | | | |
| | ___ | ___ | ___ | ___ |

2 *Market research and statistical techniques*
The purpose of market research is:

(*i*)   to determine the actual and potential field of sales;
(*ii*)   to study the methods to be used to create demand where it does not already exist, and to consider the adequacy of present methods of selling;
(*iii*)   to study the most effective means of distribution;
(*iv*)   to assess the potential purchasing power in the field of sales.

Data may be collected in a number of ways. It may involve consumer research, or perusal of trade journals and government publications such as the *Monthly Digest of Statistics*. The research may also be conducted by internal staff or by employing a specialist market research agency. The main information which market research should reveal is:

(*i*)   where the customer buys goods of the class in question;
(*ii*)   how frequently and in what quantities the goods are bought;
(*iii*)   the effect of packaging on customer decisions;
(*iv*)   the effect of price and 'discounts' on customers;
(*v*)   how customers were led to choose one brand in preference to another.

## Statistical techniques

In connection with sales forecasting statistical techniques are basically the systematic collection and evaluation of data. Attempts are made to establish significant relationships; for example, if there is an overall increase in the average national wage this should result in a fractional increase in overall sales of certain products. If there is a forecast increase in the number of orders for steel products one would expect an increase in the demand for steel. Such correlations should be constantly sought as they often give an insight into the probable trend of sales.

It should be remembered that what has occurred in the past is no guarantee of what is likely to happen in the future. Even if market research is employed, the general trade situation and likely trends should always be considered. It is usual to employ most of these methods when compiling sales forecasts; but it should be remembered that external market research is expensive and it may be found that internal information is just as reliable and far cheaper.

## Production budget

The sales forecast becomes the sales budget, and this will be shown to the production manager to enable him to establish whether optimum use is being made of the facilities available. If there is insufficient productive capacity he is able to make alternative arrangements to ensure that demand is met. These arrangements may be to:

(*a*)  purchase new plant or hire the relevant equipment;
(*b*)  introduce shift-working or increase overtime;
(*c*)  sub-contract part of the production.

If the sales forecast does not need the production capacity the excess capacity must be scrapped, or new methods of increasing sales must be found. This may involve introducing discounts for bulk sales or more extensive advertising. (Market research will probably have revealed which would be the most profitable methods of advertising.) Spare machine time (e.g. a computer) may be hired out; but this will depend to a large extent on the type of machines which are not being fully used.

## Manpower budget

This involves forecasting the number of workpeople, both direct and indirect, who will be needed to meet the production requirements. In addition to the number of people required the various grades of labour will also be listed. This will allow the personnel department to plan the necessary recruitment; or to ensure that redundancies are kept to a minimum, if the work load is to be reduced, by arranging transfers if possible when vacancies occur. Training arrangements can also be planned to ensure the minimum disruption of production.

## Plant utilisation budget

Schedules will be prepared to show the available load for each production department. By comparing these schedules with the production budget it will be possible to tell whether plant and machinery will be over- or under-loaded. As with the production budget, if overloading is likely, alternative arrangements must be made; if underloading is the case, either the plant must be scrapped or sales increased to utilise the existing plant.

## Materials budget

This will show the raw materials and components which will be necessary to meet the production estimate, together with any finished materials purchased. It will be necessary to take account of opening and closing stocks and the current policy of management in connection with stock holding (e.g. whether stocks are to be run down or built up).

## Cost of labour budget

Once the manpower budget has been prepared it will be possible to cost the various grades of labour and arrive at a labour cost budget.

## Manufacturing overhead budget

This is a relatively difficult budget to prepare, as it is necessary to apportion the fixed overheads and the fixed portion of the semi-variable overheads to the various departments on some equitable basis usually related to production. More will be said about these expenses in the next chapter, but fixed and semi-fixed expenses are those which do not vary directly with production and which are incurred regardless of the volume of production, examples being rent and rates or lease of buildings.

## Selling expenses budget

The total costs incurred in selling and distributing the company's products will be ascertained and included in the selling expenses budget. The budget is connected with the total volume of sales but a number of expenses are not directly related to sales. Advertising will form part of this budget, but in some concerns advertising has come to play such an important part of the concern's activities that a separate advertising budget is prepared. Other expenses included in the selling expenses budget will be salesmen's salaries and commission, car expenses, sales office expenses and distribution expenses, including warehousing costs and delivery costs.

The budget will normally be prepared by the sales manager after consulting the sales office manager, the advertising manager and the distribution manager.

## Administrative expense budget

This budget is concerned with the cost of the administration section of the concern and will include such expenses as office salaries and upkeep, depreciation, stationery, managing director's salary, telephones and postage. The accountant is usually responsible for preparing this budget.

## Cash budget

This has already been considered in the last chapter, but it is clear from the diagram on page 88 that nearly all the other budgets influence the cash budget, and it is usually one of the last budgets to be prepared.

## Capital expenditure budget

This budget may have a different time-span from the other budgets: indeed it should be for a much longer period if planning is to be a major concern of management. The budget will show the future expenditure on fixed assets over a period of, say, five years, broken down into perhaps yearly sections. Different emphasis might be placed on different years; years four and five might only be tentative proposals. This budget is normally subject to strict top management control as large amounts of expenditure are usually involved.

The information to prepare the capital expenditure budget will come from:

(a) the plant utilisation budget, especially if this shows overloading;
(b) requests for new types of plant and equipment;
(c) requests for new vehicles;
(d) requests for new office machinery (e.g. a computer);
(e) the main development plans of the business, which will detail the new assets which are to be purchased in order to fulfil the planned expansion (e.g. new factory to be built).

The following example illustrates the budgeting process.

The *Prudent Engineering Company Ltd.* is a small company which is engaged in the manufacture of two types of electric fans for domestic purposes. The two types of fan are known as the 'Basic' and 'De-Luxe' model. The Company, having prepared its preliminary planning strategy, is now in a position to prepare its subsidiary and master budgets for the next financial year ending 19–1.

The following are forecast for the year:

|  |  | *Cost/Unit* |
|---|---|---|
| *Raw Materials* | Material P | £1.00 |
| ,, | Q | £1·50 |
|  | Direct labour | £5·00 per hour. |

Production overheads are recovered on the basis of a rate per direct labour hour.

*Finished Product* (Content for each type of fan)

|  | *'Basic'* | *'De-Luxe'* |
|---|---|---|
| Material P | 10 units | 10 units |
| ,,   Q | 10 units | 20 units |
| Direct labour | 4 hours | 6 hours |

The balance sheet at the beginning of the year 19–1 was as follows:

|  | £ | £ | £ |
|---|---|---|---|
| *Fixed Assets* |  |  |  |
| Land and buildings |  | 50 000 |  |
| Plant and machinery | 100 000 |  |  |
| *Less* Accumulated |  |  |  |
| depreciation | 40 000 | 60 000 | 110 000 |
|  |  |  |  |
| *Current Assets* |  |  |  |
| *Stock* – finished goods | 8 000 |  |  |
| raw materials | 5 000 |  |  |
| debtors | 10 000 |  |  |
| bank | 4 000 | 27 000 |  |
|  |  |  |  |
| *Less Current Liabilities* |  |  |  |
| Creditors | 12 000 |  |  |
| Tax | 5 000 | 17 000 | 10 000 |
|  |  |  | £120 000 |
|  |  |  |  |
| *Represented by* |  | £ | £ |
| 100 000 ordinary shares of £1 each |  | 100 000 |  |
| Reserves |  | 20 000 | 120 000 |

### Finished Product

|  | *'Basic'* | *'De-Luxe'* |
|---|---|---|
| Forecast sales in units | 8 000 | 6 000 |
| Selling price per unit | £80 | £100 |
| Ending inventory required (units) | 1 000 | 500 |
| Beginning inventory available (units) | 100 | 200 |

### Direct Material

|  | P | Q |
|---|---|---|
| Beginning inventory (units) | 4 000 | 15 000 |
| Desired ending inventory (units) | 12 000 | 10 000 |

(Work-in-progress is small and may be ignored)

It is envisaged that at the volume of planned sales the following additional costs will be incurred:

|  | £ | £ |
|---|---:|---:|
| *Production Overheads* | | |
| Depreciation – plant and machinery (*fixed*) | 8 000 | |
| Supervision (*fixed*) | 15 000 | |
| Indirect labour (*variable*) | 5 000 | |
| Heating and lighting (*fixed* £1000, variable £4000) | 5 000 | |
| Power (*fixed* £1000, *variable* £5000) | 6 000 | |
| Insurance (*fixed*) | 1 000 | |
| Miscellaneous (*fixed* £500, variable £3000) | 3 500 | 43 500 |

|  | £ | £ |
|---|---:|---:|
| *Administration Overheads* | | |
| Salaries (*fixed*) | 20 000 | |
| Stationery (*variable*) | 3 000 | |
| Heating and lighting (*fixed* £500, variable £1500) | 2 000 | |
| Other expenses (*fixed* £1000, variable £7000) | 8 000 | |
| | | 33 00 |

|  | £ | £ |
|---|---:|---:|
| *Selling and Distribution Overheads* | | |
| Salaries (*fixed*) | 11 000 | |
| Commission (*variable*) | 4 000 | |
| Heat and Lighting (*fixed* £200, variable £800) | 1 000 | |
| Advertising (*variable*) | 5 000 | |
| Other expenses (*fixed* £1000, variable £3000) | 4 000 | 25 000 |

**Budgeted Cash Flows**

**Year 19–1**

*Quarters*

|  | 1 | 2 | 3 | 4 |
|---|---:|---:|---:|---:|
|  | £ | £ | £ | £ |
| Anticipated collection from debtors | 120 000 | 300 000 | 190 000 | 240 000 |
| *Payments Anticipated* | | | | |
| Materials | 100 000 | 80 000 | 80 000 | 50 000 |
| Payroll | 80 000 | 90 000 | 97 000 | 100 000 |
| Taxes | 5 000 | — | — | — |

|                           | £      | £     | £     | £     |
|---------------------------|--------|-------|-------|-------|
| Production overheads       | 8 000  | 8 375 | 6 000 | 8 000 |
| Administration overheads   | 7 000  | 6 000 | 5 000 | 5 000 |
| Selling and distribution overheads | 2 000 | 5 000 | 5 000 | 6 000 |

The following budgets would be prepared:

1  Sales budget
2  Production budget
3  Direct materials purchasing budget
4  Direct labour cost budget
5  Production overhead budget
6  Ending inventory budget
7  Cost of goods sold budget
8  Administration overhead budget
9  Selling and distribution overhead budget
10  Cash budget
11  Budgeted profit and loss account for the year
12  A projected balance sheet as at the end of the year

Note that a provision for taxation is to be made at the rate of 50 % on net profits in the profit and loss account.

**1  Sales budget**

|           | Forecast Sales in Units | Forecast Selling Price per Unit | Total Sales |
|-----------|-------------------------|---------------------------------|-------------|
| 'Basic'   | 8 000                   | £80                             | £640 000    |
| 'De-Luxe' | 6 000                   | £100                            | £600 000    |
|           | 14 000                  |                                 | £1 240 000  |

**2  Production budget** (units)

|                             | 'Basic' | 'De-Luxe' |
|-----------------------------|---------|-----------|
| Sales                       | 8 000   | 6 000     |
| *Add* planned closing stock | 1 000   | 500       |
|                             | 9 000   | 6 500     |
| *Less* existing opening stock | 100   | 200       |
| *Production required* (*units*) | 8 900 | 6 300   |

## 3  Direct materials purchasing budget

|  |  | *Material P* | | | *Material Q* |
|---|---|---|---|---|---|
|  | *Production* | *Units per* | | *Units per* | |
|  | *(Fans)* | *Fan* | *Total* | *Fan* | *Total* |
| 'Basic' | 8 900 | 10 | 89 000 | 10 | 89 000 |
| 'De-Luxe' | 6 300 | 10 | 63 000 | 20 | 126 000 |
| *Total required for production* | | | 152 000 | | 215 000 |
| *Add* planned closing stock | | | 12 000 | | 10 000 |
| | | | 164 000 | | 225 000 |
| *Less* existing opening stock | | | 4 000 | | 15 000 |
| *Purchase requirements* | | | 160 000 | | 210 000 |
| Forecast purchase price unit | | | £1·00 | | £1·50 |
| Purchases budget | | | £160 000 | | £315 000 |

£475 000

## 4  Direct labour cost budget

|  | *Units* | *Hours per Unit* | *Total Hours* | *Rate per Hour* £ | *Total Amount* £ |
|---|---|---|---|---|---|
| 'Basic' | 8 900 | 4 | 35 600 | 5 | 178 000 |
| 'De-Luxe' | 6 300 | 6 | 37 800 | 5 | 189 000 |
| | | | 73 400 | | £367 000 |

## 5  Production overhead budget

|  | £ | £ |
|---|---|---|
| *Fixed costs:* | | |
| Depreciation plant and machinery | 8 000 | |
| Supervision | 15 000 | |
| Heating and lighting | 1 000 | |
| Power | 1 000 | |
| Insurance | 1 000 | |
| Miscellaneous | 500 | |
| | | 26 500 |

|  | £ | £ |
|---|---:|---:|
| *Variable costs:* | | |
| Indirect labour | 5 000 | |
| Heating and lighting | 4 000 | |
| Power | 5 000 | |
| Miscellaneous | 3 000 | 17 000 |
| | | £43 500 |

## 6　Ending inventory budget

| | Units £ | Unit Cost £ | Total £ |
|---|---:|---:|---:|
| (a)　*Direct materials* | | | |
| P | 12 000 | 1·00 | 12 000 |
| Q | 10 000 | 1·50 | 15 000 |
| | | | £27 000 |

| | Units | Unit Cost* | £ |
|---|---:|---:|---:|
| (b)　*Finished goods* | | | |
| 'Basic' | 1 000 | 47·40 | = 47 400 |
| 'De-Luxe' | 500 | 73·60 | = 36 800 |
| | | | £84 200 |

## 7　Cost of goods sold budget

| | | £ |
|---|---:|---:|
| Opening stock (raw materials) | | 5 000 |
| *Add* purchases | | 475 000 |
| | | 480 000 |
| *Less* closing stock (raw materials) | | 27 000 |
| *Raw materials consumed* | | 453 000 |
| Direct labour | | 367 000 |
| *Prime cost* | | 820 000 |
| *Production overheads:* | £ | |
| Fixed | 26 500 | |
| Variable | 17 000 | 43 500 |
| *Budgeted production cost of finished goods* | | 863 500 |
| *Add* opening stock finished goods | | 8 000 |

|  | £ |
|---|---|
|  | 871 500 |
| *Less* closing stock finished goods | 84 200 |
| *Budgeted production cost of goods sold* | 787 300 |

| * *Computation of unit costs* | | | | | |
|---|---|---|---|---|---|
| *for finished goods* | | | 'Basic' | | 'De-Luxe' |
|  | Unit cost | Units | £ | Units | £ |
| Material P | £1·00 | 10 | 10 | 10 | 10 |
| Material Q | £1·50 | 10 | 15 | 20 | 30 |
| Direct Labour | £5·00 | 4 Hours | 20 | 6 Hours | 30 |
| Production Overhead | £0·60 | 4 Hours | 2·40 | 6 Hours | 3·60 |
|  |  |  | *£47·40 | | £73·60 |

$$\text{Production overhead rate per direct labour hour} = \frac{\text{Total production overhead}}{\text{total labour hours}}$$

$$= \frac{£43\,500}{73\,400\ (\text{hours})} \simeq £0\cdot60/\text{Hour}$$

## 8 Administration overhead budget

|  | £ | £ |
|---|---|---|
| *Fixed:* |  |  |
| Salaries | 20 000 |  |
| Heating and lighting | 500 |  |
| Other expenses | 1 000 |  |
|  |  | 21 500 |
| *Variable:* |  |  |
| Stationery | 3 000 |  |
| Heating and lighting | 1 500 |  |
| Other expenses | 7 000 | 11 500 |
|  |  | £33 000 |

## 9 Selling and distribution budget

|  | £ | £ |
|---|---|---|
| *Fixed:* |  |  |
| Salaries | 11 000 |  |
| Heating and lighting | 200 |  |
| Other expenses | 1 000 |  |
|  |  | 12 200 |

| *Variable:* | £ | £ |
|---|---|---|
| Commission | 4 000 | |
| Heating and lighting | 800 | |
| Advertising | 5 000 | |
| Other expenses | 3 000 | 12 800 |
| | | £25 000 |

## 10   Cash budget

| | *Quarters* | | | | |
|---|---|---|---|---|---|
| | 1 | 2 | 3 | 4 | **Total** |
| | £ | £ | £ | £ | |
| Opening balance | 4 000 | (78 000) | 32 625 | 29 625 | (11 750) |
| *Add* receipts | 120 000 | 300 000 | 190 000 | 240 000 | 850 000 |
| | 124 000 | 222 000 | 222 625 | 269 625 | 838 250 |
| *Less* Payments: | | | | | |
| Direct materials | 100 000 | 80 000 | 80 000 | 50 000 | 310 000 |
| Payroll | 80 000 | 90 000 | 97 000 | 100 000 | 367 000 |
| Taxes | 5 000 | — | — | — | 5 000 |
| Production overheads | 8 000 | 8 375 | 6 000 | 8 000 | 30 375 |
| Administration overheads | 7 000 | 6 000 | 5 000 | 5 000 | 23 000 |
| Selling and distribution | 2 000 | 5 000 | 5 000 | 6 000 | 18 000 |
| *Total payments* | 202 000 | 189 375 | 193 000 | 169 000 | 753 375 |
| *Closing balance* | (78 000)* | 32 625 | 29 625 | 100 625 | |

*Overdraft.

## 11   Budgeted profit and loss account for period—

| | £ | £ |
|---|---|---|
| Budgeted sales | | 1 240 000 |
| *Less:* | | |
| Budgeted production cost of sales | 787 300 | |
| Budgeted selling costs | 25 000 | |
| Budgeted administration costs | 33 000 | 845 300 |
| Budgeted profit before tax | | 394 700 |
| *Less* Provision for taxation @ 50 % | | 197 350 |
| | | £ 197 350 |

**Budgeted Balance Sheet as at 31st December 19–1**

| Fixed assets | £ | £ | £ |
|---|---|---|---|
| Land and buildings | | 50 000 | |
| Plant and machinery | 100 000 | | |
| *Less* depreciation | 48 000 | 52 000 | |
| *Current Assets* | | | 102 000 |
| Stock – finished fans | 84 200 | | |
| raw materials | 27 000 | | |
| debtors | 400 000 | | |
| bank | 100 625 | | |
| *Less current liabilities* | | 611 825 | |
| Creditors | 199 125 | | |
| Tax | 197 350 | 396 475 | 215 350 |
| | | | £317 350 |

| *Represented by shareholders' interest* | | |
|---|---|---|
| | £ | £ |
| 100 000 ordinary shares of £1 each fully paid | 100 000 | |
| Reserves (see opening balance sheet) | 20 000 | |
| Profit and loss account balance | 197 350 | 317 350 |
| *Net capital employed* | | £317 350 |

*Ascertainment of closing debtors*

| | £ |
|---|---|
| Balance at beginning | 10 000 |
| *Add* sales budget | 1 240 000 |
| | 1 250 000 |
| *Less* Cash receipts | 850 000 |
| Closing debtors | 400 000 |

| *Ascertainment of closing creditors* | | £ |
|---|---|---|
| Balance at beginning £12 000 = | | 12 000 |
| *Costs* | £ | |
| Materials | 475 000 | |
| Labour | 367 000 | |
| Production overheads (excluding depreciation) | 35 500 | |
| Administration overheads | 33 000 | |
| Selling and distribution overheads | 25 000 | 935 500 |
| | | 947 500 |

|                                                                   | £         |
| ----------------------------------------------------------------- | --------: |
| *Less payments as per cash budget* <br> (excluding tax payment)   | 748 375   |
| *Closing creditors*                                               | £199 125  |

| *Closing tax balance*        | £        |
| ---------------------------- | -------: |
| Balance at beginning         | 5 000    |
| *Add* Tax on profits for year | 197 350 |
|                              | 202 350  |
| *Less* tax paid              | 5 000    |
| Closing tax unpaid           | £197 350 |

## Flexible budgetary control

The type of budgets so far considered are known as fixed budgets, in other words the budgets are based on one level of output and sales have been equated with production, etc. If this level of output varies from the estimate, there will be large variances, most of which should be taken care of by a 'level of activity variance', but control does become difficult. Flexible budgetary control is designed to amend the budget figures as the level of activity changes. Many types of business have great difficulty in estimating sales with any accuracy because of uncontrollable external influences. For example, the plastic mackintosh industry is likely to have poor sales in a very dry summer, when conversely the soft drinks industry is likely to have bumper sales.

A flexible budget may be prepared for varying levels of output 60 %, 70 %, etc., up to 100 %. The main requirement is that expenses should be analysed into three distinct categories:

(*a*)   fixed expense, i.e. an expense which tends to be unaffected by variations in the volume of output;
(*b*)   semi-variable expense, i.e. an expense which is partly fixed and partly variable;
(*c*)   variable expense, i.e. an expense which tends to vary directly with variations in the volume of output.

Once this analysis is complete it is possible to prepare the different budgets for different levels of activity, which allows a greater degree of control to be exercised when the actual results are compared with the estimates.

An example of a flexed budget applied to a production department for control purposes is given on page 103.

## THE UNO BRICK COMPANY
## Production Department X Budget for the Period----

Budgeted level of activity: 100 000 Bricks
Actual production achieved: 80 000 Bricks
Actual activity percentage: 80%

| Expense | Budgeted Amount for 100 000 Bricks | | Flexed Budget for 80 000 Bricks | | | Actual Cost | Variances | |
|---|---|---|---|---|---|---|---|---|
| | Fixed | Variable | Fixed | Variable | Total | | Adverse | Favourable |
| | £ | £ | £ | £ | £ | £ | £ | £ |
| Direct labour | 1 000 | 7 000 | 1 000 | 5 600 | 6 600 | 7 000 | 400 | — |
| Direct materials | — | 4 000 | — | 3 200 | 3 200 | 3 600 | 400 | — |
| Production overheads: | | | | | | | | |
| Depreciation | 5 000 | — | 5 000 | — | 5 000 | 5 000 | — | — |
| Indirect materials | | | | | | | | |
| Supervision | 4 000 | — | 4 000 | — | 4 000 | 4 200 | 200 | — |
| Rates | 500 | — | 500 | — | 500 | 600 | 100 | — |
| Power | 400 | 1 600 | 400 | 1 280 | 1 680 | 1 250 | — | 430 |
| Heating and lighting | 100 | 300 | 100 | 240 | 340 | 350 | 10 | — |
| Other expenses | 1 000 | 2 100 | 1 000 | 1 680 | 2 680 | 2 400 | — | 280 |
| | 12 000 | 15 000 | 12 000 | 12 000 | 24 000 | 24 400 | 1 110 | 710 |

It should be noted that budgeted fixed costs by definition remain unchanged irrespective of the level of production, whereas variable costs will tend to vary with the level of output. Since the level of production attained was only 80 % of that budgeted it is necessary to adjust the budgeted variable costs in proportion to the level of actual activity attained in order to facilitate a fair comparison between actual costs incurred and budgeted costs.

Once the budget has been flexed in this way an analysis of variances from that budgeted can be made, and where such variances are adverse, investigations into the causes can be made and corrective action taken.

## Control

The preparation and approval of the master budget by top management is not the end of the budgetary process but merely the beginning. The whole purpose of budgeting is to establish standards with which actual performances can be compared. The budget officer should prepare a report at least once a month, showing how the actual expenses and income compare with the estimates. The principle of 'management by exception' comes into force here. Once plans have been established, management is not really interested in the fact that they are working out as expected, since this was, after all, the original intention. They are, however, interested when the plans do not work out as expected. Their role in the organisation is to take appropriate action in such cases.

The monthly budget report should therefore emphasise the main variations from the planned figures; and explanations for such variances will be required from the person responsible for incurring them. The report should also be presented promptly. Speed is probably more important than absolute accuracy, as the longer a variance is left, the more difficult it becomes to isolate and remedy.

It should always be remembered that the whole budgetary system is based on estimates – estimated sales, estimated expenses, etc. The mechanical process of bringing the data together can be carried out exactly, but the final master budget is only as good as the estimates from which it was prepared. It may well be that a variation is due to bad estimating originally and this explanation should always be considered before recriminations are made.

Although budgetary control is an invaluable exercise, since it forces management to plan for the future and it establishes responsibility for all expenses and revenues, it is costly to operate. This factor must influence the extent to which a business commits itself to budgetary control. It is also of a short-term nature, usually involving a twelve-month cycle enabling management to control current operations. Concentration on this annual cycle has the danger that strategic long-range planning may be neglected, and this could have adverse results in the future.

The more progressive organisation may use the budget to control costs for longer periods than twelve months by utilising rolling budgets, programmed budgeting. etc. particularly as a means of controlling capital expenditure. A rolling budget may cover a period of, say, three years. At the end of the first year a further year is added to the two years remaining in the original budget period, thereby bringing the overall budget period back to three years. For example, if the budget covered the years 19–1, 19–2 and 19–3 at the end of 19–1, the budget for 19–4 would be prepared and at the end of 19–2 the budget for 19–5 and so on. However, there are many organisations who have not yet come round to installing simple budgetary procedures despite their apparent benefits.

Budgetary control should be just one of the techniques used by management in planning the overall strategy of control and development of the business.

## Questions

**1** Discuss the benefits to be derived from the application of Budgetary Control.

**2** What is meant by the term 'flexible budgeting'?

**3** 'Budgetary control is an example of management by exception.' Discuss.

**4** What is meant by the 'key factor' in formulating a budget.

**5** The details overleaf apply to the budget proposals for the period 1st January 19–7 – 31st December 19–7 for the bar of the 'OK' Hotel Ltd.

*Planned Closing Stocks:*

| | |
|---|---|
| Cigarettes | 60 packets |
| Beer | 20 barrels |
| Wines | |
| X | 30 bottles |
| Y | 20 bottles |
| Z | 10 bottles |

*Labour (bar):* 6 persons gross wages £130 per week per person for 52 weeks.

*Staff meals:* 6 persons @ £6 per week per person for 52 weeks.

*Staff accommodation:* 4 persons @ £10 per week per person for 52 weeks.

|  | Cigarettes Selling Price/Packet £ | Beer Barrels | Selling Price per Barrel £ | Wines Brand | Bottles | Selling Price per Bottle £ |
|---|---|---|---|---|---|---|
| **Planned Sales** | | | | | | |
| Packets 2,000 | £1·40 | 1,800 | 60·00 | X | 400 | 2·80 |
|  |  |  |  | Y | 300 | 2·00 |
|  |  |  |  | Z | 200 | 7·10 |
| **Budgeted purchase price** | £1·00 | | 32·00 | X | | 1·60 |
|  |  |  |  | Y | | 1·40 |
|  |  |  |  | Z | | 1·20 |

**Stocks 1st January 19–7**

Cigarettes  100 packets @ £1·10 per packet
Beer  100 barrels @ £30·00 per barrel
Wines
X  10 bottles @ £1·30 per bottle
Y  10 bottles @ £1·30 per bottle
Z  20 bottles @ £3·40 per bottle

*Allocated overhead expenditure:*

| Depreciation – cutlery, glass *etc.* | 2 % of sales |
|---|---|
| Linen and uniforms | £6 per week |
| Laundry and dry cleaning | £12 per week |
| Commission | 5 % of Sales |
| Indirect supplies | 10 % of Sales |

You are required to prepare the following budgets for the Bar of the Hotel:

  (*i*)  Sales budget;
 (*ii*)  Purchasing budget;
(*iii*)  Closing stock budget (valued at purchase price);
 (*iv*)  Labour costs budget;
  (*v*)  Overhead expenditure budget;
 (*vi*)  Budgeted bar trading account.

**6**  S Limited manufactures three products, A, C and E, in two production departments, F and G, in each of which are employed two grades of labour. The cost accountant is preparing the annual budgets for 19–2 and he has asked you as his assistant to prepare, using the data given below:

(*a*)  the production budget in units for products A, C and E;
(*b*)  the direct wages budget for departments F and G with the labour costs of products A, C and E and total shown separately.

| *Data:* | | Product A | Product C | Product E |
|---|---|---|---|---|
| Finished Stocks: | | £000's | £000's | £000's |
| 1 Jan. 19–2 | | 720 | 540 | 1 800 |
| 31 Dec. 19–2 | | 600 | 570 | 1 000 |
| All stocks are valued at standard | | £ | £ | £ |
| Cost per unit | | 24 | 15 | 20 |
| Standard profit: | | % | % | % |
| Calculated as % of selling price | | 20 | 25 | 16⅔ |
| | *Total* | | | |
| Budgeted sales are: | £000's | £000's | £000's | £000's |
| South | 6 600 | 1 200 | 1 800 | 3 600 |
| Midlands | 5 100 | 1 500 | 1 200 | 2 400 |
| North | 6 380 | 1 500 | 800 | 4 080 |
| | £18 080 | £4 200 | £3 800 | £10 080 |
| *Material Loss in Production:* | 10 % | 20 % | 5 % | |

Standard labour times
per unit and standard
rates per hour:

| | | *Product* | | |
| | | A | C | E |
| | Rate | Hours | Hours | Hours |
| | £ | per unit | per unit | per unit |
| Department F | | | | |
| Grade 1 | 0·9 | 2·0 | 3·0 | 1·0 |
| Grade 2 | 0·8 | 1·5 | 2·0 | 1·5 |
| Department G | | | | |
| Grade 1 | 1·0 | 3·0 | 1·0 | 1·0 |
| Grade 2 | 0·9 | 2·0 | 1·5 | 2·5 |

ICMA

**7** The following is the last balance sheet of Dodsons Ltd. at 31st December
19–6.

## DODSONS LTD.
### Balance Sheet as at 31st 19–6

| | | Deprecia- | |
| | | tion | Net |
| *Fixed Assets* | Cost | to date | Value |
| | £ | £ | £ |
| Machinery | 8 000 | 3 200 | 4 800 |
| Motor vehicles | 4 000 | 1 600 | 2 400 |
| | 12 000 | 4 800 | 7 200 |

| | | | |
| *Current Assets* | | | |
| Stocks: | | £ | |
| Finished goods (150 units) | | 1 800 | |
| Raw materials | | 1 000 | |
| Debtors (October 19–6 £1080 + | | | |
| Nov. £720 +Dec. £900) | | 2 700 | |
| Cash and bank balances | | 1 300 | |
| | | 6 800 | |

| | £ | £ | £ |
| *Less Current Liabilities* | | | |
| Creditors for raw materials | | | |
| (November 19–6 £240 + | | | |
| December £360) | 600 | | |
| Creditors for fixed expenses | | | |
| (December) | 200 | 800 | 6 000 |
| *Net Capital Employed* | | | £13 200 |

*Represented by:*
Issued share capital:
  8 000 ordinary shares of £1 each
    fully paid

|  | £ | £ |
|---|---|---|
|  | 8 000 |  |
| *Reserves* |  |  |
| Profit and Loss Account Balance | 5 200 | 13 200 |
|  |  | £13 200 |

The plans for the next six months ending 30th June 19–7 are as follows:

(*i*)   Production will be 60 units per month for the first 4 months followed by 70 units per month for May and June.

(*ii*)  Production costs will be (per unit):

|  | £ |
|---|---|
| Direct Materials | 10 |
| Direct Labour | 8 |
| Variable Overhead | 6 |
|  | £24 |

(*iii*) Fixed overhead is £200 per month payable 1 month in arrears.

(*iv*)  Budgeted sales at a price of £36 per unit are expected to be:

|  | Jan. | Feb. | Mar. | April | May | June |
|---|---|---|---|---|---|---|
| *No. of units* | 40 | 50 | 60 | 90 | 90 | 70 |

(*v*)   Purchases of Direct Materials (Raw Materials) will be:

| Jan. | Feb. | Mar. | April | May | June |
|---|---|---|---|---|---|
| £300 | £400 | £500 | £600 | £800 | £640 |

(*vi*)  Debtors are expected to pay their accounts 3 months after they have bought the goods.

(*vii*) Creditors for raw materials bought are paid in the same month as the units are produced.

(*viii*) Direct Labour and Variable Overhead are paid in the same month as the units are produced.

(*ix*)  A machine costing £4000 will be purchased and paid for in March.

(*x*)   6000 Ordinary Shares of £1 each are to be issued at par value in May.

(*xi*)  Depreciation for the six months: machinery £900, motor vehicles £400.

Prepare the following budgets:

(*a*)   Materials stock budget;
(*b*)   Production budget in units;

(c)   Production budget in £'s;
(d)   Creditors' budget;
(e)   Debtors' budget;
(f)   Cash budget;
(g)   Cash receipts schedule;
(h)   Cash payments schedule;
(i)   Master budget–Profit and Loss Account for the six months ending 30th June 19–7;
(j)   A projcted balance sheet as at 30th June 19–7.


**8.**  (i)   How does a flexible budget differ from a fixed budget?

(ii)   From the following selected data of a department whose normal and expected work-load is 3000 hours per month,

(a)   Compile a flexible budget for activity levels of 2000; 2800 and 3600 hours of work;
(b)   Compile a fixed budget;
(c)   Calculate the departmental hourly rate for the following items.

| *Expense Headings* | *Behaviour of Expense* |
|---|---|
| Supervision: | £250 up to 2000 hours. An extra £60 for steps of 400 hours above 2000. |
| | A further £30 from 3600 hours upwards. |
| Depreciation: | £400 up to 3000 hours; £550 above 3000 hours and up to 4200 hours. |
| Consumable supplies: | £12 per 100 hours. |
| Heat and light: | £45 from 1200 to 2000 hours inclusive. |
| | £55 above 2000 hours and up to 3000 hours. |
| | £60 above 3000 hours. |
| Power: | £15 per 100 hours up to 3200 hours. |
| | £12 per 100 hours for hours above 3200. |
| Cleaning: | £30 up to 2800 hours. |
| | £40 above 2800 hours. |
| Repairs: | £75 up to 1600 hours. |
| | Additional £25 for steps of 400 hours up to 3200 hours. |
| | Additional £40 above 3200 hours. |
| Indirect wages: | £20 per 100 hours. |
| Rent and rates: | £180. |

# 8 Marginal Costing and Cost–Profit–Volume Relationships

Marginal cost may be defined as 'the variable cost of one unit of a product or a service' and marginal costing 'a principle whereby marginal costs of cost units are ascertained. Only variable costs are charged to cost units, the fixed costs attributed to a relevant period being written off in full against the contribution for that period.'

The whole subject of marginal costing has created much contention among accountants and economists. One tends to be either wholly for the system or wholly against it and much has been written on both sides of the question.

Marginal costing is a technique which enables management to consider costs in a different and, it is claimed, a more meaningful light, particularly from the point of view of the profitability of different products. A conventional costing system would allocate all costs, direct and overhead, to the units produced and would ascertain whether the sales revenue exceeded these total costs. Marginal costing differentiates between variable and fixed costs. Fixed costs are charged in total to the profit and loss account as they are the type of costs, (e.g. rent, insurance, rates, clerical costs, subscriptions) which normally relate to a specific period of time, and it is felt that they should be recovered during the current period and not depend upon recovery according to the volume of units produced during the period, as this is likely to result in under- or over-recovery.

One reason why fixed costs are eliminated is the effect which they can have on pricing policies if they are tied to recovery on a volume basis. Consider a factory incurring £2000 of fixed costs per week and producing 2000 articles. If fixed costs are recovered on a volume basis, this will result in an overhead charge of £1 per unit. Next week the fixed cost will still be £2000, but if the production is now 3000 units the fixed costs will now be recovered at a rate of £0·67; and if the following week a breakdown results in only 500 units being produced, the £2000 fixed costs will be recovered at £4 per unit. Although these are wide variations, even with minor fluctuations in output, price fixing can be a difficult problem.

## Fixed/variable costs classification

If fixed costs are eliminated from the cost computations, then we are left with variable costs, which are those costs which tend to vary in direct proportion to the number of units produced. It would, therefore, seem relatively easy to use a marginal costing system, and the advantages appear to be considerable. The main drawback is, however, in deciding which costs are fixed and which are variable. Certain costs are easily classified; obviously, all direct costs (i.e. direct materials, direct wages and direct expenses) are variable costs, and similarly the fixed costs outlined above are easily classifiable. But there are a number of overhead costs which might be called 'semi-variable' or 'semi-fixed', and unless some fairly accurate method is used to put these into their correct category the whole procedure is likely to go wrong. Examples of these semi-fixed/variable costs are power and light, inspection and repairs and maintenance.

## Methods of dividing semi-variable overheads into fixed and variable elements

There are three basic methods of producing such a division; but as we are concerned with the accuracy of the split, only the most reliable will be explained in detail. The three methods are:

(*a*) the range method;
(*b*) the scatter diagram;
(*c*) the method of least squares.

Method (*a*) relies on listing high and low levels of observed overhead costs and then using the figures to calculate a rather unscientific division between fixed and variable costs. Method (*b*) is more accurate but relies on a 'best-fit' line, in other words a line which is drawn through a number of points plotted on a graph so as to pass through as many as possible. It is therefore open to subjective manipulation by the compiler. Method (*c*) is likely to give the most accurate separation into fixed and variable elements but it is naturally the most complicated of the three, involving the use of a formula. However, it is not necessary to know the derivation of a formula before one can use it, and we shall take the formula as read and just consider how it can be applied to a specific problem. The formulae are as follows:

(*i*) $\Sigma y = na + b\Sigma x$
(*ii*) $\Sigma xy = a\Sigma x + b\Sigma x^2$

where:   x = number of units produced each month
         y = costs per month
         a = fixed costs
         b = variable costs per unit
         n = number of pairs of x and y values
         Σ = total

## Problem

The following figures for the six-month period July to December show the cost of heating and the number of units produced, heat being an integral part of the production process as well as being a general amenity.

| Month | Units Produced | Heating Costs £ |
|---|---|---|
| July | 1300 | 675 |
| August | 1600 | 750 |
| September | 1100 | 625 |
| October | 1500 | 725 |
| November | 1200 | 650 |
| December | 1700 | 775 |
| | 8400 | 4200 |

To find a and b the following procedure is followed, bearing in mind that x = number of units produced each month and y = costs per month.

| | $x$ '00 units | $y$ £ | $xy$ | $x^2$ |
|---|---|---|---|---|
| July | 13 | 6·75 | 87·75 | 169 |
| August | 16 | 7·50 | 120 | 256 |
| September | 11 | 6·25 | 68·75 | 121 |
| October | 15 | 7·25 | 108·75 | 225 |
| November | 12 | 6·50 | 78·00 | 144 |
| December | 17 | 7·75 | 131·75 | 289 |
| | 84 | 42 | 595 | 1204 |
| | $\Sigma x$ | $\Sigma y$ | $\Sigma xy$ | $\Sigma x^2$ |

Using formulae given above:

(i)   $\Sigma xy = a\Sigma x + b\Sigma x^2$
(ii)  $\Sigma y = na + b\Sigma x$

Substituting values in equations (*i*) and (*ii*) we get

(*i*)    $595 = a \times 84 + b \times 1204$
(*ii*)   $42 = 6 \times a + b \times 84$

Rearranging:

(*i*)    $595 = 84a + 1204b$
(*ii*)   $42 = 6a + 84b$

Multiplying equation (*ii*) by 14

(*i*)    $595 = 84a + 1204b$
(*ii*)   $588 = 84a + 1176b$

Subtracting (*ii*) from (*i*)

$7 = 28b$

$b = \dfrac{7}{28} = £0.25$ per *unit variable cost* (or £25 per 100 units)

Substituting for b in equation (*i*) we get

(*i*)    $595 = 84a + 1204 \times 0.25$
         $595 = 84a + 301$
∴       $84a = 294$
∴        $a = \dfrac{295}{84} = £3.50$

*OR fixed costs are 3·50 × 100 = £350 per month*

## Value of marginal costing

Having established the basic idea of marginal costing as the allocation of costs into fixed and variable, let us now see how this system can be of value to management.

If the marginal costs are deducted from the sales, the difference is known as the 'contribution'. This contribution is available to meet the pool of fixed costs, and the surplus after these have been met is net profit.

This situation can be illustrated by a simple formula.

(1)   Sales – Variable costs = Contribution
(2)   Contribution – Fixed costs = Profit
(3)   ∴ Sales – Variable costs = Fixed costs + Profit

If the result of (1) is positive, i.e. there is something available to meet fixed costs, it may be worth continuing production even though under an absorption costing system the product appears to be making a loss. Consider the example below:

**Budgeted Trading Statement for the Six Months Ending 31st December 19––**

| | Total £ | A £ | B £ | C £ |
|---|---|---|---|---|
| Prime costs and variable overheads | 15 000 | 6 000 | 5 000 | 4 000 |
| Fixed costs | 7 000 | 3 000 | 2 000 | 2 000 |
| Total cost | 22 000 | 9 000 | 7 000 | 6 000 |
| Sales | 29 000 | 14 000 | 10 000 | 5 000 |
| Profit | 7 000 | 5 000 | 3 000 | |
| Loss | | | | £1 000 |

The "Product" label spans columns A, B and C.

From this statement it would appear that, if sales of Product C cannot be increased, the only alternative would be to cease production of this product and thereby make an apparent saving of £1000. However, the £1000 loss might well be due to the manner in which fixed overhead costs have been apportioned between the products. As this is usually a very arbitrary decision a much more revealing picture is shown if the statement is produced on a marginal costing basis. This is shown below.

**Marginal Trading Statement for the Six Months Ending 31st December 19––**

| | Total £ | A £ | B £ | C £ |
|---|---|---|---|---|
| Sales | 29 000 | 14 000 | 10 000 | 5 000 |
| Less Variable costs | 15 000 | 6 000 | 5 000 | 4 000 |
| Contribution | 14 000 | 8 000 | 5 000 | 1 000 |
| Less Fixed costs | 7 000 | | | |
| Profit | £7 000 | | | |

It will be seen that Product C makes a contribution to the fixed costs of £1000.

If Product C is eliminated this is likely to have little effect on the fixed costs. These will, therefore, now have to be borne by the other two products and the profit is reduced by £1000 from £7000 to £6000.

|  | | *Product* | |
|  | *Total* | A | B |
|  | £ | £ | £ |
| Sales | 24 000 | 14 000 | 10 000 |
| *Less* Variable costs | 11 000 | 6 000 | 5 000 |
| Contribution | 13 000 | 8 000 | 5 000 |
| *Less* Fixed costs | 7 000 | | |
| Profit | £6 000 | | |

## Advantages and disadvantages of marginal costing

*Advantages*
1 It is not necessary to allocate fixed overhead expenses to cost centres and problems of over- and under-recovery of overheads are eliminated.
2 Management, when concerned with price fixing, finds the marginal cost statement much easier to understand.
3 Marginal costs per unit are not generally affected by changes in volume of output.
4 The contribution which each product makes towards fixed overheads and profits is easily ascertained. This is useful in times of a trade recession, when maximisation of profit is not always possible and any orders which cover marginal costs are worth having.
5 The exclusion of fixed overhead costs from stock and work in progress valuations gives more uniform and realistic figures.

*Disadvantages*
1 The allocation of semi-variable costs into their variable and fixed element is a complicated procedure if accuracy is required.
2 Short-term pricing may take account of the contribution of individual products and production of some products may continue when the contribution is insufficient to meet the fixed overheads. This can, however, only be a temporary measure as in the long run all fixed overheads must be covered and a reasonable margin obtained over and above total costs.

3   Although it is not necessary to allocate fixed overheads, it is still necessary to allocate variable overheads to cost centres.

4   Difficulties arise in the contracting industries such as shipbuilding. It is often necessary to value work in progress at total cost and calculate a profit element to appear in the annual accounts in order to avoid large fluctuations in profits which would occur if profit was only recorded when the revenue was received (i.e. on completion of the contract). Under a marginal costing system this valuation would be very difficult.

### Cost−profit−volume relationships

It is vitally necessary that management should be aware of the effect of volume of output upon profits. This is particularly so when a new product is being introduced or there is a slump in the industry resulting in reduced sales. Once costs have been grouped into fixed and variable, then it is possible to show the relationship between sales and output, and more specifically at what output total costs equal sales. At this point there will be neither profits nor losses, and this is known as the break-even point.

We can use the simple relationship already established:

$$\text{Sales} - \text{Variable costs} = \text{Fixed costs} + \text{Profit}$$

to produce a formula which will calculate this break-even point. Units required to break-even =

$$\frac{\text{Fixed costs}}{\text{Selling price} - \text{Variable costs per unit}}$$

If the sales revenue needed to break-even is required, then it can be found by the formula:

$$\frac{\text{Fixed costs} \times \text{Sales}}{\text{Sales} - \text{Variable costs}}$$

Let see how these formulae work on a practical question. During a particular year the following estimates were made:

Fixed costs, £15 000
Prime costs, £3 per unit
Variable overheads, £2 per unit
Number of units to be produced, 10 000
Selling price per unit, £8.

How many units must be produced to break-even?
*Formula:*

$$\frac{FC}{SP - VCU}$$

$$= \frac{£15\,000}{£8 - £5} = \frac{£15\,000}{£3} = 5000 \text{ units}$$

The equivalent sales revenue needed to break-even may be found by multiplying the units figure above by the selling price, in other words $5000 \times £8 = £40\,000$. It may also be found by the formula:

$$\frac{FC \times S}{S - VC} = \frac{£15\,000 \times £80\,000}{£80\,000 - £50\,000} = \frac{£120\,000}{£3} = £40\,000$$

The significance of these figures, i.e. 5000 units and £40 000 sales revenue, is that the company must achieve this sales level before it starts to make a profit. If these figures are not achieved a loss will occur.

It is generally easier for management to appreciate the significance of cost–profit–volume relationships if they are presented in graphical form. This is known as a break-even chart and preparation of such a chart is fairly straightforward (see Fig. 8.1). The left-hand vertical side

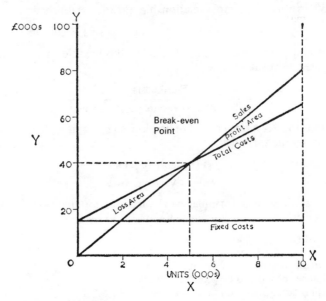

**Fig. 8.1**   Break-even chart I

of the chart is known as the Y axis and the horizontal side at the bottom is the X axis.

It is usual to show costs and revenues on the Y axis and volume either in units or £'s on the X axis. Capacity in percentage terms may be an alternative X axis notation.

The figures already given will now be plotted on such a chart (see Fig. 8.1).

**Preparation**

1   The fixed cost line is firstly drawn in at £15 000. This will be horizontal as fixed costs do not vary with volume of output.

2   The total cost line can now be plotted. This represents an increase in costs of £5 for each unit produced (note that the line starts at the fixed cost point on the Y axis).

3   The sales revenue at £8 per unit is then plotted.

4   The break-even point lies on the intersection of the total sales and total cost line. Losses are measured to the left of the break-even point, the amount of loss in £'s at any point being equal to the difference between the total cost line and the total sales line. Profits are measured to the right of the point, the amount being calculated in a similar manner.

Another method of presenting this information is by using the contribution concept already considered. This is illustrated in Fig. 8.2 using the same figures as in the last chart.

It is claimed that this type of chart reveals more clearly the effects of fixed overheads on the volume of sales.

It will be appreciated that the information which can be shown on such a chart is extremely varied. Consider the very composite chart (Fig. 8.3) overleaf.

The desired profit could be further split into the amount needed to finance the capital of the concern − debenture interest, preference share dividend, ordinary dividend and retained earnings.

Two important points revealed by the conventional break-even chart are the 'margin of safety' and the 'angle of incidence'.

*Margin of safety*

This is the difference between the total sales figures and the amount of sales at break-even point. It may be expressed as a percentage based either on units or £ value. It is important that there should be a reasonable margin of safety, because otherwise a reduced level of

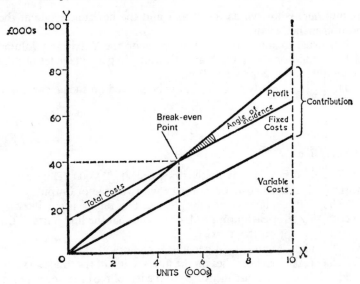

**Fig. 8.2**  Break-even chart II

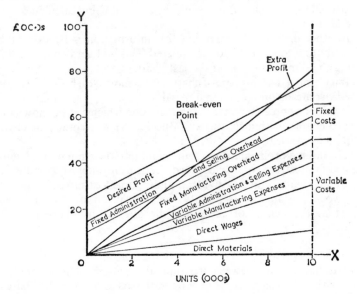

**Fig. 8.3**  Break-even chart III

output might mean that the firm was unable to break-even and losses were incurred. Consider the following situation:

|  | Firm A | Firm B |
|---|---|---|
|  | £ | £ |
| Total sales | 50 000 | 80 000 |
| Break-even point | 30 000 | 64 000 |
| Margin of safety | £20 000 | £16 000 |
| Margin of safety as a percentage of sales | 40% | 20% |

If the rate of profit earned on sales above break-even point is the same, Company A is in a much stronger position than Company B to withstand a fall in sales. A low percentage usually indicates a high level of fixed costs which requires a high level of activity to cover them.

If we refer to the information contained in Fig. 8.1, we see that the margin of safety expressed in £'s is £80 000 − £40 000 = £40 000 and expressed in units 10 000 − 5000 = 5000. This gives a percentage of 50%, i.e.:

$$\frac{\text{Sales} - \text{Sales at break-even point}}{\text{Sales}} \times 100$$

$$= \frac{£40\,000}{£80\,000} \times 100$$

$$= 50\%$$

This is a highly satisfactory margin.

*Angle of incidence*

This is the angle formed at break-even point by the sales line cutting the total cost line (see Fig. 8.2). The aim should be to have as large an angle as possible at this point. The size of the angle shows the rate of profit earned after break-even, and a large angle will mean a high rate of profit accruing after this point.

**Profit−volume chart**

This type of chart (Fig. 8.4) is sometimes used in place of or in addition to a break-even chart. Profits and losses are shown on the vertical scale and units or percentage of capacity are shown on the horizontal scale. The profits and losses at various sales levels are then plotted on the chart and where this line crosses the horizontal zero line this is the break-even point.

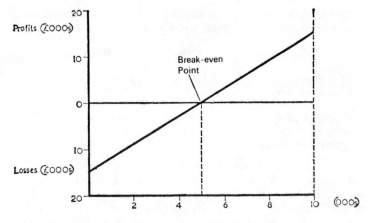

**Fig. 8.4**  Profit-volume chart

The original example would be presented on such a chart as Fig. 8.4 above.

The advantage of such a chart is that it is possible to read off the profit or loss at any given level of production, but it does not show how costs vary with any given activity.

Management are able to use break-even analysis for short-term planning on the assumption that market prices are established and that moderate changes in output will not affect the price. In the long run other factors may be taken into account; for example, it may be decided to sacrifice immediate profits by producing beyond the point of maximum profit, in order to secure a market that will yield greater profits when additional capacity is available.

### Limitations of break-even analysis

One of the basic faults of the simple break-even chart is that it is assumed that the total sales line and the total cost line are straight (i.e. linear). It is unlikely to be the case in practice, as there will come a point when the addition of variable factors of production to a given fixed factor will result in reduced efficiency. This follows from the economists' Law of Diminishing Returns. The total cost line is likely, therefore, to have an increasing slope as more is produced. It may also follow that at low levels of production, efficiency may be increasing, thus causing the slope of the total cost curve to be decreasing at that particular level of production.

When the sales line is plotted as a straight line it is assumed that it will not be necessary to decrease the unit price in order to achieve more sales; but in a competitive market such action may very well be necessary and this will cause the sales curve to decrease its slope as sales increase.

If these two factors are taken into account the chart may look like Fig. 8.5 below.

It will be observed that there are two break-even points at OA and OB. This is due to having curved lines instead of the usual straight ones. Optimum output (i.e. the output at which maximum profitability will be achieved), is where the sales curve and total cost curve are farthest apart (i.e. where the difference between total expenses and total sales is greatest).

Although fixed costs have so far always been shown as a straight line, even these will vary as production increases. Such costs will normally remain unchanged until a certain limit of capacity is reached and when they do change it will be in definite jumps or steps, rather than gradually. For example, if capacity is increased by the purchase of a new factory, then there will be an immediate rise in fixed costs to take account of the increased rates, heating, depreciation, etc. However, as the main use of break-even analysis is for short-term

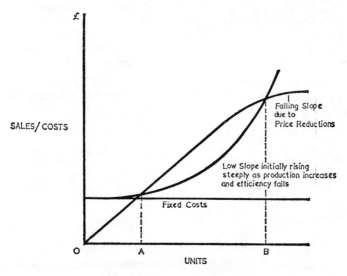

**Fig. 8.5** Break-even chart V

planning it is permissible to show fixed costs as being unchanged throughout the short term.

Despite these limitations, the simple break-even chart does enable cost–volume–profit relationships to be clearly shown. And as the normal business will be working within a limited range of production the straight lines, although only approximating to the actual position, will be sufficiently accurate to provide adequate information for management's decision-making.

## Product mix choices under resource constraints

In any organisation there may be constraints imposed which limit profit maximisation. Examples are production capacity constraints, scarcity of labour or materials, shortage of capital and so on.

If, for example, there is a production capacity constraint and the firm has a choice of manufacturing several different types of product whose total demand exceeds the production capacity then the firm must choose which products to manufacture.

Suppose, for example, that a firm has the choice of making product X or product Y; the demand for each product exceeds the company's production capacity, and the following details apply:

| Product | X | Y |
|---|---|---|
| Process time | 4 hours | 2 hours |
| Selling price per unit | £5 | £8 |
| Variable costs per unit | £3 | £6 |
| Fixed costs per month | £15 000 | |
| Available production capacity | 40 000 hours | |

In reaching a decision as to which product to make, it is necessary to compute the contribution per limiting factor for each product – in this case the contribution made by each product per hour.

| | X | Y |
|---|---|---|
| Selling price | £5 | £8 |
| Variable costs | 3 | 6 |
| Contribution per unit | 2 | 2 |
| Process time | 4 hours | 2 hours |
| Contribution per hour | £0·50 | £1·00 |

It will be seen that, although the contribution per unit for each product is the same in this case, and, therefore, we might think it would make no difference which product we chose to produce, we would be wrong, since on the basis of contribution per hour Y gives the greater contribution; hence the correct decision will be to use all the manufacturing capacity in producing Y. This can easily be verified as follows:

| Product | X | Y |
|---|---|---|
| Total hours available | 40 000 hours | 40 000 hours |
| Contribution per hour | £0·50 | £1·00 |
| Total contribution | £20 000 | £40 000 |
| *Less* fixed costs | 15 000 | 15 000 |
| | | |
| *Profit* | £5 000 | £25 000 |

## Linear programming where there are two or more variables

Where there is more than one variable it is necessary to use a more dynamic approach in determining the optimum product mix. This technique is known as 'Linear Programming' and results in the solution of an optimal plan.

If there are only two variables then the problem can be solved by using the Linear Programming graphical approach, but where there are three or more variables the Linear Programming is best solved by the 'simplex procedure'. This is beyond the scope of this book, but is described in *Operational Research* (Teach Yourself Books).

The following example illustrates the procedure using the graphical approach.

A company makes two similar sub-assemblies P and Q, which are marketed at £28·40 and £38·30 each respectively.

Each sub-assembly requires the following components.

| | *Sub-Assembly* | |
|---|---|---|
| Component | P | Q |
| a | 5 | 2 |
| b | 12 | 14 |
| c | 5 | 10 |
| d | 4 | 6 |

Labour and variable overhead costs are as follows:

| | P | Q |
|---|---|---|
| | £ | £ |
| Labour | 0·80 | 1·10 |
| Variable overheads | 1·50 | 1·80 |

In the assembly programme the following stock constraints apply:

| Component | Stock | Cost per Component £ |
|---|---|---|
| a | 240 | 0·5 |
| b | 840 | 1·0 |
| c | 400 | 1·2 |
| d | 324 | 0·4 |

Determine, using the Linear Programming approach,

(a) The production schedule of assemblies which will maximise contribution.
(b) The maximum contribution obtainable under the above constraints.
(c) The quantities of each component remaining, if any, after the manufacturing programme is complete.

Before we can formulate the problem into a linear programming model the following preliminary work is necessary in order to ascertain the contribution per assembly.

### Material Costs per Sub-Assembly

| Sub-Assembly P Component | No. | Cost £ | Cost per Sub-Assembly £ |
|---|---|---|---|
| a | 5 | 0·5 | 2·50 |
| b | 12 | 1·0 | 12·00 |
| c | 5 | 1·2 | 6·00 |
| d | 4 | 0·4 | 1·60 |
| Total material cost | | | £22·10 |

| Sub-Assembly Q Component | No. | Cost £ | Cost per Sub-Assembly £ |
|---|---|---|---|
| a | 2 | 0·5 | 1·00 |
| b | 14 | 1·0 | 14·00 |
| c | 10 | 1·2 | 12·00 |
| d | 6 | 0·4 | 2·40 |
| Total material cost | | | £29·40 |

Ascertainment of Contribution per Sub-Assembly

| Sub-Assembly | P | Q |
|---|---|---|
| | £ | £ |
| Selling price | 28·40 | 38·30 |
| | | |
| *Variable Costs:* | | |
| Materials | 22·10 | 29·40 |
| Labour | 0·80 | 1·10 |
| Variable overheads | 1·50 | 1·80 |
| | | |
| Total variable costs | 24·40 | 32·30 |
| | | |
| Contribution per sub-assembly | £4·00 | £6·00 |

It is now necessary to formulate the details in the form of mathematical equations which express the problem to be solved. It should be noted that the equations express linear relationships and therefore, as will be seen later, can be shown as straight lines on a graph.

If we let $x$ represent the number of sub-assemblies P to be produced and $y$ represent the number of sub-assemblies Q to be produced then for component $a$ the following equation applies.

|  | Sub-Assemblies | | |
|---|---|---|---|
| Component | P | Q | Stock |
| $a$ | $5x + 2y$ | $\leqslant$ | $240$ |

Thus, if we produce $x$ sub-assemblies P we shall use up $5x$ units of component $a$, and if we produce $y$ sub-assemblies Q we shall use up $2y$ units of components $a$; but the total components used of $a$ cannot exceed the constraint of 240 units in stock.

Similar equations are then formulated for the remaining components giving the following equations:

|  |  | Sub-Assembly | | |
|---|---|---|---|---|
|  | Component | P | Q | Stock |
| (1) | $a$ | $5x + 2y$ | $\leqslant$ | $240$ |
| (2) | $b$ | $12x + 14y$ | $\leqslant$ | $840$ |
| (3) | $c$ | $5x + 10y$ | $\leqslant$ | $400$ |
| (4) | $d$ | $4x + 6y$ | $\leqslant$ | $324$ |
| (5) | | $x \geqslant 0$ | | |
| (6) | | $y \geqslant 0$ | | |

(7) Objective Function $C_{max} = 4x + 6y$
where C = contribution.

Equations (5) and (6) are merely stating that we cannot have negative values for $x$ and $y$ which in this problem would be illogical, therefore we can ignore them in our solution.

Equation (7) sets out the objective of the exercise, that is, to ascertain the number of each sub-assembly which should be made to maximise the contribution; in other words to arrive at the optimal plan without violating the stock constraints. It will be remembered that the contributions are £4 for P and £6 for Q.

In order to carry out the graphical solution to this problem, equations (1–4) are restated as follows:

(1)    $5x + 2y = 240$
(2)   $12x + 14y = 840$
(3)    $5x + 10y = 400$
(4)    $4x + 6y = 324$
(7)    Objective function $C_{max} = 4x + 6y$

Equation (1) can now be represented by a straight line, viz.:

Since $$5x + 2y = 240$$

∴
$$\text{if } x = 0 \text{ then } y = 120$$
$$\text{if } y = 0 \text{ then } x = 48$$

It is now possible to plot the above values on a graph and to draw a straight line through the points (see Fig. 8.6).

The line depicting equation (1) shows the boundaries within which the values of $x$ and $y$ must be kept. Thus if equation (1) were the only constraint, then any values of $x$ and $y$ to the left of the line would be permissible, but values to the right of the line would violate the stock constraint of 240 units of component $a$.

The same procedure is carried out for equation (2) viz.:

$$12x + 14y = 840$$
$$\text{If } x = 0 \text{ then } y = 60$$
$$\text{If } y = 0 \text{ then } x = 70$$

The values are then plotted in the same graph and a straight line drawn through the points, see Fig. 8.7.

Fig. 8.7 now shows that the choice is further restricted by the equation (2) constraint and shows the feasibility area shown by the shaded area on the graphs; we can therefore select any values of $x$ and $y$ which lie within the shaded area.

The same procedure is carried out for the equation (3) and (4). Fig. 8.8 shows the four equations depicted by straight lines. The

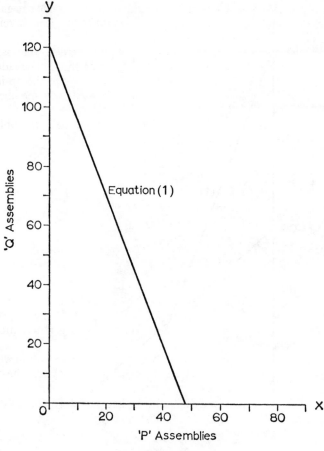

**Fig 8.6**

shaded area represents the feasibility area. Any choice of x and y units must be made within this area. It is obvious that there is a wide choice that can be made, that is to say, there are a variety of permutations; but such a choice would not necessarily lead to the solution which maximises contribution.

In order to arrive at the optimum solution it is necessary to make use of equation (7) which describes the contribution made by

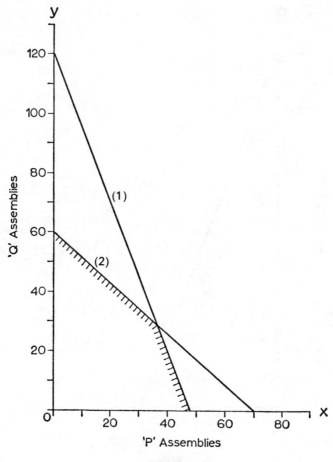

**Fig. 8.7**

producing $x$ units of P and $y$ units of Q.

(7)   Objective function $C_{max.} = 4x + 6y$

Again this linear equation can be represented by a straight line whose slope is determined by the coefficients of $x$ and $y$. No matter what values we give to $x$ and $y$ the slope of the line will remain constant. Therefore, we can append any value to C without altering the slope of the line.

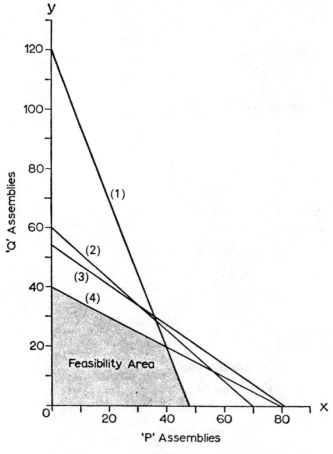

**Fig. 8.8**

Since we want a value which will allow us to plot the equation on the graph we will try values of C which will enable us to do this.

Thus, if we choose the value £ 60 to represent C then we have (7)
£ 60 = 4x + 6y

$\therefore$ if x = 0  y = 10
if y = 0  x = 15

Equation (7) is then plotted on the graph (see Fig. 8.9).

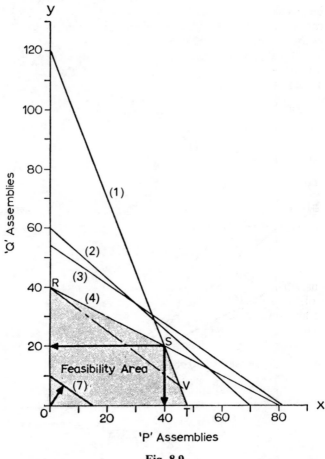

**Fig. 8.9**

If we now push the line of equation (7) further out from the origin it will mean that we can make more of $x$ and $y$, and the more units we make of $x$ and $y$ the greater will be the contribution; but we can only push the contribution line (7) as far as the extremities allowed by the shaded area RSTO. In pushing out this line from the origin it is essential that the same slope is maintained. RV represents the contribution line being pushed out as far as R but this would not represent the optimal solution. The optimal solution is where the line can be pushed out to the full extremities of the feasibility region, in this case at the point S. Hence the optimum solution is at S where the values are $x = 40$ and $y = 20$.

The optimal plan is therefore to make 40 sub-assemblies P, and 20 sub-assemblies Q.

The maximum contribution obtainable without violating the stock constraints is given by substituting the values for $x$ and $y$ in equation (7).

(7)  $C_{max} = 4x + 6y$
$\therefore$    Contribution $C = 4 \times 40 + 6 \times 20$
*Total contribution* $= 160 + 120 = £280$

*Stock Left Over*

| Components | Assembly P Make | Assembly Q Make | Total Used | Actual Stock | Remainder |
|---|---|---|---|---|---|
| a | $40 \times 5 = 200$ | $20 \times 2 = 40$ | 240 | 240 | NIL |
| b | $40 \times 12 = 480$ | $20 \times 14 = 280$ | 760 | 840 | 80 |
| c | $40 \times 5 = 200$ | $20 \times 10 = 200$ | 400 | 400 | NIL |
| d | $40 \times 4 = 160$ | $20 \times 6 = 120$ | 280 | 324 | 44 |

Thus, all the stock of components $a$ and $c$ are used in the plan but 80 units of $b$ and 44 units of $d$ remain unused.

The above shows that under the optimal plan none of the stock constraints have been violated.

### Summary

Historical, marginal and standard costing systems are not mutually exclusive, and you may have, and in a large organisation you should have, all three systems in operation.

Marginal costing will aid the initial decision, of whether to increase production or make or buy a component.

Standard costing will allow targets to be established, and historical costing will enable the actual results to be compared with the predetermined standards.

### Questions

1  Explain in your own words the meaning of marginal cost.
2  Distinguish between total absorption costing and marginal costing.
3  In what particular areas is marginal costing particularly suitable?
4  Derive the formula for ascertaining (*i*) the 'contribution' and (*ii*) the 'break-even point'.

**5**  In what circumstances might a firm be willing to sell at a price below total cost?

**6**  Give the formula for calculating sales at break-even point and number of units at break-even point.

**7**  Prepare a break-even chart from the following information for a period:

Selling price: £5 per unit
Total production capacity: 5000 units
Fixed overheads: £5000
Variable costs per unit: £3

**8**  What is the margin of safety? Calculate the margin in units from the figures in the last question.

**9**  From the information contained in question 7 prepare a profit volume chart and explain its significance.

**10**  What are the limitations of break-even analysis?

**11**  The Jolson Brick Company manufacturers a standard rustic brick for the building industry, the production capacity for the year is 100 000 standard bricks. The selling price per brick is £0·80, variable costs per brick are £0·30. The fixed costs of the company are £30 000 per annum. You are required to:

(*i*)  Draw a break-even chart depicting the above data.

(*ii*)  Determine from your chart

(*a*)  the break-even point in terms of £ sales and bricks;

(*b*)  the factor of safety expressed in terms of bricks.

(*iii*)  Verify your results obtained in (*ii*) by calculation.

**12**

(*i*)  From the data in question 11 draw up a profit–volume chart for the Jolson Company.

(*ii*)  Compute the profit–volume ratio.

(*iii*)  If the selling price were reduced to £0·75 per brick and the variable costs increased to £0·35 per brick, ascertain by calculation:

(*a*)  the new break-even point;

(*b*)  the new factor of safety;

(*c*)  the new profit–volume rato.

**13**  The Tudor Engineering Company is at present working at full capacity and is likely to be working at this capacity in the ensuing year.

Management is considering concentrating on four products, A, B, C and D, the forecast demand for next year is as follows:

Product A    2000 units
Product B    1000 units
Product C    5000 units
Product D    8000 units

Owing to the state of the finance market the Directors have prohibited further capital expenditure required for increasing the Company's production capacity.

The relevant costs, selling prices and process times pertaining to these four products are as follows:

| Product | A | B | C | D |
|---|---|---|---|---|
| | £ | £ | £ | £ |
| Selling price/unit | 100 | 80 | 150 | 152 |
| Variable costs price/unit | 40 | 50 | 70 | 80 |
| Process time *in hours* per unit | 5 | 5 | 8 | 9 |

The budgeted fixed overheads for the year are £400 000.
The total production capacity for the year is 86 000 hours.

(*i*) On what products should the company concentrate in order to maximise its profits within the production constraint?
(*ii*) Prepare a schedule showing the production plan which maximises profits and show the maximum profit attainable.

**14** A factory manufactures two qualities of a product known as 'Basic' quality and 'De-luxe' quality. Both qualities require two processes known as Process (1) and Process (2). The following data shows the processing times required for each product:

| | Process – Hours per Unit | |
|---|---|---|
| | Process (1) | Process (2) |
| 'Basic' | 2 | 4 |
| 'De-luxe' | 3 | 1 |

The hours available in each process are:

| | |
|---|---|
| Process (1) | 6000 hours |
| Process (2) | 8000 hours |

The selling prices and variable costs are:

| | 'Basic' | 'De-luxe' |
|---|---|---|
| | £ | £ |
| Selling price | 10 | 15 |
| Variable cost | 5 | 9 |

Using the graphical linear programming approach, determine the manufacturing mix which will maximise the total contribution towards fixed overheads and profit.

# 9 Accounting Ratios

## Ratios used in financial analysis and interpretation of accounts

The published accounts of a concern may be used by different people for different purposes. They are, of course, primarily an account of the stewardship function of management which they are obliged to prepare for the owners of the company, the shareholders. However, the accounts will also prove invaluable to the financial analyst who is acting as an investment adviser or to the bank manager who has been requested to give a loan or overdraft facilities to the company, or even to the prospective creditor of the company to enable him to assess the creditworthiness of the company before selling goods to them. Management will also be able to ascertain meaningful ratios from the published accounts. (However, they also have access to unpublished information which may, from their point of view, be even more valuable.) Management ratios will be considered in the next chapter.

## Limitations

Over-emphasis of a single ratio should be avoided and it is essential to look at the following points when considering individual ratios. Firstly, how does the particular ratio fit in with the trend over the past few years? Secondly, how does the ratio compare with other ratios obtained from the same information? Finally, what influence does the type of business activity have on the ratio? For example, we might expect a low current assets to fixed assets ratio if we were considering the accounts of a market stallholder, where the only fixed asset might be a motor vehicle for transporting his stock; but such a ratio would not be acceptable for a motor-car manufacturer.

## Ratios obtained from the balance sheet

We will use the following balance sheet to illustrate the various ratios:

**Balance Sheet as at 31st December 19—**

| | £ | | £ | £ |
|---|---|---|---|---|
| 80 000 ordinary | | *Fixed Assets* | | |
| shares (£1) | 80 000 | | | |
| 5% preference | | | | |
| shares (£1) | 60 000 | Buildings | 100 000 | |
| General reserve | 10 000 | Plant and machinery | 50 000 | |
| Profit and loss a/c. | | | | |
| balance | 10 000 | Fixtures and fittings | 30 000 | |
| | 160 000 | | | 180 000 |
| 10% Debentures | 60 000 | | | |
| *Current Liabilities* | | *Current Assets* | | |
| | £ | | | |
| Creditors | 38 000 | Stock | 35 000 | |
| Taxation | 17 000 | Debtors | 45 000 | |
| Dividend | 11 000 | Bank | 26 000 | |
| | 66 000 | | | 106 000 |
| | £286 000 | | | £286 000 |

## Share valuation

Although there are a number of methods which may be adopted to
value shares we shall use the 'asset valuation' method. This involves
calculating the total equity of the company, in other words that part
of the capital which has been subscribed for by the ordinary
shareholders plus retained earnings.

In our example we have:

| | £ |
|---|---|
| Ordinary shares of £1 each | 80 000 |
| General reserve | 10 000 |
| Profit and loss account balance | 10 000 |
| Equity | £100 000 |

Asset value of 1 ordinary share $\dfrac{£100\,000}{80\,000} = £1 \cdot 25$

The same result will occur if the current liabilities, debentures and
preference shares are deducted from the total assets. The benefit of
doing the calculation in this way is that the assets can be valued on a
realistic basis rather than as shown in the balance sheet. Thus some of
the fixed assets, such as buildings, may be worth more than the
balance sheet figure; and account can also be taken of the fact that
current assets must be used effectively if their full value is to be taken

in the calculation. For example, a large cash balance accumulated for no particular purpose cannot be said to be effectively employed in the business, and this fact would be taken into account when arriving at the total asset figure for the computation.

The computed figure may be compared with the actual Stock Exchange quotation, if the company is quoted; but this can only be a very general guide, as stock market prices are influenced by many external factors which are not directly related to the performance of companies.

### Liquidity ratios

It is possible for a concern to be earning a high rate of profit yet still encounter difficulties in meeting its day-to-day commitments. This is known as 'over-trading'.

The two ratios to ascertain the availability of funds are:

(*a*) current ratio;
(*b*) quick ratio or liquid ratio.

The current ratio assesses the overall working capital position and is found by:

$$\frac{\text{Current assets}}{\text{Current liabilities}}$$

In our example this would be:

$$\frac{\pounds 106\,000}{\pounds 66\,000} = 1 \cdot 6 : 1$$

This result might be said to be rather low as the 'ideal' ratio is reckoned to be nearer to 2 : 1. However, high ratios may be the result of poor investment policies or too large a holding of stock; and it is necessary to consider carefully the type of business under analysis and also the result of the other ratio concerned with liquidity, in other words the 'quick ratio'.

The quick ratio demonstrates the ability of the concern to meet its immediate commitments. It is frequently called the 'acid test ratio'. Stock may take a large share of the total current assets, yet in an emergency it will probably be difficult to transform it quickly into cash and if it has to be sold under such circumstances it is likely to yield far less than its book value. To calculate the quick ratio, stock is taken away from the total current assets to give liquid assets.

In our example this will result in

$$\frac{£71\,000}{£66\,000} = 1·07:1$$

This ratio should generally be at least 1:1 and if it is below this figure immediate steps should be taken to correct it.

It can be very damaging to the future activities of the business if it cannot pay its immediate liabilities. Creditors will be less willing in the future to sell goods to the company on credit and in extreme cases of insolvency the company may be forced into liquidation.

### Net current assets to fixed assets

As already mentioned this ratio will depend upon the type of business being analysed. It is most useful if it is compared with the same ratio ascertained for other businesses involved in the same type of activity. However, comparisons may be misleading due to different policies adopted by different managements, for example frequent revaluation of fixed assets by one company, or different depreciation rates being used by different companies.

Our example would yield:

$$\frac{£106\,000}{£180\,000} = 0·59:1$$

### Proprietors' ratio

The proprietor should provide sufficient capital to cover the fixed assets and some part of the working capital. If this is not done, then reliance will have to be placed on outside financing and this may involve undesirable conditions being imposed by the lenders.

The proprietors' ratio is:

$$\frac{\text{Capital employed}}{\text{Liabilities (short- and long-term)}}$$

The capital employed for the purpose of this ratio comprises the original capital, all types of share being included, plus the amounts which have been retained in the business for future expansion.

Our example gives us:

$$\frac{£160\,000}{£126\,000} = 1·27:1$$

(i.e. Current liabilities + Debentures)

Subsequent calculation of this ratio will reveal whether there has been an increase or decrease in the funds being supplied by outsiders or whether finance is being provided from internal sources.

## Capital employed to fixed assets

Ideally the owners of the business should 'cover' all the fixed assets and part of the current assets. This was outlined for the last ratio. The capital employed to fixed assets ratio reveals whether any parts of the fixed assets are owned by debenture holders or other creditors.

In our example the ratio is:

$$\frac{£160\,000}{£180\,000} = 0.89:1$$

which does in fact mean that some of the fixed assets have been financed by outside lenders.

## Gearing ratio

Gearing has already been considered in some detail in Chapter 3 and therefore we shall simply calculate the ratio for our particular company.

$$\text{Capital gearing ratio} = \frac{\text{Ordinary share capital}}{\text{Fixed interest capital}}$$

$$= \frac{£80\,000}{£120\,000} = 0.66:1$$

This low ratio shows our company to be highly geared, in other words it has a high proportion of fixed interest capital. This will mean that equity earnings will rise and fall faster than, and hence disproportionately to, variations in total profits.

## Ratios utilising the trading account and profit and loss account

These ratios are often termed operating ratios and we shall use the following Trading Account and Profit and Loss Account in conjunction with the balance sheet already given.

**Trading Account for the Year Ending 31st December 19—**

|  | £ | £ |  | £ |
|---|---|---|---|---|
| Opening stock | 15 000 |  | Sales | 365 000 |
| Purchases | 315 000 |  |  |  |
|  |  | 330 000 |  |  |
| *Less* Closing stock |  | 35 000 |  |  |
|  |  | 295 000 |  |  |
| Gross profit c/d |  | 70 000 |  |  |
|  |  | 365 000 |  | 365 000 |

**Profit and Loss Account for the Year Ending 31st December 19—**

|  | £ |  | £ |
|---|---|---|---|
| Administration expenses | 12 000 | Gross profit b/d | 70 000 |
| Selling expenses | 8 000 |  |  |
| Distribution expenses | 5 000 |  |  |
| Financial expenses | 10 000 |  |  |
| Net profit c/f | 35 000 |  |  |
|  | £ 70 000 |  | £ 70 000 |

**Profit and Loss Appropriation Account for the Year Ending 31st December 19—**

|  | £ |  | £ |
|---|---|---|---|
| Dividend | 11 000 | Net profit b/d | 35 000 |
| Transfer to reserve | 2 000 | Balance brought |  |
| Taxation | 17 000 | forward | 5 000 |
| Balance carried to balance sheet | 10 000 |  |  |
|  | £ 40 000 |  | £ 40 000 |

## Credit sales to debtors ratio

This ratio reveals how quickly the cash is being received from credit sales. The ratio should have a definite relationship to the period of credit allowed to customers; thus, if customers are allowed 30 days to pay, then this would mean a ratio of 12 : 1 (i.e. 365 days divided by 30).

In our example sales are £365 000 and debtors £45 000. The ratio is:

$$\frac{£365\,000}{£45\,000} = 8:1$$

which is an average ratio indicating that debtors pay their accounts reasonably quickly.

To establish the average collection period the sales are divided by 365 to obtain the average daily sales and this is then divided into the debtors to give the average collection period:

$$\frac{\text{Debtors}}{\text{Sales} \div 365} = \frac{£45\,000}{£365\,000 \div 365}$$

$$= 45 \text{ days}$$

It is obviously of great benefit to the business if money can be collected as quickly as possible. This period of just over six weeks would normally be quite satisfactory.

### Purchases to creditors ratio

A similar ratio can be calculated for creditors. This will show on average how quickly the business is settling its own debts.

The ratio is:

$$\frac{\text{Purchases}}{\text{Creditors}} = \frac{£315\,000}{£38\,000} = 8 \cdot 3:1$$

The average payment period is found by:

$$\frac{\text{Creditors}}{\text{Purchases} \div 365} = \frac{£38\,000}{£315\,000 \div 365} = 44 \text{ days}$$

Both of the last two ratios reveal relatively short intervals for payment of creditors and receiving money from debtors, but this will be influenced by discounts given for prompt payment both by the business and by its creditors.

### Sales to fixed assets

This ratio shows the efficiency achieved in the use of fixed assets. It is particularly useful for comparison purposes to ascertain whether the sales per £1 of fixed assets is increasing or decreasing over a period. In our example:

$$\frac{\text{Sales}}{\text{Fixed assets}} = \frac{\pounds\,365\,000}{\pounds\,180\,000} = 2:1$$

Each £1 of fixed assets is producing over £2 of sales. This is a satisfactory position and comparison with previous periods will show whether the trend is favourable or otherwise.

## Gross profit ratio

This reveals the average mark-up on the cost of goods available for sale. It is essential that this percentage should be sufficiently high to bear the overhead charges and still make a net profit, but it may be influenced by market factors, particularly competition, which will tend to make the rate of mark-up an important management decision. Our example gives us:

$$\frac{\text{Gross profit}}{\text{Sales}} = \frac{\pounds\,70\,000}{\pounds\,365\,000} \times \frac{100}{1} = 19\% \; approx.$$

If, however, a number of different products are made such an average can be misleading. This was shown in the example in Chapter 1 when only one of the three products manufactured had the same net profit as the average net profit, and the average was in fact masking a product making a substantial loss.

## Net profit ratio

In this ratio the net profit is substituted for gross profit:

$$\frac{\text{Net profit}}{\text{Sales}} = \frac{\pounds\,35\,000}{\pounds\,365\,000} \times \frac{100}{1} = 9\cdot6\%$$

## Stock turnover ratio

Here we are concerned with the number of times the average stock is turned over during the year. This indicates how the stock is flowing through the business and is valuable as a guide to present activities compared with past events. If the ratio is increasing this usually means that business is expanding and if it is decreasing, then vice versa. Care must be taken when using the ratio because of the effect which opening and closing stocks have upon it.

The method of calculation is:

$$\frac{\text{Cost of sales}}{\text{Average stock}}$$

Cost of sales in our example consists of:

| | | |
|---|---|---|
| Opening stock | £15 000 | |
| Purchases | £315 000 | |
| | | £330 000 |
| *Less* Closing stock | | £35 000 |
| Cost of sales | | £295 000 |

Average stock is found as follows:

$$\frac{\text{Opening stock} + \text{Closing stock}}{2}$$

i.e.

$$\frac{£15\,000 + £35\,000}{2} = £25\,000$$

Turnover ratio is therefore:

$$\frac{£295\,000}{£25\,000} = \text{approximately 12 times}$$

This means roughly that the stock is completely turned over on average once a month, and also that the stock-holding period is 4 weeks or more. The influence of opening and closing stocks can be illustrated by the following example.

If the cost of sales remained the same in the next period, but it was decided to hold a stock of £35 000 throughout the year, then the ratio falls to:

$$\frac{£295\,000}{£35\,000} = \text{approximately 8 times}$$

The *cost* of holding such stock is an important point which should always be borne in mind. This cost is made up of the interest being lost on the capital tied up in the stock, together with warehouse and storage expenses incurred.

Careful control should be maintained over stock levels, and only sufficient stocks should be held to ensure that production requirements will be met without undue delays.

**Expense ratios**

Here we are concerned with the ratio of various overhead expenses to sales – administration expenses to sales, selling expneses to sales, distribution expenses to sales and financial expenses to sales. By observing the trends in these ratios and the relationships between them it is possible to spot significant changes and assess what action management has taken and should take.

In our example, the ratios are:

%

Administration expenses to sales $\dfrac{£12\,000}{£365\,000} = 1:30$    3·3

Selling expenses to sales $\dfrac{£8\,000}{£365\,000} = 1:45$    2·2

Distribution expenses to sales $\dfrac{£5\,000}{£356\,000} = 1:73$    1·4

Financial expenses to sales $\dfrac{£10\,000}{£365\,000} = 1:36$    2·7

**Financial ratios for the investor**

It will now be necessary for us to assume a market price for the shares of our company. Let us say the current stock market price is £1·50p per £1 share. We can now calculate a number of important ratios from the investor's point of view.

**Dividend yield**    The rate of dividend on ordinary shares is found by deducting the preference share dividend: £60 000 × 5% = £3000 from the total dividend paid, that is £11 000. This leaves £8000 for the ordinary shares, which is a rate of 10% on the £80 000 ordinary share capital.

By dividing the dividend rate by the market price a more realistic yield is achieved. This is found by:

$$\frac{\text{Par value of share} \times \text{Dividend \%}}{\text{Market value}}$$

In our example:

$$\frac{£1 \times 10\%}{£1·5} = 6·7\%$$

**Dividend cover** Here we are concerned with how many times the dividend is covered by earnings. This is important to the investor as he can ensure that management are not paying out all earnings or reducing capital (i.e. previous earnings retained) but are pursuing a prudent policy of ploughing back some part of the year's profits. The formula is:

$$\frac{\text{Profits (after tax)} - \text{Preference dividend}}{\text{Dividend on ordinary shares}}$$

$$= \frac{£35\,000 - £17\,000 - £3000}{£8000}$$

$$= \frac{£15\,000}{£8000} = 1 \cdot 875 \text{ times covered}$$

**Price earnings ratio** This ratio has come to the fore in recent years as a measure of the relationship between the current market price of the share and earnings.

The *earnings per share* will be the amount available for the ordinary shareholder, either to be paid out as a dividend or retained in the business to promote future growth. The formula is:

$$\frac{\text{Attributable profit (after tax)} - \text{Preference dividend}}{\text{Number of ordinary shares}}$$

In our example this gives us:

$$\frac{£18\,000 - £3000}{80\,000} = \frac{£15\,000}{80\,000} = £0 \cdot 19$$

The price earnings ratio is found by:

$$\frac{\text{Market price per share}}{\text{Earnings per share}} = \frac{£1 \cdot 5}{£0 \cdot 19} = 8$$

Any price earnings ratio should be compared with the ratio for other firms in the same industry.

### Profitability ratio–profit to capital employed

It is probably true to say that this should be the first ratio which the financial analyst or investor calculates, as it may be said to be the ultimate test of business efficiency. It forms the basis of the pyramid structure of ratios used by the Centre for Interfirm Comparisons and is known as the 'primary ratio'.

The term 'capital employed' is unfortunately subject to many different interpretations. We have already considered one interpretation earlier in this chapter, that of equity capital plus retained earnings. When using it to form a measure of profitability it is usual to calculate it by taking the current liabilities from the total assets. More, however, will be said about this important ratio in the next chapter, as it forms an important part of management control by ratios.

Profit is also subject to controversy. Should the profits used in the calculation be before or after tax? Those in favour of using a net profit figure after tax claim that it represents a more realistic figure of the amount available for financing and remunerating the capital. Those supporting the net profit before tax concept point out that their profit figure gives a fairer indication of the actual performance of the assets which have been utilised to produce the profit. Also the tax charge of each company is affected by individual circumstances such as variations in capital allowances or even by differing skills in taxation management. Tax rates are subject to change from period to period, making comparisons over such periods difficult if tax is taken into account in the return-on-capital-employed computation. We shall produce both versions from our figures.

1 Return on capital employed (after tax):

$$\frac{\text{Profit (after tax)}}{\text{Assets} - \text{Current liabilities}} = \frac{\pounds 18\,000}{\pounds 286\,000 - \pounds 66\,000}$$

$$= \frac{\pounds 18\,000}{\pounds 220\,000} \times \frac{100}{1} = 8\cdot 2\,\%$$

2 Return on capital employed (before tax):

$$\frac{\text{Profit}}{\text{Assets} - \text{Current liabilities}} = \frac{\pounds 35\,000}{\pounds 220\,000} \times \frac{100}{1} = 15\cdot 9\,\%$$

The significance of these figures will be considered in the next chapter. However, it might be said here that if a reasonable rate of return cannot be earned on the capital, then it would be better employed elsewhere.

There is a direct relationship between the rate of return on capital employed and the ratio of net profit to sales. We calculated this ratio earlier in this chapter to be 9·6 %.

The net assets (i.e. Assets − Current liabilities) have generated

$\pounds 365\,000$ of sales or have turned over $\dfrac{\pounds 365\,000}{\pounds 220\,000} = 1\cdot 66$ times.

If we now link these two ratios (i.e. $1.66 \times 9.6\%$) we have the return on capital employed of $15.9\%$ originally calculated.

## Conclusion

Ratio analysis has a number of limitations which have already been considered, and ratios in themselves cannot provide answers for management or investors; but they do highlight trends and allow comparisons to be made, and when applied intelligently can be a valuable tool.

## Questions

**1** Explain what you understand by the term 'over-trading'.

**2** How is the 'quick ratio' or 'acid test' ratio calculated and what is its significance?

**3** Explain the importance of the proprietors' ratio.

**4** Give the formula for calculating the average period in which debtors pay their accounts.

**5** What factors are likely to affect the gross profit ratio?

**6** How is the dividend yield calculated?

**7** Outline the advantages and disadvantages of calculating the return on capital employed using the profit before tax is deducted.

**8** From Question 10, Chapter 4:

(*i*) Compute the following ratios for years 19–6 and 19–7.

   (*a*) Rate of turnover of stocks;
   (*b*) Net profit after tax to net capital employed;
   (*c*) Credit period given;
   (*d*) Working capital ratio;
   (*e*) Liquidity ratio;
   (*f*) Net worth of an ordinary share.

(*ii*) Write a concise report on the financial position of the company making any recommendations you think would be advantageous to the company.

# 10 Uniform Costing and Interfirm Comparisons

## Uniform costing

Uniform costing may be defined as the use by several undertakings of the same basic costing methods and techniques.

It is most usefully employed by large business organisations which have a number of factories spread over a wide area, manufacturing the same type of product under similar conditions or operating the same type of service. It may also be used by trade associations when processes are standardised and easily identifiable.

The concept of uniform costing is not a new one; indeed the first scheme using such a system was introduced in the United States of America at the end of the last century. Perhaps the most famous scheme in Britain is that of the Federation of Master Printers which was first operated in 1913; and since then a number of other industries have used the technique.

In order to ensure that uniform costing will be of value, it is first necessary to establish that comparisons between different firms in an industry are in fact possible. This means that the following matters will have to be considered:

(a) the type of costing system to be used (i.e. contract, job, batch or process costing, or some combination if that is more suitable);
(b) the methods of overhead recovery;
(c) the methods of depreciation;
(d) the definition of terms such as 'direct costs' and 'indirect costs';
(e) the designing of a suitable cost classification coding system;
(f) the system of stores pricing and valuation of year-end stocks and work in progress, including the treatment of scrap and obsolete stores;
(g) the design of suitable statement forms which can be easily completed from existing records;
(h) the methods of remunerating labour, including standard bonus schemes;
(i) a standard unit of production;
(j) the inclusion of charges for rent and interest on capital, even though premises for example are actually owned by the concern.

The technique of uniform costing is not just restricted to industrial concerns. Local authorities for example have a comprehensive system of cost comparisons for different services by which one local authority is able to compare the cost of services such as housing, education, police, etc. with all the other major authorities in the country. The information is produced by the Chartered Institute of Public Finance and Accountancy on an annual basis; and a standard accounting system is recommended by the former body to ensure that the costs are compiled on an equitable basis and can in fact be compared.

The advantages of uniform costing are:

1   Constant attention will be paid to the best methods of ascertaining and presenting cost data within the particular industry.
2   Better operating efficiency is possible because of the stimulation of the competitive spirit and a deeper understanding of the role of costing and of its value to the organisation.
3   Components and materials can be standardised, and pricing policies may be determined on a more realistic basis.

The main difficulties are:

1   The problem of standardisation of terms is not easy to overcome as the methods and needs of each firm will be different.
2   The adaptation of a firm's present costing system to suit a standard costing system may be expensive.
3   It is often difficult to persuade firms to disclose confidential information to the central collection agency, for fear that it will be disclosed to competitors.
4   There are many factors which affect different firms in different ways. For example, geographical location of the firm may increase or reduce its costs; or the available supply of labour may affect decisions on mechanisation and automation.

Tremendous interest has been shown in the establishment of uniform costing over a wide field of industrial activities since the Centre for Interfirm Comparisons began in 1959. The work of the Centre is described below.

## Interfirm comparisons

(The author wishes to acknowledge with thanks the help given by the Centre for Interfirm Comparison in the preparation of this section, and particularly Mr L. Taylor Harrington, its Director.)

An interfirm comparison scheme is intended to show the management of each firm taking part how its profitability and productivity compares with that of other firms in the same industry; in what respects the firm is weaker or stronger than its competitors; and what specific questions of policy or performance should be tackled if the firm's profitability and productivity are to be raised.

In 1959 an organisation known as the Centre for Interfirm Comparison Limited was set up by the British Institute of Management in association with the British Productivity Council, to meet the demand of industry and trade for an expert body to conduct interfirm comparisons on a confidential basis as a service to management. It was established as a separate company, although it is a non-profit-making organisation, in order that its services should not be confined to members of its sponsoring organisations but should be made widely available to industry and trade. To date (1985) the Centre has worked in over 100 different sectors.

The major aims of the Centre are:

1  To undertake interfirm comparisons (IFCs) by direct arrangement with individual firms.
2  To offer a special service to trade associations, acting on their behalf as a 'neutral' expert organisation for the promotion and conduct of interfirm comparisons among their members.
3  To carry out research into performance measurement and comparison.
4  To offer its international connections to British firms wishing to compare their efficiency and costs with their opposite numbers in such countries as Germany, France, Switzerland, Holland, Belgium and the United States.
5  To help to introduce management ratio systems within companies and other organisations as an aid to internal planning and control.
6  To provide advice and training to organisations overseas which wish to undertake interfirm comparisons, productivity studies, etc.

In recent years the Centre has developed the work to cover the public and voluntary sectors, and has also conducted confidential statistical and financial surveys for various organisations concerned with industry and trade.

## Independent external yardstick

There are three standards by which to measure the performance of a firm – its past performance, budgets and interfirm comparisons. Comparisons with the past have the disadvantage that the economic climate and the state of technology is constantly changing. It is therefore impossible to know with certainty whether a change over time is due to change in efficiency or to economic and technological changes. The disadvantage of comparisons with budgets is that even the best budgets depend on the estimates of the executives who compile them, with all the limitations that such an approach implies.

With interfirm comparisons there is the outstanding advantage that a comparison is made between the performance of a firm with that of other firms operating in the same competitive conditions during the same period of time. Interfirm comparisons therefore provide an independent external yardstick against which to assess the performance of a company.

In theory, there are two possible approaches to the conduct of an interfirm comparison – by using the services of such organisations as the Centre, or by 'doing-it-yourself'. The major drawback of the 'do-it-yourself' approach is its reliance on published information from other companies. The Centre estimates, for instance, that only 10–20 % of the information used in its comparisons could be calculated from published accounts, and that even this information is unlikely to have been arrived at on a comparable basis. A further disadvantage inherent in the use of published information is that the terminology, the definitions and the valuation principles of different accountants are not standard. Divisions of large organisations do not have to publish accounts, and it has been estimated that about 75 % of all limited companies are exempt, under the Companies Act 1985, from disclosing some of the information required by that act. Few firms take account of an inflation factor in their published data, and it is well known that the once-a-year balance sheet may be drawn up at a time which is not typical of the year as a whole. All these disadvantages are avoided in a properly organised interfirm comparison.

## Individual report

A comparison organised by the Centre goes through a number of stages. First, a group of firms, which are sufficiently comparable and sufficiently numerous to make a comparison between them worth while, is built up by the Centre, usually acting with the close co-operation of the relevant trade associations. In many comparisons the next stage is to visit each of the participating firms to discover more about its mode of operating, and to find out what information about its activities it can readily provide.

With this information, the staff of the Centre will then devise a set of ratios which on the one hand provides the firms with the information that they want, while on the other does not put inordinate demands upon the accounts and other departments to provide the necessary basic information. The Centre then sends a questionnaire to participating firms which when completed provides all the information required. As well as the questionnaire, participants are sent definitions of all terms used so that each can be sure that the figures have been arrived at on a strictly comparable basis. When the questionnaires are returned to the Centre they are checked and, if necessary, the figures amended after discussion with the firms concerned.

A general report is then prepared and sent to each participating firm. This report will contain all the ratios for each firm, together with background information which enables the participant to compare his firm with those firms most similar to his own. If there are general conclusions to be drawn from the figures as a whole, these are incorporated in this report.

Senior members of the Centre's staff then write an individual report which interprets for each individual participant the conclusions which it seems he should draw from the figures in the general report. Often these reports are then discussed at follow-up meetings at the firm between members of their top management team and senior personnel from the Centre.

## Confidentiality and cost

The Centre is completely independent and no information supplied to it by companies is passed to any other organisation. The results of interfirm comparisons are made available to participating companies only. In the reports, the comparative data showing the figures for participating firms do not, of course, appear under the name of the firm, but under code numbers. The data are expressed in ratio, percentage and similar statistical forms (rather than as absolute figures), which reduces the possibility of identification.

It is impossible to quote in advance a price for the service because it will vary according to the amount of time and expense incurred in building up the comparison group, the amount of detail to be covered by the comparison, whether firms need to be visited (for example, to discuss the arrangements for, or the results of, the comparison), and the amount of individual written interpretation provided. However, for each comparison scheme a definite fee is quoted before companies are asked to commit themselves to participate.

*Industries and trades, etc., already covered by the Centre*
It was stated above that the first stage of a comparison was to build up a group of participants. However, in many industries such groups already exist, and interested firms can therefore expect to receive the results of comparisons that much sooner.

The following list shows the industries, trades, services and professions in which the Centre for Interfirm Comparison has prepared IFC schemes:

Adoption services
Aluminium anodisers
Aluminium home improvement
  systems
Bedding manufacture
Biscuit manufacture
Blanket manufacture
Book publishers
Book publishers' distribution
Breweries: managed Houses
Builders' merchants
Building and civil engineering
Bulk liquid haulage contractors
Carpet manufacture
    (a) woven
    (b) tufted
Chemical manufacture*
Clothing manufacture
Cold rolled sections manufacture
Colour makers
Computing bureaux
Corn and agricultural merchants
Cotton spinning
Crane manufacture
Decorators' merchants
Distribution (manufacturers)*
Domestic central heating
  equipment manufacture
Drop forgers
Electrical contractors
Electrical/electronic product
  manufacturers
Electrical engineering
Engineers' tool manufacture

English woollen and worsted
  industry
Express carriers
Finance houses
Flexible package manufacture
Food manufacture
Food distribution
Forgemasters
Fork lift truck manufacture
Gauge and tool manufacture
Glass container manufacture
Hand tool manufacture
Housing associations
Industry in New Towns
Ironfoundries
Joinery manufacture
Leather dressing
Libraries   (a) Public
            (b) Academic
Local authority services
Machine tool importers
Machine tool manufacture
Mains cable manufacture
Maintenance costs*
Mechanical engineering*
Narrow fabric manufacture
Non-ferrous foundries
Nylon hose dyeing
Painting and decorating
  contractors
Paintmakers
Paper manufacture
Paper sack manufacture
Pharmaceutical manufacture

* Covering various types and size groups

Pipework contractors
Plastics moulding
Pump manufacture
Radio and electronic component
   manufacture
Rayon weaving
Residential homes for the elderly
Resin manufacture
Road haulage*
Rubber manufacture*
Scientific instrument
   manufacture
Scottish woollen industry
Secondary aluminium ingots
Shirt manufacture

Soft drinks manufacture
Solicitors
Steel stockholders
Structural steelwork
Tank and industrial plant
   manufacture
Throwsters
Tie manufacture
Timber importers
Timber merchants
Valve manufacture (mechanical)
Vending machine operators
Veterinary practices
Warp knitting

\* Covering various types and size groups.

## An example of IFC

The following is a much condensed example of an IFC in a light engineering industry. In the actual comparison about thirty-five firms took part. Some forty ratios with a considerable amount of background information were provided to participants. The 'pyramid' of ratios presented on page 156 shows the set of the *major* management ratios covered by the IFC, and explains why the individual ratios were chosen.

The ratio of operating profit/operating assets is selected as the primary ratio because it reflects the earning power of the operations of a business. A favourable ratio will indicate that a company is using its resources effectively, and will put it into a strong competitive position.

The relationship between a firm's operating profit and its operating assets depends first of all on two other important relationships (ratios) – namely between its operating profit and its sales, and between its sales and its operating assets.

Ratio 2 shows *what* profit margin has been earned on sales, while ratio 3 shows *how often* the margin has been earned on assets in the year. Ratio 3 shows how many times assets have been turned over in a year. Ratio 3a indicates the assets required per £1000 of sales.

Thus the return on operating assets of a firm depends on the relationship between its ratios 2 and 3, and this in turn depends on the relationships between its sales and its profits (and therefore its costs), and between its sales and its assets.

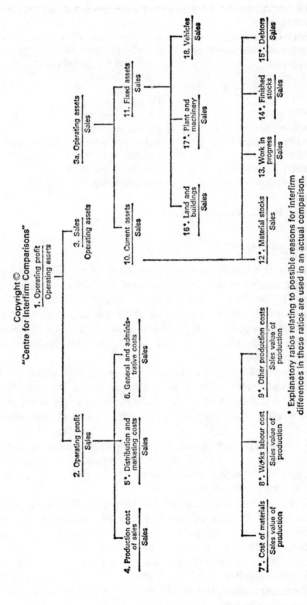

* Explanatory ratios relating to possible reasons for interfirm differences in these ratios are used in an actual comparison.

**Fig 10.1** 'Pyramid' of ratios for general management

Table 10.1, on page 158, shows the ratios of a light engineering firm for two years.

This looks like a success story: return on assets (ratio 1) has gone up from 8·7 to 10·8 % due to a rise both in the firm's profit on sales (ratio 2) and its turnover of assets (ratio 3). The former has improved because the fall in the firm's production cost ratio 4 has been greater than the rise in its marketing and distribution cost ratio 5. Ratio 4 in turn has improved as a result of falls in the firm's material and works labour cost ratios 7 and 8.

As to the firm's asset utilisation ratios, there has been an improvement on both the current and fixed asset sides (ratios 10 and 11). The rise in the debtors ratio 15 is more than off-set by falls in the materials stock, work in progress and finished stock ratios 12, 13 and 14. Furthermore, the two major fixed asset investment ratios 16 and 17 have improved.

But the firm's illusion of success was shattered when it compared its ratios with those of other light engineering firms of its kind. Table 10.2, on page 159, is an extract from the results – it gives the figures of only seven of the thirty-five participating firms. Our firm's figures are shown under letter E.

As Table 10.2 shows, this year the firm's profit on assets is well below that of four other firms and this is due to both its profit on sales (ratio 2) and turnover of assets (ratio 3) being relatively low. The firm's profit on sales (ratio 2) is relatively low mainly because both its production cost ratio 4 and its general and administrative cost ratio 6 are comparatively high, even though they compared well with the firm's previous year's figures. Firm E's distribution and marketing cost ratio 5 on the other hand, which had risen during the last year, is the lowest of all; this might reflect an insufficient marketing effort. The firm's production cost ratio 4 is comparatively high because although its materials and works labour cost ratios 7 and 8 have improved, it now turns out that both these ratios, and also its other production costs ratio are higher than those of firms A to D.

As to the utilisation of current asset investment, the firm's work in progress ratio 13 is higher (less favourable) than those of firms A to D, even though it had improved in comparison with the previous period. Its finished stock investment ratio 14, on the other hand, is almost the lowest of all; this however, is not necessarily a favourable indication, since greater emphasis on stock production of standard products or components might help the firm to manufacture more economically.

| Ratios | Last year | This year |
|---|---|---|
| *Return on assets* | | |
| 1. Operating profit/Operating assets (%) | 8·7 | 10·8 |
| *Profit margin on sales and turnover of assets* | | |
| 2. Operating profit/Sales (%) | 8·9 | 10·7 |
| 3. Sales/Operating assets (times per year) | 0·97 | 1·01 |
| *Departmental costs* (as percentage of sales) | | |
| 4. Production cost of sales | 77·4 | 75·4 |
| 5. Distribution and marketing costs | 4·6 | 4·9 |
| 6. General and administrative costs | 9·1 | 9·0 |
| *Production costs* (as a percentage of sales value of production) | | |
| 7. Materials costs | 34·7 | 33·1 |
| 8. Works labour costs | 27·4 | 26·8 |
| 9. Other production costs | 15·3 | 15·5 |
| *General asset utilisation* (£s per £1,000 of sales) | | |
| 3a. Operating assets | 1,031 | 990 |
| 10. Current assets | 582 | 549 |
| 11. Fixed assets | 449 | 441 |
| *Current asset utilisation* (£s per £1,000 of sales) | | |
| 12. Material stocks | 101 | 100 |
| 13. Work in progress | 215 | 188 |
| 14. Finished stocks | 53 | 44 |
| 15. Debtors | 213 | 217 |
| *Fixed asset utilisation* (£s per £1,000 of sales) | | |
| 16. Land and buildings | 206 | 201 |
| 17. Plant, machinery and works equipment | 237 | 233 |
| 18. Vehicles | 6 | 7 |

**Table 10.1** The firm's own figures

| Ratios | A | B | C | D | E | F | G |
|---|---|---|---|---|---|---|---|
| *Return on assets* | | | | | | | |
| 1. Operating profit/ Operating assets (%) | 25·1 | 23·9 | 18·9 | 13·2 | 10·8 | 4·3 | 3·5 |
| *Profit margin on sales and turnover of assets* | | | | | | | |
| 2. Operating profit/ Sales (%) | 19·0 | 19·9 | 15·1 | 11·5 | 10·7 | 4·7 | 3·6 |
| 3. Sales/Operating assets (times per year) | 1·32 | 1·20 | 1·25 | 1·15 | 1·01 | 0·92 | 0·98 |
| *Departmental costs (as percentage of sales)* | | | | | | | |
| 4. Production cost of sales | 62·8 | 63·5 | 71·1 | 71·9 | 75·4 | 80·2 | 80·9 |
| 5. Distribution and marketing costs | 11·4 | 12·6 | 6·6 | 6·9 | 4·9 | 5·6 | 6·1 |
| 6. General and administrative costs | 6·8 | 4·0 | 7·2 | 9·7 | 9·0 | 9·5 | 9·4 |
| *Production costs (as a percentage of sales value of production)* | | | | | | | |
| 7. Materials costs | 32·0 | 28·7 | 32·9 | 31·6 | 33·1 | 35·8 | 33·8 |
| 8. Works labour costs | 16·5 | 22·1 | 24·2 | 25·1 | 26·8 | 28·9 | 29·2 |
| 9. Other production costs | 14·3 | 12·7 | 14·0 | 15·2 | 15·5 | 15·5 | 17·9 |
| *General asset utilisation (£s per £1,000 of sales)* | | | | | | | |
| 3a. Operating assets | 758 | 833 | 800 | 864 | 990 | 1,081 | 1,016 |
| 10. Current assets | 465 | 481 | 412 | 474 | 549 | 608 | 543 |
| 11. Fixed assets | 293 | 352 | 388 | 390 | 441 | 473 | 473 |
| *Current asset utilisation (£s per £1,000 of sales)* | | | | | | | |
| 12. Material stocks | 80 | 110 | 71 | 92 | 100 | 102 | 96 |
| 13. Work in progress | 43 | 40 | 63 | 101 | 188 | 215 | 220 |
| 14. Finished stocks | 132 | 102 | 57 | 75 | 44 | 67 | 19 |
| 15. Debtors | 210 | 229 | 221 | 206 | 217 | 224 | 208 |
| *Fixed asset utilisation (£s per £1,000 of sales)* | | | | | | | |
| 16. Land and buildings | 130 | 158 | 194 | 174 | 201 | 244 | 241 |
| 17. Plant, machinery and works equipment | 160 | 189 | 190 | 213 | 233 | 220 | 225 |
| 18. Vehicles | 3 | 5 | 4 | 3 | 7 | 9 | 7 |

**Table 10.2** The Interfirm Comparison – reproduced by permission of the Centre for Interfirm Comparison Ltd.

The firm's fixed asset investment ratio 11 is comparatively unfavourable, mainly because both its land and buildings ratio 16 and its plant investment ratio 17 (which had improved) are considerably higher than those of firms A to D.

In the actual IFC, firm E received a detailed report relating both to the above ratios and the additional ratios mentioned at the foot of page 159 (some eighty ratios were covered in all); the report discussed the policy and performance factors underlying the firm's position in the IFC, highlighted its weaknesses and strengths, and indicated the directions in which improvements should be made.

### What does this example show?

**IFC – a better basis for judgement**   Comparisons between two years may create a feeling of false security. Only an interfirm comparison could show that the results achieved by this firm were not good enough.

**IFC – a guide to action**   Our firm can draw specific conclusions from the comparison because the figures compared were carefully selected with a definite plan in mind: it was known that the comparative figures were wanted by managing directors as an aid in the overall direction of their businesses. Accordingly, ratios were chosen which would indicate to each firm how its return on capital compared with that of the others, and to help those with a comparatively low return on capital to narrow down systematically the possible reasons for this. Aided by the Centre's report, our firm will now investigate the reasons why its production costs, work in progress and plant investment ratios are relatively unfavourable.

**IFC – ratios express key relationships**   Ratios are used for comparison because they provide a better basis for judgment than their underlying figures. For instance, a firm may make a hundred of its products in one month and a hundred and twenty in the subsequent month. This is a sign of improvement *only if* the costs of the resources used in making these products have not increased at the same or even a higher rate. Only ratios can express this relationship between output and resources used, and other key relationships of importance to management.

**IFC – security**   Clearly ratios such as those used in the example do not disclose the actual figures of participating firms. A firm's sales may have been £100 000 with a capital of £50 000, or £20 000 with a capital of £10 000; but in either case its ratio of sales to capital will be 2:1 or its 'turnover' of capital two times.

On page 162 you will find an alternative presentation of interfirm comparison.

## What the comparison shows firm 6

Suppose you are the managing director of firm 6 in Table 10.3 shown on page 162; what does the comparison show you?

1   First and most important, the comparison gives you for the first time an objective yardstick of your firm's overall success – as indicated by the standing of your operating profit/operating assets ratio against that of other firms.

The comparison of this primary ratio shows that your firm's overall success and effectiveness is *less* than that of the majority of the others, since your return on assets is only 7·9 % against the median of 11·3 %.
2   What is the cause of your low operating profit/operating assets? Comparison of ratios 2 and 3 shows that the reason is your low operating profit/sales – your figure of 6·1 % is the third lowest of the figures shown. On the other hand, your turnover of assets, ratio 3, is the fastest of any firm. It therefore seems that you should first of all investigate the cost ratios which determine your operating profit/sales.
3   Looking at the departmental cost ratios, you find that your production cost, ratio 4, is high; your distribution and marketing cost, ratio 5, is below average; and your administration cost, ratio 6, is above average.
4   The causes of your high ratio 4 are shown by ratios 7 and 8 to be your high materials and labour costs. In the actual comparison, you have access to more detailed comparative data which throws further light on these points – it shows (*a*) that your high materials cost is related to your high materials waste ratio, and (*b*) that your high works labour cost is caused, not by high wages and costs per employee, but by low volume of output per employee.
5   Turning to the asset utilisation ratios you see that your fast turnover of total operating assets (ratio 3) is expressed in a different way by ratio 3*a*, which shows that you have the lowest figure of total operating assets per £1000 of sales. You will see from ratio 11 that this is because you have the lowest figure of fixed assets in relation to sales. This is, in turn, mainly due to your low plant and machinery

**Table 10.3** An alternative presentation of interfirm comparison – prepared by permission of the Centre for the Interfirm Comparison Ltd

| Ratios | Firms 1 | 2 | 3 | 4 | 5 | 6 | 7 | 8 | 9 | Median* |
|---|---|---|---|---|---|---|---|---|---|---|
| 1. Operating profit/Operating assets | 20.2 | 17.9 | 14.3 | 13.3 | 11.3 | 7.9 | 3.9 | 3.1 | 7.4 | 11.3 |
| 2. Operating profit/Sales | 18.2 | 14.9 | 13.1 | 11.9 | 10.9 | 6.1 | 7.6 | 3.1 | 3.8 | 10.9 |
| 3. Sales/Operating assets (times) | 1.11 | 1.20 | 1.09 | 1.12 | 1.04 | 1.30 | 0.98 | 1.25 | 0.81 | 1.11 |
| *Departmental Costs* (as a percentage of sales) | | | | | | | | | | |
| 4. Production costs | 71.3 | 77.1 | 77.4 | 79.6 | 79.4 | 84.2 | 82.5 | 89.5 | 84.3 | 79.6 |
| 5. Distribution and marketing costs | 4.9 | 3.7 | 4.1 | 2.2 | 3.3 | 2.9 | 4.4 | 3.3 | 3.6 | 3.6 |
| 6. Administrative costs | 5.6 | 4.3 | 5.4 | 6.3 | 6.4 | 6.8 | 5.7 | 4.1 | 8.3 | 5.7 |
| *Production costs* (as a percentage of sales value of production) | | | | | | | | | | |
| 7. Materials cost | 46.9 | 53.0 | 51.0 | 50.8 | 56.2 | 55.3 | 56.3 | 56.5 | 51.7 | 53.0 |
| 8. Works labour cost | 10.4 | 9.8 | 7.3 | 10.1 | 9.2 | 12.3 | 8.2 | 16.1 | 14.7 | 10.1 |
| 9. Production overheads | 14.0 | 14.3 | 19.1 | 18.7 | 14.0 | 16.6 | 18.0 | 16.9 | 17.9 | 16.9 |
| *Asset Utilisation* (£s per £1,000 of sales) | | | | | | | | | | |
| 3a. Total operating assets | 899 | 833 | 918 | 893 | 960 | 770 | 1,019 | 798 | 1,233 | 899 |
| 10. Current assets | 328 | 384 | 400 | 351 | 379 | 404 | 589 | 423 | 430 | 400 |
| 11. Fixed assets | 571 | 449 | 518 | 542 | 581 | 366 | 430 | 375 | 803 | 518 |
| *Current asset utilisation* (£s per £1,000 of sales) | | | | | | | | | | |
| 12. Material stocks | 58 | 73 | 43 | 58 | 86 | 65 | 129 | 80 | 68 | 68 |
| 13. Work in progress | 51 | 90 | 104 | 63 | 44 | 114 | 164 | 122 | 135 | 104 |
| 14. Finished stocks | 66 | 94 | 123 | 63 | 118 | 77 | 147 | 60 | 84 | 84 |
| 15. Debtors | 153 | 127 | 130 | 167 | 131 | 148 | 149 | 161 | 143 | 148 |
| *Fixed asset utilisation* (£s per £1,000 of sales) | | | | | | | | | | |
| 16. Land and buildings | 240 | 87 | 102 | 143 | 156 | 88 | 47 | 73 | 299 | 102 |
| 17. Plant and machinery | 316 | 343 | 407 | 389 | 413 | 267 | 363 | 289 | 486 | 363 |
| 18. Vehicles | 15 | 19 | 9 | 10 | 12 | 11 | 20 | 13 | 18 | 13 |

*The median is the middle figure for each ratio

ratio (ratio 17). Incidentally, the fixed asset figures used in this comparison are based upon comparable valuations.

The more detailed data available (not shown in this table) indicate that the average age of your plant is greater than that of most other firms; and that your value of plant and machinery per works employee is below the average. The comparison therefore suggests that your low labour productivity (a major cause of your high production costs) may be due to the fact that your plant is not sufficiently up-to-date.

6 Your current asset utilisation ratios (ratios 12 to 15) show that most of your current asset items are about average – with the exception of your work in progress, ratio 13, which is above the average. This seems to provide another indication of the need for altering your production arrangements so as to allow a faster throughput.

*Summary – the scope for improvement, measured in ratios and absolute figures*

If you were able to achieve materials and labour cost ratios equal to the medians, while retaining your present production overheads ratio and the same ratios for your other departmental costs, your profit to sales ratio would improve to 10·6 %.

In order to achieve your improved labour cost ratio, you might have to spend more on new plant. Supposing you increased your plant value (which at the moment is £267 per £1000 of sales) by 50 %, then your fixed assets ratio would increase to £499. However, you should be able to improve your work in progress figure to the median, giving a lower current asset ratio (ratio 10) of £394. Your rate of turnover of operating assets (ratio 3) would then become 1·12 times. Because of your increased investment in plant and machinery, your depreciation would go up, and the effect of this would be to increase your production overheads ratio to 17·6 %; your profit margin on sales would then become 9·6 % and your return on assets 10·8 % – in other words, nearly three percentage points higher than it is now.

In terms of absolute figures: your present sales volume is £2 million. At the same volume of sales, your new profit ratio would mean a profit of £192 000 – an improvement of £70 000 on your present profits.

## Return on capital employed – problems

We have already considered a number of problems in connection with the definition of the term 'capital employed'. Let us review the various possible definitions:

1   *Total gross capital employed*   This is the sum of the issued share capital, reserves, loans and current liabilities – in other words, the total fixed and current assets.
2   *Total net capital employed*   This is the most popular and acceptable definition. It can be found by either adding together the share capital, reserves and loans or by deducting current liabilities from total assets.
3   *Total shareholders' capital employed*   This is represented by the sum of issued capital plus reserves.
4   *Total equity capital employed*   This is the sum of issued ordinary share capital and reserves.

Your choice of definition is likely to depend upon the purpose for which the capital employed figure is to be used; but no matter how it is calculated there are two important points to bear in mind.

First, as one is attempting to establish a rate of return on the capital employed in the business, it is essential that all the assets used for the calculation are in fact being usefully employed. For example, if a large cash balance has been allowed to accumulate or there has been a sudden influx of cash due to a share issue, such excessive balances are obviously not being usefully employed in the business and until they are (for example, by the purchase of new plant or stocks), they should be excluded from the computation. If the second point considered below is also adopted, intangible assets such as good will must also be eliminated.

The second consideration is the value to be placed on the assets when calculating the return. The figures which appear in the balance sheet rarely reflect the true value of the fixed assets being employed. This is primarily due to the conservative approach of the financial accountant in valuing assets at the lower of cost or market value.

Consider a company whose balance sheet figures reveal that the net capital employed totals £100 000 and the net profit before tax is £20 000. This will give a rate of return on the capital employed of 20%:

$$\frac{£20\,000}{£100\,000} \times \frac{100}{1} = 20\%$$

But assume that the assets include land which was purchased for £10 000 twenty-five years ago and is still shown at that figure in the balance sheet. Obviously the current value of the land will be much more than £10 000 and a conservative estimate might put the value at

£100 000. This means that the real value of the capital employed by our company is at least £190 000. This has a drastic effect on the rate of return, reducing it from 20 % to just over 10 %.

It is essential, therefore, to use some method by which all the assets of a company can be measured at current values. This is not an easy task and more will be said about the problems involved in a later chapter.

It is to be hoped, however, that the introduction of an agreed form of accounting for inflation will eliminate this problem. Great care should be exercised when using published rates of return on capital employed to ensure that the basis for the calculation is known and deficiencies in the basis are noted.

# 11 Capital Investment Appraisal

The process of budgeting for capital expenditure decisions is a vital part of policy-making and top management usually assumes direct responsibility for the authorisation of all but the smallest capital investment sums.

The main reasons why these decisions should be the concern of top management are:

1   The sums involved in capital investment are usually very substantial.
2   Once decisions have been made the resources of the firm are likely to be tied up for some considerable time in the particular project to which the capital investment relates.
3   The future of the firm may depend on a single investment decision and it may be very difficult to reverse the effects of a bad decision.
4   Capital budgeting is a long-term function and the farther into the future that plans are made the more uncertain are the results.

## The main influences affecting the capital investment decision

These will fall into three main categories:
(a)   the future net increase in income or the future net saving in costs;
(b)   the net amount of the investment;
(c)   a satisfactory rate of return.

All these categories are related and it is probably necessary for management to decide first the minimum acceptable rate of return, rejecting at once any project which does not meet this rate.

An immediate difficulty is to decide what rate of return on the capital expenditure is acceptable. If the money has to be borrowed in order to finance the project, the rate of return should obviously be at least sufficient to finance the cost of such borrowings. It is, however, necessary to take account of the increased risk factor because we are dealing with the uncertain future. There are a number of factors which can turn an apparently successful investment project into a 'white elephant' over a very short period. For example, technological innovation may make the investment obsolete, or there may be a change of fashion which can have equally disastrous results on the firm's earnings. In these circumstances a company may decide to increase the cost of capital by a risk factor to obtain the minimum acceptable rate of return. A different factor may be used for different classes of investments.

Although it has been stated that capital expenditure should be capable of generating a satisfactory return, this is not possible in all cases. Most firms undertake capital expenditure which will definitely not yield any direct monetary returns, as in the provision of a medical centre or sports pavilion. This type of project will, no doubt, benefit the firm indirectly by improving the morale of employees but the immediate effect on profits will be to reduce them. The returns from 'normal' profitable projects must therefore be loaded with a factor which will offset the cost of the non-profit-earning projects.

## Methods of evaluating investment decisions

The appraisal of capital projects may take one of two forms or a combination of the two. The first and perhaps the simplest is to evaluate two or more alternatives, and then select the one which yields the highest return after taking into account individual circumstances relating to that particular decision (e.g. the chance of obsolescence). The second is to evaluate a single project from the point of view of overall profitability and the possibility of achieving an acceptable rate of return.

The principal methods employed for evaluating capital projects are explained below.

**1 Total income methods (rate of return on original investment)** This involves expressing the total expected income from a project as a percentage of its capital cost. Example:

Cost, £300 000
Depreciation to be at rate of £60 000 per year
Life of asset, five years
Annual income before depreciation:

|  |  | £ |
|---|---|---|
| *Year* | 1 | 80 000 |
| „ | 2 | 100 000 |
| „ | 3 | 100 000 |
| „ | 4 | 120 000 |
| „ | 5 | 120 000 |
|  |  | £520 000 |

|                                   | £       |
|-----------------------------------|---------|
| Total forecast income             | 520 000 |
| *Less* Depreciation, i.e. 100%    | 300 000 |
| Net income after providing depreciation | £220 000 |

Total return on the original investment is:

$$\frac{£220\,000}{£300\,000} \times 100 = 73\%$$

To calculate an average net return per annum, the average income per annum is found by:

$$\frac{£220\,000}{5} = £44\,000 \text{ per annum}$$

This gives an average return of

$$\frac{£44\,000}{£300\,000} \times 100 = 14 \cdot 7\%$$

It is now widely accepted that this method has many defects. It takes no account of time or the interest value of money, and it is based on a five-yearly average of income rather than actual income each year.

**2   Rate of return on average investment**   This method makes some attempt to take account of the time element but its operation is open to question.

It is recognised that during the life of the asset, provision must be made for depreciation. As this involves no actual cash outlay it means that each year additional cash becomes available for reinvestment or for use as working capital.

The mechanics of the calculation involve dividing the original investment by two to give an average investment over the period, which assumes that the amount recovered in the form of depreciation will be used effectively in the business. In the above example this will give

$$\frac{£300\,000}{2} = £150\,000$$

The rate of return on average investment now becomes

$$\frac{£44\,000}{£150\,000} \times 100 = 29 \cdot 3\%$$

This rate will obviously be twice the previous rate since the cost of the original investment has been halved.

The only merits of these two methods of appraisal are that the method of calculation is simple and they permit the immediate elimination of any project which shows a lower rate of return than the business is earning on the rest of the capital employed. Some comparisons may be possible between different projects, but even these may be fallacious because of the different distributions of the income over the period.

**3  Pay back period**  This method attempts to measure the time it will take the expected income to equal the original cost of the investment. Once again, no attempt is made to discount future income to present values. Taking the figures already considered:

|  | *Income before Depreciation* | *Cumulative Income* |
|---|---|---|
|  | £ | £ |
| Year 1 | 80 000 | 80 000 |
| „ 2 | 100 000 | 180 000 |
| „ 3 | 100 000 | 280 000 ⎱ |
| „ 4 | 120 000 | 400 000 ⎰ |

It will be seen that the whole cost of the original investment – £300 000 – is recovered during year 4.

The main value of this method is again the question of elimination of projects with too long a pay-back period. All figures showing future income are of necessity estimates. The longer the period the more likely the estimates are to be unreliable. There is always the danger that in our fast-changing technical environment the investment may become obsolete long before its normal working life is over. Therefore the quicker the cost can be recovered the smaller the effect of obsolescence. Again, if the concern is likely to suffer from a shortage of cash, the quicker outlays are recovered, the better for the concern.

The main disadvantage of this method is that, if it is used in isolation, total earnings are ignored. This could mean that an investment was rejected in favour of another project because of an unfavourable pay back period, when in fact its *total earnings* might be much higher, over the expected life of the asset.

**4  Discounted cash flow**  The main drawback with all the methods so far considered is that no account has been taken of the fact that future income is worth less than income received today. The concept has nothing to do with inflation reducing the value of money, but with the fact that a person who forgoes spending money immediately expects to receive a reward for his his action. The reward takes the form of interest.

Consider an investment made today of £100 which is to receive interest at 5% per annum. The value of this investment in twelve months' time will therefore be:

|  | £ |
|---|---|
| Original investment | 100 |
| One year's interest | 5 |
|  | £105 |

In two years' time the value of the investment will be:

|  | £ |
|---|---|
| Value at end of Year 1 | 105 |
| *Add* One year's interest at 5% p.a. on £105 = | 5·25 |
| Value at end of Year 2 | £110·25 |

This addition of 5% interest each year to the balance at the beginning of the year is known as 'compounding'.

Let us now look at the opposite side of the coin. If a sum of £105 is to be received in twelve months' time, then if it is discounted at 5% p.a. the present value of that £105 is £100, viz.:

|  | £ |
|---|---|
| Value in twelve months' time | 105 |
| *Less* 5% discount | 5 |
| Present value | £100 |

It should be noted that the rate of discount in the above example is really 4·71%. This is because, in practice, to discount £105 by 5% does not mean 'take £105 and deduct 5% from it', but rather to decide the sum which, if invested now at 5% will produce £105 in one year's time. This will become clear when the formula for calculating the present value of a future sum is considered below.

It has already been mentioned that, when using compound interest, if the value of the £100 is required in two years' time, then the 5% is applied not only to the principal but also to the interest earned after the first year.

The initial interest amount is found by the formula: $1 + R$ where $R$ = rate of interest:

$$1 + \frac{5}{100} = 1.05$$

The standard formula for calculating compound interest is: $A = P(1 + R)^n$, when $A$ = amount, $P$ = principal, $R$ = rate of interest and $n$ = number of years.

The present value of a £ due in twelve months' time is found by using the reciprocal of the first formula:

$$\frac{1}{1.05} = 0.952.$$

To obtain the present value of a future sum the formula is:

$$V = \frac{1}{(1 + R)^n} \text{ or } (1 + R)^{-n}$$

in other words the reciprocal of the first formula.

Consider £100 invested for three years at 5% per annum:

*Rate of Interest*

| | |
|---|---|
| End of Year 1 £100 × 1.05 | = £105 |
| „ „ „ 2 £100 × (1.05 × 1.05) | = £110.25 |
| „ „ „ 3 £100 × (1.05 × 1.05 × 1.05) | = £115.763 |

Using these figures the discounting factor for each year is:

$$\text{Year } 1 \quad \frac{1}{1.05} = 0.952$$

$$\text{„} \quad 2 \quad \left(\frac{1}{1.05}\right)^2 = 0.907$$

$$\text{„} \quad 3 \quad \left(\frac{1}{1.05}\right)^3 = 0.864$$

If the figure of £110.25 (the amount of £100 for two years at 5%) is multiplied by the discounting factor for Year 2 we have $110.25 \times 0.907 = £100$, in other words the original principal sum.

It is not necessary to work out the discounting factors each time as they can be found from tables similar to the ones produced at the end of this chapter (pp. 186–7).

(*a*)  *The internal rate of return* (*or Yield*)  If it is desired to compare the rate of return of related investments, both the investment and the expected cash income should be on a present value basis.

In order to equate the cash income which it is expected will be generated by the investment with the cost of the investment, the income must be discounted at a suitable rate. The procedure for finding the suitable rate is on a trial and error basis involving the use of the tables at the end of this chapter.

Let us restate our original problem:

*Cost of investment, £300 000*

|  |  |  |  | £ |
|--|--|--|--|--|
| *Expected income Year* | | 1 | | 80 000 |
| ,, | ,, | ,, | 2 | 100 000 |
| ,, | ,, | ,, | 3 | 100 000 |
| ,, | ,, | ,, | 4 | 120 000 |
| ,, | ,, | ,, | 5 | 120 000 |
| | | | | £520 000 |

We shall first have to take an arbitrary rate of discount and apply it to the income for each year. (For this simple illustration it is assumed that all income is received at the end of each year, and that the expenditure is regarded as having been made on 31st December of the base year, i.e. Year 0.) Let us try a rate of 15%.

From the tables the multiplying factor for Years 1 to 5 at a rate of 15% is:

| End of Year | | | 1 | 0·870 |
|--|--|--|--|--|
| ,, | ,, | ,, | 2 | 0·756 |
| ,, | ,, | ,, | 3 | 0·658 |
| ,, | ,, | ,, | 4 | 0·572 |
| ,, | ,, | ,, | 5 | 0·497 |

We now apply these factors to the income for each year:

| Year | Cash flow | Discounting factor | Present value |
|--|--|--|--|
| | £ | 15% | £ |
| 1 | 80 000 | 0·870 | 69 600 |
| 2 | 100 000 | 0·756 | 75 600 |
| 3 | 100 000 | 0·658 | 65 800 |
| 4 | 120 000 | 0·572 | 68 640 |
| 5 | 120 000 | 0·497 | 59 640 |
| | £520 000 | | £339 280 |

As the original cost of the investment is £300 000 the rate of 15 % is too low. Let us try 22 %.

| Year | Cash flow | Discounting factor | Present value |
|---|---|---|---|
| | £ | 22 % | £ |
| 1 | 80 000 | 0·820 | 65 600 |
| 2 | 100 000 | 0·672 | 67 200 |
| 3 | 100 000 | 0·551 | 55 100 |
| 4 | 120 000 | 0·451 | 54 120 |
| 5 | 120 000 | 0·370 | 44 400 |
| | £520 000 | | £286 420 |

A rate of 22 % is obviously too high, so we now know that the rate lies somewhere between 15 % and 22 %. Let us try 20 %.
(N.B. See page 238 for method of arriving at true rate of interest by interpolation.)

| Year | Cash flow | Discounting factor | Present value |
|---|---|---|---|
| | £ | 20 % | £ |
| 1 | 80 000 | 0·833 | 66 640 |
| 2 | 100 000 | 0·694 | 69 400 |
| 3 | 100 000 | 0·579 | 57 900 |
| 4 | 120 000 | 0·482 | 57 840 |
| 5 | 120 000 | 0·402 | 48 240 |
| | £520 000 | | £300 020 |

This is as near as we shall be able to get using whole number interest figures, which means that the discounted rate of return for our example is 20 %. This may be compared with an alternative project to ascertain which will yield the better return, and all other things being equal the project yielding the highest return will be the one adopted.

(b) *The net present value* An alternative form of calculation is possible if a minimum acceptable rate of return is laid down. If the cash income from each alternative project is discounted at the minimum rate of return, the project which yields the highest excess value (on a present value basis) is the most acceptable.

Let us assume that the required minimum rate of return before tax is 16%.

The present value is calculated as above.

| Year | Cash flow | Discounting factor 16% | Present value |
|------|-----------|------------------------|---------------|
| | £ | | £ |
| 1 | 80 000 | 0·862 | 68 960 |
| 2 | 100 000 | 0·743 | 74 300 |
| 3 | 100 000 | 0·641 | 64 100 |
| 4 | 120 000 | 0·552 | 66 240 |
| 5 | 120 000 | 0·476 | 57 120 |
| | £520 000 | | 330 720 |
| | | *Less* Cost | 300 000 |
| | | Net present value | £30 720 |

The net present value of alternative projects which also cost £300 000, would be computed at a rate of 16%, and if they were all less than £30 720 the above project would be adopted.

It is also possible to calculate an index which gives the present value of a capital project per £1 invested. This is known as the 'profitability index', and for the above project it would be

$$\frac{£330\,720}{£300\,000} = 110\%$$

Those projects with the highest index are the most profitable. Any project with an index below 100 would not be profitable since the discounted cash flows would be less than the original investment.

The advantages of using a discounting technique over the older and less sophisticated methods are fairly easy to appreciate; but even so it has its own pitfalls of which the reader should be aware.

Problems arise when attempting to compare two projects which have either different lives or different capital outlays. Consider first the choice between two projects which have different lives.

**Example 1**   A and B are two projects each costing £1000 but the cash flow from A occurs at the end of Year 1 and is £1130. The cash flow from B occurs over three years at a rate of £416 per year.

The rate of return or yield calculation is as follows:

| Year | | Cash flow £ | Discounting factor | Present value £ |
|---|---|---|---|---|
| **A** | 1 | 1130 | **A** 13% 0·885 | 1000 |
| **B** | 1 | 416 | **B** 12% 0·893 | 372 |
| | 2 | 416 | 0·797 | 332 |
| | 3 | 416 | 0·712 | 296 |
| | | | | £1000 |

If the yield method is used to assess the two alternatives, project A would appear to be the better alternative as it yields 13% as against project B's 12%.

Net present value calculation:

Assume that the minimum acceptable rate of return is 10%.

| Year | Cash flow A £ | B £ | Discounting factor 10% | Present value A £ | B £ |
|---|---|---|---|---|---|
| 1 | 1130 | 416 | 0·909 | 1027 | 378 |
| 2 | | 416 | 0·826 | | 344 |
| 3 | | 416 | 0·751 | | 312 |
| | | | | 1027 | 1034 |
| | | *Less* Capital cost | | 1000 | 1000 |
| | | *Net* present value | | £27 | £34 |

With this method of evaluation, project B shows the better return, having a net present value of £7 over that of A. A gives a net present value of £27 over one year. B gives a net present value of £34 over three years; the most appropriate choice, therefore, will depend on what use is to be made of the cash flows. The yield method is only valid if it is assumed that there are other opportunities available offering a return higher than the firm's cost of capital. The profitability index for the two alternatives are project A $\frac{£1027}{£1000} = 100.27\%$ and project B $\frac{£1034}{£1000} = 100.34\%$, which again shows a preference for project B.

**Example 2** A and B are two projects, A costing £3000 and B £16 000. The cash flow from A for two years is £2010 each year and from B £10 470 each year. The yield calculation will reveal the following:

| Year | | Cash flow £ | Discounting factor **A** 22% | Present value £ |
|---|---|---|---|---|
| **A** | 1 | 2 010 | 0·820 | 1 650 |
| | 2 | 2 010 | 0·672 | 1 350 |
| | | | | 3 000 |
| | | | **B** 20% | |
| **B** | 1 | 10 470 | 0·833 | 8 724 |
| | 2 | 10 470 | 0·694 | 7 266 |
| | | | | 15 990 |
| | | | *i.e. approximately* | £16 000 |

According to the yield method project A is to be preferred, having a yield of 22% as against project B's 20%.

The net present value method, applying our 10% required minimum, gives us the following:

| Year | Cash flow **A** £ | **B** £ | Discounting factor 10% | Present value **A** £ | **B** £ |
|---|---|---|---|---|---|
| 1 | 2 010 | 10 470 | 0·909 | 1 827 | 9 517 |
| 2 | 2 010 | 10 470 | 0·826 | 1 660 | 8 648 |
| | | | | 3 487 | 18 165 |
| | | | *Less* Capital cost | 3 000 | 16 000 |
| | | | *Net* Present value | £487 | £2 165 |

Using this method, project B is obviously the better alternative.

However, if we apply the profitability index to the two projects, project A has an index of 116% and project B 113%, indicating that project A is again to be preferred.

The profitability index will give a more accurate ranking of alternatives than both the yield and NPV methods, provided that the annual cash flows from the alternative projects can be reinvested at the minimum rate of return.

## Effect of taxation on investment decisions

The evaluation of competing projects is concerned primarily with the movement of funds over the period of the investment. Basic accounting concepts of matching expenses with revenues etc. do not enter into the decision. It is when cash is spent and when cash is received that is of prime importance.

These cash flows are affected by the timing of taxation payments and the rate at which capital allowances may be offset against tax liabilities.

In recent years company taxation has been subject to numerous changes and amendments, particularly in the field of capital allowances. It would seem unwise, therefore, to set out the current position, as this is likely to be out of date in a very short time. However, the general effect of taxation on cash flows can be illustrated with a simple example which ignores such current possibilities as special rates for development areas, 100% allowances in the first year, and so forth.

Assume that new plant is purchased for £1600, for which the appropriate capital allowance is 20% per annum on the reducing balance method. The rate of tax is 50%. The capital allowances will, therefore, be as follows:

|  | £ | Tax saved |
|---|---|---|
| *Year* 1 | | |
| Cost of plant | 1600 | |
| *Less* capital allowance (20%) | 320 × 50% = | £160 |
| | 1280 | |
| *Year* 2 | | |
| *Less* capital allowance (20%) | 256 × 50% = | £128 |
| | 1024 | |
| *Year* 3 | | |
| *Less* capital allowance (20%) | 205 × 50% = | £103 |
| | 819 | |

If we now assume that this new plant brings in additional cash flows (net) of £1000 per year for the first two years and £500 for the remaining years, then the project evaluation will be as below for the first four years, assuming a discount factor of 10%. (As tax is normally paid several months after the profit has been earned, the tax on profit and savings on tax allowances in Year 1 will not affect cash flows until Year 2, and so on.)

| 1 | 2 | 3 | 4 | 5 | 6 | 7 |
|---|---|---|---|---|---|---|
| Year | Cash inflow | Tax at 50% | Tax saved by allowances | Net cash flow $(2-3+4)$ | Discount factor 10% | Present value |
| | £ | £ | £ | £ | £ | £ |
| 1 | 1000 | | | 1000 | 0·909 | 909 |
| 2 | 1000 | 500 | 160 | 660 | 0·826 | 545 |
| 3 | 500 | 500 | 128 | 128 | 0·751 | 96 |
| 4 | 500 | 250 | 103 | 353 | 0·683 | 241 |

– and so on for the life of the project. The total present values will be reduced by the original capital cost of £1600 to give the excess present value of the project at a discount rate of 10%.


## Uncertainty

This chapter has outlined the different methods of evaluating alternative investments. The analysis of data has concentrated on the costs involved in different projects and the associated returns. The need for the application of sound principles has been emphasised throughout and little regard has so far been paid to the accuracy of the data which has been manipulated. It will no doubt occur to the reader that much of the data is based on forecasts, for example sales volume, production costs, administration costs, financial costs and selling prices. It may be asked whether the effort involved in evaluating proposed investment decisions is worth while, bearing in mind the effects of errors in the forecasts on the final outcome of the investment. This question is similar to that posed in the chapter on budgeting, when it was pointed out that to have some form of analysed information upon which to base decisions, even if not one hundred per cent accurate, was better than having no information at all. After all, business exists in a world of uncertainty and a large number of decisions made today are substantially affected by the events of tomorrow.

With reference to the capital investment decision, there would appear to be four areas which may be affected by errors in data. These are (1) the discount rate, (2) the project lifetime, (3) the initial outlay, (4) the project's return. Management's main concern will be with *critical variables*, in other words those factors which are critical to the success of the decision or which, if a variation does occur, have a more than proportionate effect on the final outcome.

Various techniques have been developed to isolate these critical variables and attach probabilities to various expectations concerning them. A generic term for these methods is *sensitivity analysis* and although the detailed operation of this type of analysis is beyond the scope of this book, some of the basic principles are considered.

The use of probability allows management to look at a number of possible outcomes when a probability of the event occurring is attached to the individual critical variables.

**Expected values**
Instead of assuming a single net present value the calculations are made on the basis of three types of situation:

(*a*)  Best possible
(*b*)  Most probable
(*c*)  Worst possible

The likelihood of these situations occurring are then assigned a probability. (Remember all the individual probabilities must add up to 1.) The result of applying the probabilities gives an expected value:

*Example*

| Outcome | | NPV £ | Probability | Expected value £ |
|---|---|---|---|---|
| (*a*) | Best possible | 17 850 | .3 | 5 355 |
| (*b*) | Most probable | 13 000 | .6 | 7 800 |
| (*c*) | Worst possible | 9 750 | .1 | 975 |
| | | | 1.0 | 14 130 |

Once again there is no certainty in the value of £14 130 but at least some of the risk element has been incorporated in its calculation.

**Decision trees**
It is possible to illustrate the use of probability within an individual appraisal by the use of decision trees.

## Example

Mufte Ltd. are considering buying a new machine for £20 000 and with a three-year life its likely cash inflows have been forecast as follows:

| Year | Cash £ | Probability |
|------|--------|-------------|
| 1 | 3 000 | .4 |
| | 5 000 | .6 |
| 2 | 16 000 | .5 |
| | 18 000 | .5 |
| 3 | 28 000 | .3 |
| | 23 000 | .7 |

From this data the following decision tree can be constructed.

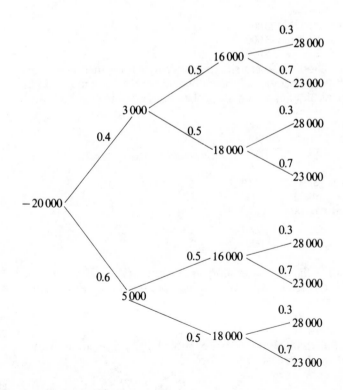

It is now possible to calculate the NPVs for each of the 'paths'. Assuming that the cut off rate is 15% we have the following:

| Path | Year | Cash flow | Discount factor 15% | NPV |
|------|------|-----------|---------------------|-----|
|      |      | £         |                     | £   |
| 1    | 0    | (20 000)  | 1                   | (20 000) |
|      | 1    | 3 000     | .870                | 2 610 |
|      | 2    | 16 000    | .756                | 12 096 |
|      | 3    | 28 000    | .658                | 18 424 |
|      |      |           |                     | 13 130 |
| 2    | 0    | (20 000)  | 1                   | (20 000) |
|      | 1    | 3 000     | .870                | 2 610 |
|      | 2    | 16 000    | .756                | 12 096 |
|      | 3    | 23 000    | .658                | 15 134 |
|      |      |           |                     | 9 840 |
| 3    | 0    | (20 000)  | 1                   | (20 000) |
|      | 1    | 3 000     | .870                | 2 610 |
|      | 2    | 18 000    | .756                | 13 608 |
|      | 3    | 28 000    | .658                | 18 424 |
|      |      |           |                     | 14 642 |
| 4    | 0    | (20 000)  | 1                   | (20 000) |
|      | 1    | 3 000     | .870                | 2 610 |
|      | 2    | 18 000    | .756                | 13 608 |
|      | 3    | 23 000    | .658                | 15 134 |
|      |      |           |                     | 11 352 |
| 5    | 0    | (20 000)  | 1                   | (20 000) |
|      | 1    | 5 000     | .870                | 4 350 |
|      | 2    | 16 000    | .756                | 12 096 |
|      | 3    | 28 000    | .658                | 18 424 |
|      |      |           |                     | 14 870 |
| 6    | 0    | (20 000)  | 1                   | (20 000) |
|      | 1    | 5 000     | .870                | 4 350 |
|      | 2    | 16 000    | .756                | 12 096 |
|      | 3    | 23 000    | .658                | 15 134 |
|      |      |           |                     | 11 580 |

| Path | Year | Cash flow | Discount factor 15% | NPV |
|------|------|-----------|---------------------|-----|
|      |      | £         |                     | £   |
| 7    | 0    | (20 000)  | 1                   | (20 000) |
|      | 1    | 5 000     | .870                | 4 350 |
|      | 2    | 18 000    | .756                | 13 608 |
|      | 3    | 28 000    | .658                | 18 424 |
|      |      |           |                     | 16 382 |
| 8    | 0    | (20 000)  | 1                   | (20 000) |
|      | 1    | 5 000     | .870                | 4 350 |
|      | 2    | 18 000    | .756                | 13 608 |
|      | 3    | 23 000    | .658                | 15 134 |
|      |      |           |                     | 13 092 |

## Probabilities

*Path*
1  $0.4 \times 0.5 \times 0.3 = 0.06$
2  $0.4 \times 0.5 \times 0.7 = 0.14$
3  $0.4 \times 0.5 \times 0.3 = 0.06$
4  $0.4 \times 0.5 \times 0.7 = 0.14$
5  $0.6 \times 0.5 \times 0.3 = 0.09$
6  $0.6 \times 0.5 \times 0.7 = 0.21$
7  $0.6 \times 0.5 \times 0.3 = 0.09$
8  $0.6 \times 0.5 \times 0.7 = 0.21$

## Expected value

| Path | NPV | Probability | Expected value |
|------|-----|-------------|----------------|
|      |     | £           |                |
| 1    | 13 130 | 0.06     | 787.8 |
| 2    | 9 840  | 0.14     | 1 377.6 |
| 3    | 14 642 | 0.06     | 878.5 |
| 4    | 11 352 | 0.14     | 1 589.3 |
| 5    | 14 870 | 0.09     | 1 338.3 |
| 6    | 11 580 | 0.21     | 2 431.8 |
| 7    | 16 382 | 0.09     | 1 474.4 |
| 8    | 13 092 | 0.21     | 2 749.3 |
|      |        | 1.00     | 12 627 |

The expected surplus over the initial investment is therefore £12 627. Obviously, if the number of probabilities exceeds two per event or the number of years is over three, diagrammatic presentation becomes difficult. However, it is relatively simple for larger problems to be handled by the computer using the same basic principles as illustrated above.

## Questions

**1** Discuss the critical areas in arriving at the capital budgeting decision.
**2** Discuss the advantages/disadvantages of the main techniques used in capital budgeting.
**3** John Brown, the works director, is concerned with the problem of replacing one of the semi-automatic machines in the machine shop. The machine is used for the production of small nuts and bolts of varying sizes.

There are three similar types of machine on the market, the 'Alpha', 'Sigma' and 'Omega', each costing £20 000 each. Tim Smith, the accountant, has prepared the forecast cash flows as follows:

| Machine type<br>Initial outlay | 'Alpha'<br>£20 000 | 'Sigma'<br>£20 000 | 'Omega'<br>£20 000 |
|---|---|---|---|
| Cash inflows | | | |
| End of Year 1 | 3 000 | 5 000 | 6 000 |
| 2 | 4 000 | 6 000 | 6 000 |
| 3 | 7 000 | 6 000 | 6 500 |
| 4 | 8 000 | 4 000 | 4 000 |
| 5 | 8 500 | 4 000 | 1 000 |
| | £30 500 | £25 000 | £23 500 |

The cost of capital is estimated at 10%.
Compare the various alternatives under each of the following methods of capital investment appraisal:

(a) Pay back;
(b) Average rate of return based on original investment;
(c) Net present value;
(d) The internal rate of return i.e. true yield method for the machine having the highest net present value.

The machines will have no scrap value after their useful lives have expired.
**4** Three possible alternative projects A, B and C would each involve a capital outlay of £1000. The following table shows the expected earnings.

| Project | 1 | 2 | 3 | 4 | 5 |
|---|---|---|---|---|---|
| | £ | £ | £ | £ | £ |
| A | 200 | 500 | 500 | 400 | |
| B | 500 | 500 | 300 | 100 | |
| C | 300 | 400 | 400 | 400 | 300 |

*Years*

The projects will have nil realisable value after their useful life.

You are required to compare the alternative projects by using the following methods of capital investment appraisal:

(*a*) Pay back;
(*b*) Average rate of return on original investment;
(*c*) Net present value.

The cost of capital is 8%.

**5** Progressive Ltd. is a manufacturing company which uses a variety of machines for its production programme. One of the machines has now to be replaced and the management of the company are considering which of two alternative machines should be acquired.

Details of the two machines (each of which has an estimated life of five years) and of the expected net cash inflows directly referable to each machine are as follows:

|  | Machine X | Machine Y |
|---|---|---|
| Cost | £25 000 | £30 000 |
| *Net Cash Inflows:* | | |
| End of Year | 4 000 | 6 000 |
| 2 | 8 000 | 12 000 |
| 3 | 10 000 | 10 000 |
| 4 | 5 000 | 6 000 |
| 5 | 4 000 | 4 000 |
| Estimated trade-in value at end of Year 5 | 3 000 | 5 000 |

(*a*) Calculate which of the two machines is likely to yield the better return (based on discounted present value), using (*i*) 10% and (*ii*) 15% as the required rate.

(*b*) By interpolation ascertain the true internal rate of return for each machine.

(*c*) Having determined from (*b*) which machine should be acquired, indicate which of the alternative methods given below should be adopted for the acquisition:

(*i*) an immediate purchase for cash, the necessary funds being obtained from a bank loan at an interest rate of 12% per annum;

(*ii*) purchase for 20% (of the cash price) as deposit, the balance being payable by five annual instalments of £6720 each;

(*iii*) leasing the machine for five years, at an annual rental of 25% of the cash price.

(1) Use a discount rate of 12% for comparing the alternative methods of finance in (*c*) above.

(2)   Except where otherwise stated, assume that all inflows and outflows of cash take place at the end of the appropriate years.

(3)   Ignore taxation.

(4)   The following table shows the present value of £1, using the rates of interest and the relevant years required by the question.

|  | 10% | 12% | 15% |
|---|---|---|---|
| End of 1 Year | 0·9091 | 0·8929 | 0·8696 |
| „ 2 Years | 0·8264 | 0·7972 | 0·7561 |
| „ 3 Years | 0·7513 | 0·7118 | 0·6575 |
| „ 4 Years | 0·6830 | 0·6355 | 0·5718 |
| „ 5 Years | 0·6209 | 0·5674 | 0·4972 |

**Table 11.1** Present value factors—present value of £1

| Year hence | 4% | 5% | 6% | 7% | 8% | 9% | 10% | 11% | 12% | 13% | 14% | 15% | 16% |
|---|---|---|---|---|---|---|---|---|---|---|---|---|---|
| 1 | 0·962 | 0·952 | 0·943 | 0·935 | 0·926 | 0·917 | 0·909 | 0·901 | 0·893 | 0·885 | 0·877 | 0·870 | 0·862 |
| 2 | 0·925 | 0·907 | 0·890 | 0·873 | 0·857 | 0·841 | 0·826 | 0·812 | 0·797 | 0·783 | 0·769 | 0·756 | 0·743 |
| 3 | 0·889 | 0·864 | 0·840 | 0·816 | 0·794 | 0·772 | 0·751 | 0·731 | 0·712 | 0·693 | 0·675 | 0·658 | 0·641 |
| 4 | 0·855 | 0·823 | 0·792 | 0·763 | 0·735 | 0·708 | 0·683 | 0·659 | 0·636 | 0·613 | 0·592 | 0·572 | 0·552 |
| 5 | 0·822 | 0·784 | 0·747 | 0·713 | 0·681 | 0·650 | 0·621 | 0·594 | 0·567 | 0·543 | 0·519 | 0·497 | 0·476 |
| 6 | 0·790 | 0·746 | 0·705 | 0·666 | 0·630 | 0·596 | 0·564 | 0·535 | 0·507 | 0·480 | 0·456 | 0·432 | 0·410 |
| 7 | 0·760 | 0·711 | 0·665 | 0·623 | 0·583 | 0·547 | 0·513 | 0·482 | 0·452 | 0·425 | 0·400 | 0·376 | 0·354 |
| 8 | 0·731 | 0·677 | 0·627 | 0·582 | 0·540 | 0·502 | 0·467 | 0·434 | 0·404 | 0·376 | 0·351 | 0·327 | 0·305 |
| 9 | 0·703 | 0·645 | 0·592 | 0·544 | 0·500 | 0·460 | 0·424 | 0·391 | 0·361 | 0·333 | 0·308 | 0·284 | 0·263 |
| 10 | 0·676 | 0·614 | 0·558 | 0·508 | 0·463 | 0·422 | 0·386 | 0·352 | 0·322 | 0·295 | 0·270 | 0·247 | 0·227 |
| 11 | 0·650 | 0·585 | 0·527 | 0·475 | 0·429 | 0·388 | 0·350 | 0·317 | 0·287 | 0·261 | 0·237 | 0·215 | 0·195 |
| 12 | 0·625 | 0·557 | 0·497 | 0·444 | 0·397 | 0·356 | 0·319 | 0·286 | 0·257 | 0·231 | 0·208 | 0·187 | 0·168 |
| 13 | 0·601 | 0·530 | 0·469 | 0·415 | 0·368 | 0·326 | 0·290 | 0·258 | 0·229 | 0·204 | 0·182 | 0·163 | 0·145 |
| 14 | 0·577 | 0·505 | 0·442 | 0·388 | 0·340 | 0·299 | 0·263 | 0·232 | 0·205 | 0·181 | 0·160 | 0·141 | 0·125 |
| 15 | 0·555 | 0·481 | 0·417 | 0·362 | 0·315 | 0·276 | 0·239 | 0·209 | 0·183 | 0·160 | 0·140 | 0·123 | 0·108 |
| 16 | 0·534 | 0·458 | 0·394 | 0·339 | 0·292 | 0·252 | 0·218 | 0·188 | 0·163 | 0·142 | 0·123 | 0·107 | 0·093 |
| 17 | 0·513 | 0·436 | 0·371 | 0·317 | 0·270 | 0·231 | 0·198 | 0·170 | 0·146 | 0·125 | 0·108 | 0·093 | 0·080 |
| 18 | 0·494 | 0·416 | 0·350 | 0·296 | 0·250 | 0·212 | 0·180 | 0·153 | 0·130 | 0·111 | 0·095 | 0·081 | 0·069 |
| 19 | 0·475 | 0·396 | 0·331 | 0·277 | 0·232 | 0·196 | 0·164 | 0·138 | 0·116 | 0·098 | 0·083 | 0·070 | 0·060 |
| 20 | 0·456 | 0·377 | 0·312 | 0·258 | 0·215 | 0·178 | 0·149 | 0·124 | 0·104 | 0·087 | 0·073 | 0·061 | 0·051 |

| Year hence | 17% | 18% | 19% | 20% | 22% | 24% | 25% | 26% | 28% | 30% | 35% | 40% | 45% |
|---|---|---|---|---|---|---|---|---|---|---|---|---|---|
| 1 | 0·855 | 0·847 | 0·840 | 0·833 | 0·820 | 0·806 | 0·800 | 0·794 | 0·781 | 0·769 | 0·741 | 0·714 | 0·690 |
| 2 | 0·731 | 0·718 | 0·706 | 0·694 | 0·672 | 0·650 | 0·640 | 0·630 | 0·610 | 0·592 | 0·549 | 0·510 | 0·476 |
| 3 | 0·624 | 0·609 | 0·593 | 0·579 | 0·551 | 0·524 | 0·512 | 0·500 | 0·477 | 0·455 | 0·406 | 0·364 | 0·328 |
| 4 | 0·534 | 0·516 | 0·499 | 0·482 | 0·451 | 0·423 | 0·410 | 0·397 | 0·373 | 0·350 | 0·301 | 0·260 | 0·226 |
| 5 | 0·456 | 0·437 | 0·419 | 0·402 | 0·370 | 0·341 | 0·328 | 0·315 | 0·291 | 0·269 | 0·223 | 0·186 | 0·156 |
| 6 | 0·390 | 0·370 | 0·352 | 0·335 | 0·303 | 0·275 | 0·262 | 0·250 | 0·227 | 0·207 | 0·165 | 0·133 | 0·108 |
| 7 | 0·333 | 0·314 | 0·296 | 0·279 | 0·249 | 0·222 | 0·210 | 0·198 | 0·178 | 0·159 | 0·122 | 0·095 | 0·074 |
| 8 | 0·285 | 0·266 | 0·249 | 0·233 | 0·204 | 0·179 | 0·168 | 0·157 | 0·139 | 0·123 | 0·091 | 0·068 | 0·051 |
| 9 | 0·243 | 0·225 | 0·209 | 0·194 | 0·167 | 0·144 | 0·134 | 0·125 | 0·108 | 0·094 | 0·067 | 0·048 | 0·035 |
| 10 | 0·208 | 0·191 | 0·176 | 0·162 | 0·137 | 0·116 | 0·107 | 0·099 | 0·085 | 0·073 | 0·050 | 0·035 | 0·024 |
| 11 | 0·178 | 0·162 | 0·148 | 0·135 | 0·112 | 0·094 | 0·086 | 0·079 | 0·066 | 0·056 | 0·037 | 0·025 | 0·017 |
| 12 | 0·152 | 0·137 | 0·124 | 0·112 | 0·092 | 0·076 | 0·062 | 0·062 | 0·052 | 0·043 | 0·027 | 0·018 | 0·012 |
| 13 | 0·130 | 0·116 | 0·104 | 0·093 | 0·075 | 0·061 | 0·055 | 0·050 | 0·040 | 0·033 | 0·020 | 0·013 | 0·008 |
| 14 | 0·111 | 0·099 | 0·088 | 0·078 | 0·062 | 0·049 | 0·044 | 0·039 | 0·032 | 0·025 | 0·015 | 0·009 | 0·006 |
| 15 | 0·095 | 0·084 | 0·074 | 0·065 | 0·051 | 0·040 | 0·035 | 0·031 | 0·025 | 0·020 | 0·011 | 0·006 | 0·004 |
| 16 | 0·081 | 0·071 | 0·062 | 0·054 | 0·042 | 0·032 | 0·028 | 0·025 | 0·019 | 0·015 | 0·008 | 0·005 | 0·003 |
| 17 | 0·069 | 0·060 | 0·052 | 0·045 | 0·034 | 0·026 | 0·023 | 0·020 | 0·015 | 0·012 | 0·006 | 0·003 | 0·002 |
| 18 | 0·059 | 0·051 | 0·044 | 0·038 | 0·028 | 0·021 | 0·018 | 0·016 | 0·012 | 0·009 | 0·005 | 0·002 | 0·001 |
| 19 | 0·043 | 0·043 | 0·037 | 0·031 | 0·023 | 0·017 | 0·014 | 0·012 | 0·009 | 0·007 | 0·003 | 0·002 | 0·001 |
| 20 | 0·037 | 0·037 | 0·031 | 0·026 | 0·019 | 0·014 | 0·012 | 0·010 | 0·007 | 0·005 | 0·002 | 0·001 | 0·001 |

*Formula:*

$$\frac{1}{(1+i)^n}$$

where $i$ is the rate of interest expressed as a decimal and $n$ the number of years.

# 12 Accounting for Price Level Changes

## Introduction

In recent years inflation has seriously affected the measurement of profit and the value of assets which have been based on historical cost accounting.

If you had an asset in your balance sheet which you purchased for £100 twenty years ago and you continued to show it in your balance sheet at that figure twenty years later, you would be deluding yourself, since its real value would be considerably less than you paid for it originally.

Profit in the simple case is nothing more than the difference between two net worth values between two consecutive periods of time.

If we let $K_n$ = Net Worth (or closing capital) at the end of the period and let $K_{n-1}$ = Net Worth (opening capital) at the beginning of the period then profit = $K_n - K_{n-1}$.

Since $K$ = Net Worth = Total Assets − (Current Liabilities + Long Term Loans) we can readily see that profit is inextricably bound up with the value we place on the assets.

*Example*

Joe Smith, a retailer, has the following assets and liabilities at 1st January 19–4.

| | | | |
|---|---|---|---|
| Freehold shop premises | £20 000 | Debtors | £500 |
| Motor van | £5 000 | Bank and cash | £400 |
| Stock | £2 000 | Creditors | £600 |

At the end of the year he had the following:

| | | | |
|---|---|---|---|
| Freehold premises | £20 000 | Debtors | £1 700 |
| Motor van | | Bank and cash | £1 600 |
| (less depreciation) | £4 000 | Creditors | £200 |
| Stock | £1 800 | Long term loan | £1 000 |

His net worth at the beginning of the year $K_{n-1}$ is as follows:

| Assets | £ |
|---|---|
| Freehold shop | 20 000 |
| Motor van | 5 000 |
| Stock | 2 000 |
| Debtors | 500 |
| Bank and cash | 400 |
| Total Assets | 27 900 |
| Less Current Liabilities | |
| Creditors | 600 |
| Net worth $K_{n-1}$ at 1st Jan 19–4 | £27 300 |

His net worth $K_n$ at the end of the 31st December 19–4 is as follows:

| Assets | £ |
|---|---|
| Freehold shop | 20 000 |
| Motor van (less depreciation) | 4 000 |
| Stock | 1 800 |
| Debtors | 1 700 |
| Bank and cash | 1 600 |
| | 29 100 |
| Less | |
| Long-term loan | 1 000 |
| Creditors | 200 |
| | 1 200 |
| Net worth at 31st Dec. 19–4 $K_n$ | 27 900 |

We can now calculate his profit since it is merely the difference between the two net worth values, viz:

$$\text{Net profit} = K_n - K_{n-1}$$
$$= £27\,900 - £27\,300$$
$$= £600$$

It is obvious that the value we place on the assets and liabilities is the determinant of profit measurement. If, for example, we undervalue the assets at the end of the year our profits will be less. Conversely, if we overvalue them then our profits will be overstated. The major problem is how should we value them.

## Inflation

In times of inflation if we are using historical acquisition costs to value our assets then we will find that profits will be overstated and balance sheet values undervalued. This is a serious situation since there will be a danger that we shall draw excessive amounts from the business, thinking that we have made these actual profits. The same will apply to companies since they will be paying dividends out of profits which have not in fact been earned. This will result in severe cash flow problems at a later date.

*Example*

Suppose we purchase 1 000 'widgets' for £1 each for cash on 1 January and subsequently sell half of them at the end of the year for £1·50 each for cash, having invested £1 000 capital in the business on 1st January. Assuming no other transactions and using historical cost-based accounts, the balance sheet as at 1st January and 31st December together with the income statement is as follows:

**Balance Sheet as at 1st January 19—**

| | £ | | £ |
|---|---|---|---|
| Capital (Net worth) | 1 000 | Cash | 1 000 |

**Income Statement (Profit & Loss A/c) for year ending 31st December 19—**

| | £ | | £ |
|---|---|---|---|
| Purchases at 1st Jan | 1 000 | Sales at 31st Dec | |
| *Less* Closing stock | | | |
| 500 × £1 | 500 | 500 × £1·50 = | 750 |
| Cost of sales | 500 | | |
| Profit | 250 | | |
| | 750 | | 750 |

**Balance Sheet as at 31st December 19—**

| | £ | | £ | £ |
|---|---|---|---|---|
| *Capital* | | | | |
| Balance at 1st Jan | 1000 | Current assets | | |
| *Add* Net profit | 250 | Stock | 500 | |
| Net worth | 1250 | Cash | 750 | 1250 |
| | 1250 | | | 1250 |

Suppose now that at the time we sold the 'widgets', which was at the end of the year, the purchase price of 'widgets' (i.e. the replacement cost) was £2 per 'widget' and inflation was the cause of the fact that the index of prices was 100 at 1st January and 200 at 31st December.

If we adjusted our profit statement and balance sheet for the effects of the price change we would arrive at the following:

### Income Statement (Adjusted) for year ending 31st December 19—

| | £ | | £ |
|---|---|---|---|
| Purchases 1st Jan $1\,000 \times \dfrac{200}{100} = 2\,000$ | | Sales at 31st Dec | |
| *Less* Closing stock $500 \times \dfrac{200}{100} = 1\,000$ | | $500 \times £1.50 =$ | 750 |
| Cost of sales | 1 000 | | |
| Loss | (250) | | |
| | 750 | | 750 |

### Balance Sheet as at 31st December (Adjusted)

| | £ | | £ | £ |
|---|---|---|---|---|
| *Capital A/c:* | | | | |
| $1\,000 \times \dfrac{200}{100} =$ | 2 000 | *Current Assets* | | |
| *Less* Net loss | (250) | Stock | 1000 | |
| Net worth | 1 750 | Cash | 750 | 1750 |
| | 1750 | | | 1750 |

If we now compare the unadjusted statements with the inflation adjusted statements we can discern the following:

(a)   Under historical cost accounting profits are overstated.
(b)   Balance sheet values are understated in the historical cost balance sheet.

Suppose our trader had drawn out for private purposes the £250 profit which he thought he had made by referring to his historical cost income statement. He would then have had a reduced cash position of

£500 in his balance sheet. If he wished to continue as a going concern he would now need £1000 cash (500 × £2) to replenish his stocks, but he has only £500 cash left in the business for replenishment purposes. Therefore he cannot replenish the stocks he has sold. He has, in fact, by using the historical cost statement, run into a cash flow problem, and a serious erosion of capital.

To sum up, inflation results in severe cash flow problems where accounts are prepared on a historical cost basis resulting in firms overstating their profits. This in turn has misled firms into paying out excessive dividends to shareholders. Furthermore, the impact of inflation has resulted in serious erosion of capital. For example, since depreciation calculated on historical cost values will be less than if calculated on current replacement costs then there will be an undercharging for depreciation resulting in an overstatement of profit. Subsequently, the company will not have the cash resources to replace their assets when it is necessary to do so and if it is to continue as a going concern it is vital that assets are replaced.

Since balance sheet values are understated the net worth of the company is also under valued, the true worth being in some cases much higher. This has resulted in a spate of take-over bids and subsequent asset stripping with many workers being made redundant, with all the social implications.

It can, therefore, be seen that inflation has serious implications for accountants and accounting measurement, and the accountancy professional bodies have sought to wrestle with the problem.

## Historical background

The professional accountancy bodies have, since the early 1970s, been most concerned about the impact of inflation on accounting. On 17th January 1973 the Accounting Standards Committee, ASC, representing the views of the major professional accounting bodies, issued an exposure draft entitled *Accounting for Changes in the Purchasing Power of Money*.

This exposure draft was crystallised into a *Provisional Statement of Standard Accounting Practice, PSSAP 7*, which was promulgated in May 1974. This recommended that a supplementary statement should be attached to companies' published accounts in the form of adjusted historical accounts adjusted by means of a general price index such as, for example, the retail price index (RPI). The accounts were to be adjusted by means of an index which related to the change in the purchasing power of money. Taking a simple example, if net profit is the difference between two net worth values between two consecutive periods of time, viz:

Profit $= K_n - K_{n-1}$

where $K_n$ $=$ Net worth at end of period

$K_{n-1}$ $=$ Net worth at beginning of period

and the historical unadjusted accounts showed $K_{n-1} = £20\,000$ and $K_n = £30\,000$ then assuming no drawings and no additional capital introduced during the period then the historical net profit will be:

$$\text{Profit} = K_n - K_{n-1}$$
$$= £30\,000 - £20\,000$$
$$= £10\,000$$

Now let us assume that the RPI as at $K_{n-1}$ equals 100 and at $K_n$ it rose to 120. If the accounts were adjusted to take into account the fall in the purchasing power of money, and if we assume $K_n$ to be already in terms of current purchasing power, it would be necessary to adjust $K_{n-1}$ in terms of current purchasing power at $K_n$, otherwise we would be trying to subtract dissimilar units of purchasing power which would make nonsense of the number system as we know it, in other words it would be like – to use an analogy – subtracting kangaroos from elephants.

If we therefore adjust $K_n - 1$ in terms of current purchasing power at $K_n$, it would mean adjusting all the assets fixed and current and all the liabilities – long term and current by the index.

Taking the above example:

$K_{n-1} = £20\,000$ would be adjusted as follows:

$$£20\,000 \times \frac{\text{RPI at } K_n}{\text{RPI at } K_{n-1}}$$

$$£20\,000 \times \frac{120}{100} = £24\,000$$

Therefore net profit in terms of current purchasing power would be:

$$\text{Net Profit} = K_n - K_{n-1}$$
$$= £30\,000 - £24\,000$$
$$= £6\,000$$

The above result shows that historical cost profit $= £10\,000$ was over-stated when we compare it with the current purchase power profit of $£6000$.

PSSAP 7 included adjustments for gains or losses on net monetary assets. Net monetary assets are debtors, and bank balances less creditors. In addition, the long-term loans received by a firm would result in monetary gains during inflation.

For example, if a company has in its balance sheet £100 000 worth of 10% debentures which were issued on 1st January 19–3 assuming the same rate of inflation given above then at 3rd December 19–3 the company will have made a monetary gain of $\frac{120}{100} \times 100\,000 - 100\,000$

$= £20\,000$, because if the company were to redeem the debentures on 31st December 19–3 it would in reality be paying back in *real* terms £20 000 less than if it had repaid them immediately on 1 January 19–3. The same would apply to gains on creditors. Conversely, if the firm had held cash and/or debtors over a long period these would result in monetary losses.

*Example:* A firm has held £10 000 cash and £2000 of debtors since January 19–3 until 31st December 19–3. The inflation rate as before would result in a monetary loss viz:

$$\text{Monetary loss} = £12\,000 \times \frac{120}{100} - 12\,000$$
$$= £14\,400 - 12\,000$$
$$= £2400$$

### Criticism of PSSAP 7

The major defect with PSSAP 7 is that it uses a general price index to adjust the assets. To take an example:

Suppose a television retailer has a stock of 100 colour televisions which he bought on 1st January 19–3 for £100 each and, for simplicity, suppose the stock remains unsold on 31st December 19–3.

$$\text{Adjusting for inflation } 10\,000 \times \frac{120}{100} = £12\,000$$

Under PSSAP 7 he would value the stock in his balance sheet at £12 000. But suppose the actual replacement costs of the same colour television sets were falling so that the same sets would now cost only £80 to be replaced, then the balance sheet value of his ten sets valued at current replacement cost should be shown at $100 \times £80 = £8000$.

Since the net worth would include the stock of TV sets, under PSSAP 7 he would be overvaluing his stock and therefore overvaluing his net worth and hence his profits.

The vital point is that for many assets such as plant and machinery the specific replacement costs applicable to that asset will rarely coincide with the general price index and therefore adjusting assets using a general price index rather than a specific price index could produce dangerous results.

A simple example of adjusting accounts for current purchasing power is given:

## Example

Joe Bloggs commenced business on 1st January 19–3. His historical balance sheets as at 1st January 19–3 and 31st December 19–3 together with an historical cost profit and loss account were as follows:

### Balance Sheet as at 1st January 19–3 (based on historical cost)

|  | 19–3 1st Jan £ | 19–3 31st Dec £ |  | 19–3 1st Jan £ | 19–3 31st Dec £ |
|---|---|---|---|---|---|
| Capital (net worth) | 1500 | 1800 | Plant & machinery (cost) | 1500 | 1500 |
| Creditors | 500 | 700 | Stock at cost | — | 250 |
| Accruals | — | 125 | Bank | 500 | 875 |
|  | 2000 | 2625 |  | 2000 | 2625 |

### Income Statement for year ending 31st December 19–3

| | | |
|---|---|---|
| Sales | | 2500 |
| Purchases | 1500 | |
| *Less* | | |
| Closing stock | 250 | |
| Historical cost of sales | | 1250 |
| Gross profit | | 1250 |
| *Less* | | |
| Sundry Expenses paid on 31st December | 825 | |
| *Add* owing from 31st December | 125 | 950 |
| Historical net profit | | £300 |

*Assumptions:*
Retail Price Index 1st January     100
Retail Price Index 31st December   110
All sales took place on 31st December
All purchases took place on 1st
   January

*Required:* Adjust the final accounts on a current purchasing power basis.

## Solution

### JOE BLOGGS

**Trading and Profit and Loss Account (Current Purchasing Power)
For Year Ending 31st December 19–3**

|  | £ | £ |
|---|---|---|
| Sales already in terms of CPP at 31st December |  | 2 500 |
| Purchases $1500 \times \dfrac{110}{100} =$ | 1650 |  |
| *Less* |  |  |
| Closing stock $250 \times \dfrac{110}{100} =$ | 275 |  |
| CPP Cost of sales |  | 1375 |
| Gross profit at CPP |  | 1125 |
| *Less* |  |  |
| Expenses at CPP 31st December | 825 |  |
| *Add* |  |  |
| Accruals occurring at 31st December | 125 | 950 |
|  |  | 175 |
| *Gain on net monetary assets |  | 150 |
| *Net Profit at CPP* |  | 325 |

*\*Ascertainment of Gains and Losses on Net Monetary Assets*

Opening net monetary assets:

| at 1st January | £ | £ | £ | £ |
|---|---|---|---|---|
| Debtors | | | | |
| Cash | 500 | | | |

$$500 \times \frac{110}{100} = \quad 550$$

| *Less* Creditors | 500 | $\times \dfrac{110}{100} =$ | 550 | — |
|---|---|---|---|---|

*Add* Sales at CPP 31st December                                     2500

Value of opening net monetary assets in terms of CPP
at 31st December                                              (a) 2500

|  | £ |
|---|---|
| Purchases $1500 \times \dfrac{110}{100}$ | 1650 |
| Expenses & accruals already at CPP 31st December | 950 |

*Add*

| *Closing net monetary assets* | £ | | | |
|---|---|---|---|---|
| Debtors (actual) | — | | | |
| Cash     „ | 875 | | | |
| | 875 | | | |
| *Less* Creditor & accruals | 825 | | 50 | (b) 2650 |

Gain on net monetary assets       (a) − (b)      £150\*

## Current Purchasing Power Balance Sheet as at 31st December 19–3

| | | | | | |
|---|---|---|---|---|---|
| Capital $1500 \times \dfrac{110}{100} =$ | 1650 | *Fixed Assets* | | | |
| | | Plant and Machinery | $1500 \times \dfrac{110}{100}$ | 1650 | |
| *Add* Net Profit (CPP) | 325 | | | | |
| *Net Worth at CPP* | 1975 | *Current Assets* | | £ | |
| | | Stock $250 \times \dfrac{110}{100}$ | | 275 | |

| Current Liabilities | £ | | Bank (Actual) | 875 | 1150 |
|---|---|---|---|---|---|
| Creditors (Actual) | 700 | | | | |
| Accruals (Actual) | 125 | 825 | | | |
| | | £2800 | | | £2800 |

Let us prove that our CPP profit fits in with our accounting model previously stated.

$$\text{Profit} = K_n - K_{n-1}$$

Adjusting $K_{n-1} = £1500$ in historical terms to CPP at 31st December gives:

$$£1500 \times \frac{110}{100} = £1650$$

$K_n$ in terms of CPP at 31st December (see CPP balance sheet) = £1975

Therefore CPP Profit $= K_n - K_{n-1}$
$= 1975 - 1650$

$= £325$ which is precisely the figure we get by adjusting the historical income statement for CPP.

## Further historical background

In September 1975 the Sandilands Report under the chairmanship of Sir Francis Sandilands rejected PSSAP 7 and recommended instead that published accounts should be drawn up in accordance with the principles of current cost accounting using specific price indices specific to a particular asset.

Early in 1976 the Inflation Accounting Steering Group (IASG) under the chairmanship of Douglas Morpeth was set up to consider current cost accounting and on 30th November, 1976 and through this groups's deliberations there was published an exposure draft ED 18, known as 'Current Cost Accounting' for consideration by the accounting profession. The ASC under the chairmanship of William Hyde set up a sub-committee to reconsider ED 18. In November 1977, based upon this sub-committee's recommendations, the ASC published the Hyde Guidelines *Inflation Accounting – An Interim Recommendation*.

On 30th April 1979 a new exposure draft based on 'Current Cost Accounting' was issued by the ASC and, after some consideration by the accounting profession at large, culminated in the publication of *Statement on Standard Accounting Practice No. 16 – SSAP* 16 in March 1980 and at the time of going to press, SSAP 16 is still operative. However, Exposure Draft 35, 'Accounting for the Effects of Changing Prices', which differs fundamentally from SSAP 16, was issued in July 1984, with December 1984 as the final date for comments. This has subsequently been withdrawn and SSAP 16 is likely to follow the same fate. Final agreement on the inflation accountancy problem would still seem to be some way off. However, it is proposed to deal in outline with what is meant by current cost accounting and to deal with a simple example although the example will not deal with the gearing adjustment or monetary adjustment as laid down by SSAP 16.

There are four possible adjustments in arriving at current cost profit which is derived by adjusting the historical cost profit before interest and tax.

(a)   A depreciation adjustment which is the difference between depreciation charged at historic cost and the proportion of the value to the business of fixed assets consumed in the period.

(b)   A cost of sales adjustment – COSA being the difference between the historical cost and the 'value to the business' of stock consumed during the period.

(c)   A monetary working capital adjustment – MWCA which allows for the impact of price level changes on the monetary working capital.

(d)   A gearing adjustment which allows for the benefits of gearing.

'*Value to the business*'
The Sandilands Report stated that there are only three alternative bases of valuation of an asset:

(i)     The current purchase price, in other words the cost of replacing it, the replacement cost, RC.

(ii)    The current disposal value or net realisable value, NRV.

(iii)   The net present value of future cash flows expected to be generated by that asset in the future, PV.

It can therefore be seen that the valuation of an asset can either be its current replacement cost, RC, or its net realisable value, NRV, or its present value of expected future earnings, PV. It is therefore possible to have six outcomes as follows:

- (i)   NRV > PV > RC
- (ii)  NRV > RC > PV
- (iii) PV > RC > NRV
- (iv)  PV > NRV > RC
- (v)   RC > PV > NRV
- (vi)  RC > NRV > PV

The problem is selecting the correct one to use.

The main criteria is that the value of an asset as propounded by Professor J. C. Bonbright in his book *The Valuation of Property* 'is the greatest loss which would be sustained by the business if it were deprived of that asset'.

Let us take, for instance, (iii) above as our example – PV > RC > NRV. Prima facie it would appear that, since PV > RC > NRV, the greatest loss would be the present value but, in fact, providing the firm could purchase a similar asset on the market, then it would be able to restore the status quo. The greatest loss therefore would be the cash outflow required to replace the asset, in other words, the replacement cost. Therefore, in situation (iii) RC would be the value to be placed on the existing asset. In fact, in all the six possibilities the correct valuation would be as follows:

|       | Situation       | Correct Valuation |
|-------|-----------------|-------------------|
| (i)   | NRV > PV > RC   | RC                |
| (ii)  | NRV > RC > PV   | RC                |
| (iii) | PV > RC > NRV   | RC                |
| (iv)  | PV > NRV > RC   | RC                |
| (v)   | RC > PV > NRV   | PV                |
| (vi)  | RC > NRV > PV   | NRV               |

In the majority of cases the correct valuation will be RC.

### Example

A milling machine is expected to generate a present value of future cash flows of £20 000 during its useful life. If it were sold its net realisable value would be £8000 and its current replacement would be £10 000.

We therefore have the following situation:

(iii)  PV > RC > NRV
       £20 000 > £10 000 > £8000

It follows that the value to the business is RC of £10000 and therefore the milling machine should be valued at £10000 in the balance sheet.

A simple example of current cost accounting is now illustrated.

Joe Bloggs commenced business on 1st January 19–3. His historical balance sheets at 1st January 19–3 and 31st December 19–3 and his income statement for the year ended 31st December 19–3 prepared on an historical basis are as follows:

### Balance Sheet as at 1st January 19–3

|  | 19–3 1 Jan £ | 19–3 31 Dec £ |  | 19–3 1 Jan £ | 19–3 31 Dec £ |
|---|---|---|---|---|---|
| Capital (net worth) | 1500 | 1800 | Plant and machinery (at cost) | 1500 | 1500 |
| Creditors | 500 | 700 | Stock (at cost) | — | 250 |
| Accruals | — | 125 | Bank | 500 | 875 |
|  | 2000 | 2625 |  | 2000 | 2625 |

### Income Statement for Year Ending 31st December 19–3

|  | £ | £ |
|---|---|---|
| Sales |  | 2500 |
| Purchases | 1500 |  |
| *Less* closing stock | 250 |  |
| Historical cost of sales |  | 1250 |
| Gross profit |  | 1250 |

| *Less* | £ |  |
|---|---|---|
| Sundry expenses paid 31st December | 825 |  |
| *Add* owing from 31st December | 125 | 950 |
| *Historical Net Profit* |  | 300 |

*Assumptions*

(i)  Specific price index for stock at 31st December 19–3 – 120.
(ii)  Specific price index for plant and machinery at 31st December 19–3 – 150.

(*iii*) All purchases were made on 1st January 19–3.
(*iv*) All sales took place on 31st December 19–3.
 (*v*) Specific price indices when purchased were:
Plant and Machinery    100
Purchases                     100

*Required*

 (*i*) A current cost income statement for the year ending 31st December
19–3.
(*ii*) A current cost balance sheet as at 31st December 19–3.

## Solution

### JOE BLOGGS

### Income Statement for Year Ending 31st December 19–3

|  | £ | £ |
|---|---|---|
| Sales |  | 2500 |
| *Less* historical cost of sales | 1250 |  |
| *Add* cost of sales adjustment COSA: |  |  |
| RC – HC |  |  |
| $\dfrac{120}{100} \times 1250 - 1250 =$ | 250 |  |
| Current cost of sales |  | 1500 |
| Current gross profit |  | 1000 |
| *Less* |  |  |
| Sundry Expenses at current cost | 825 |  |
| *Add* accruals at current cost | 125 | 950 |
| *Net Profit at Current Cost* |  | 50 |

### JOE BLOGGS

### Current Cost Balance Sheet as at 31st December 19–3

|  | £ |  |  | £ |
|---|---|---|---|---|
| Capital a/c bal. at |  |  |  |  |
| 1st Jan | 1500 | *Fixed Assets* |  |  |
| *Add* net profit | 50 | Plant and | | |
|  |  | machinery | $1500 \times \dfrac{150}{100}$ | 2250 |

| *Net Worth* | | 1550 | | | |
|---|---|---|---|---|---|
| ** Revaluation Reserve | | 750 | *Current assets* | £ | |
| (Plant and machinery) | | | | | |
| * Holding gain on | 50 | | Stock | | |
| stock | | | $250 \times \dfrac{120}{100}$ | 300 | |
| Cost of sales | | | | | |
| adjustment | 250 | 300 | | | |
| | | | Bank (Actual) | 875 | 1175 |

| *Current liabilities* | | | | | |
|---|---|---|---|---|---|
| Creditors (actual) | 700 | | | | |
| Accruals (actual) | 125 | 825 | | | |
| | | £3425 | | | £3425 |

\* Holding gain on stock = CRC − HC
$$300 - 250$$
$$= £50$$

\*\* Revaluation reserve − Plant and machinery:
CRC − HC
$$2250 - 1500 = £750$$

Comparison of Joe Bloggs profits under the different profit measurements.

| | HC | CPP | CRC |
|---|---|---|---|
| | £ | £ | £ |
| Net Profit | 300 | 325 | 50 |

If we compare the historical cost profits with current cost profits we see that profits are overstated by a considerable amount. Furthermore, the balance sheet values are less under historical costs where compared with current costs.

The major objective of current cost accounting is that of capital maintenance, in other words to stop the erosion of the firm's capital by overstating profits. This conserves the resources invested in the firm's assets, thereby allowing it to continue to function as a going concern. This is particularly so in relation to depreciation of fixed assets.

Suppose we have a machine which was purchased on 1st January 19–0 for £10 000 and, at the end of the year, its current replacement cost was £18 000. If the firm depreciates the machine at 20% per annum on an historical basis, the depreciation charge against profits would be 20% × £10 000 = £2000, thus reducing profits by this amount. If, however, we were more realistic we should charge depreciation on the current replacement cost which would be $20\%$ $\times £18\,000 = £3600$. Thus depreciation on an historical cost basis is inadequate and results in excessive profits and inadequate provisions for depreciation on fixed assets and, if the firm is to continue indefinitely into the future as a going concern, it will at some time have to replace its assets and will have to have adequate funds available for replacement.

The charging of depreciation on a current cost basis goes a long way in conserving the resources necessary at some time in the future for replacement of assets, therefore ensuring the maintenance of capital invested in the firm's operating capacity.

As mentioned previously, the inflation accounting debate is a continuing one but this chapter has explored the two principal methods available, that is indexation using a general price index and the current cost system.

# Suggested Answers

## Chapter 1

**1** Refer to page 1. **2** Refer to page 2. **3** Refer to page 2. **4** Refer to page 3. **5** Refer to page 4. **6** The management accountant. **7** The role of the management accountant is to assist management to fulfil the objectives of the business by providing relevant information to aid decision-making. **8** Men, Machines, Materials, Money. **9** Budgetary control ensures that responsibilities for revenue and expenditure are established. A comparison is then possible between actual and budgeted figures, enabling differences to be analysed and corrective action taken where appropriate. **10** Capital Investment Decision.

## Chapter 2

**1** Total claims and liabilities £10 000. **2** Owner's claims £6000. **3** Assets = Liabilities + Shareholders' Equity. **4** Refer to page 17. **5** Refer to page 16. **6** Refer to page 13. **7** Refer to page 17. **8** Refer to page 16. **9** Refer to page 16.

**10** JOE PIPER (GROCER)

(*i*)

**Balance Sheet as at 1st July 19–8**

|  | £ |  | £ |
|---|---|---|---|
| | | *Current asset* | |
| Capital – J. Piper | 20 000 | Bank | 20 000 |
| | £20 000 | | £20 000 |

(*ii*)

**Balance Sheet as at 2nd July 19–8**

|  | £ |  | £ |
|---|---|---|---|
| | | *Fixed assets* | |
| Capital – J. Piper | 20 000 | Freehold shop | 10 000 |
| | | *Current asset* | |
| | | Bank | 10 000 |
| | £20 000 | | £20 000 |

(*iii*) **Balance Sheet as at 5th July 19–8**

|  | £ |  | £ | £ | £ |
|---|---|---|---|---|---|
| Capital – J. Piper | 20 000 | *Fixed assets* |  |  |  |
|  |  | Freehold |  |  |  |
|  |  | shop |  | 10 000 |  |
| *Current liabilities* |  | Fixtures |  |  |  |
| Creditor – J. Brown | 800 | and |  |  |  |
|  |  | fittings | 200 |  |  |
|  |  | *Add* |  |  |  |
|  |  | Instal- |  |  |  |
|  |  | lation | 20 | 220 | 10 220 |
|  |  |  |  |  |  |
|  |  | *Current assets* |  |  |  |
|  |  | Stock – |  |  |  |
|  |  | groceries |  | 800 |  |
|  |  | Bank |  | 9 780 | 10 580 |
|  | £20 800 |  |  |  | £20 800 |

(*iv*) **Balance Sheet as at 8th July 19–8**

|  | £ | £ |  | £ | £ |
|---|---|---|---|---|---|
| Capital | 20 000 |  | *Fixed assets* |  |  |
| *Add* net profit |  |  | Freehold |  |  |
| retained | 100 | 20 100 | shop | 10 000 |  |
|  |  |  | Fixtures and |  |  |
| *Current liabilities* |  |  | fittings | 220 |  |
| Creditor – J. Brown |  | 800 | Motor van | 500 | 10 720 |
|  |  |  |  |  |  |
|  |  |  | *Current assets* |  |  |
|  |  |  | Stock – |  |  |
|  |  |  | groceries | 600 |  |
|  |  |  | Debtor — |  |  |
|  |  |  | L. Crowther | 300 |  |
|  |  |  | Bank | 9 280 | 10 180 |
|  |  | £20 900 |  |  | £20 900 |

# Chapter 3

**1** Refer to pages 31–3. **2** The effect of high gearing on the earnings per ordinary share depends upon the level of earnings attained. If earnings are sufficiently high, the benefits of gearing will be apparent in increasing the earnings per share. The danger is that with a high geared capital structure, earnings will not reach a high enough level to permit the benefits of gearing to be realised. Where earnings over the years are subject to wide fluctuations the earnings per share in a highly geared company will also fluctuate, whereas in a low geared company such fluctuations will not have such a dramatic effect on the earnings per share. Hence a low geared company will tend to give greater stability of earnings per share.

**3** (i)

| | | *Structure* | |
|---|---|---|---|
| | | (1) | (2) |
| Gearing Ratio = $\dfrac{\text{Equity}}{\text{Debt}}$ | | $\dfrac{90\,000}{10\,000}$ | $\dfrac{20\,000}{80\,000}$ |
| | = | 9 : 1 | 0·25 |

Therefore structure (2) is relatively more highly geared than structure (1).

(ii)  (a)  **Earnings before interest and tax £ 50 000**

| | *Structure* (1) £ | *Structure* (2) £ |
|---|---|---|
| Earnings before interest and tax | 50 000 | 50 000 |
| Debenture interest – 6 % | 600 | 3 000 |
| | 49 400 | 47 000 |
| Corporation tax     52 % | 25 688 | 24 440 |
| | 23 712 | 22 560 |
| Preference dividend – 8 % | — | 2 400 |
| Earnings attributable to ordinary shareholders | £23 712 | £20 160 |
| No. of ordinary shares | 90 000 | 20 000 |
| Earnings per ordinary share | £0·26347 | £1·008 |
| Rate of return per £1 share         (a) | 26·34 % | (a)  100.8 % |

(ii)  (b)  **Earnings before interest and tax £ 10 000**

| | *Structure* (1) £ | *Structure* (2) £ |
|---|---|---|
| Earnings before interest and tax | 10 000 | 10 000 |
| Debenture interest – 6 % | 600 | 3 000 |
| | 9 400 | 7 000 |
| Corporation tax     52 % | 4 888 | 3 640 |
| | 4 512 | 3 360 |
| Preference dividend – 8 % | — | 2 400 |
| Earnings attributable to ordinary shareholders | £4 512 | £960 |

| (*ii*) (*c*) | | Structure (1) | | Structure (2) |
|---|---|---|---|---|
| | | £ | | £ |
| No. of ordinary shares | | 90 000 | | 20 000 |
| Earnings per ordinary share | | £0·05013 | | £0·0480 |
| Rate of return per £1 share | (*b*) | 5·01% | (*b*) | 4·8% |
| Reduction in rate of return (*a*) − (*b*) | | 21·3% | | 96% |

**4** Refer to page 34.

## Chapter 4

**1** Refer to page 36. **2** Refer to page 37. **3** Refer to page 37.
**4** Working capital is generally defined as the excess of current assets over current liabilities. For example, firm X has the following current assets and current liabilities:

| | £ | £ |
|---|---|---|
| *Current assets* | | |
| Stock | 50 000 | |
| Debtors | 10 000 | |
| Cash at bank | 20 000 | |
| Cash in hand | 1 000 | 81 000 |
| *Current liabilities* | | |
| Creditors | 50 000 | |
| Tax owing | 2 000 | 52 000 |
| | | £29 000 |

Hence the firm's working capital is £29 000.

Working capital is vitally important to a company since it relies on working capital to meet the day-to-day expenses of the business, e.g. wages, payments to creditors, payment of rates etc. If the company cannot generate sufficient working capital to meet these day-to-day costs it will be unable to maintain or expand its volume of output and therefore will be in a state of decline eventually culminating in insolvency. **5** Refer to page 39. **6** Since depreciation is charged against profits to arrive at a net profit it is essential when preparing sources and application of funds statements to add back the depreciation to this net profit since we are dealing with *cash flow*. Depreciation is merely a book-keeping entry and does not in fact involve an outflow of cash since the outflow of cash took place at a time when the asset to which the depreciation applies was purchased. Therefore, when we are dealing with cash flow it is the net profit *before* depreciation which we take as being a source of funds. **7** Refer to page 39. **8** Refer to pages 45–6.

**9** Cash budgets are usually prepared for a period of twelve months to give an overall picture of the cash position, but more frequent statements will be required for control purposes. Such statements may be prepared on a daily or weekly basis.

**10** **Sources and Application of Funds Statement for 19–7**

|  |  | £ |
|---|---|---|
| Balance of cash at beginning of 19–6 |  | 25 000 |
| *Sources of increase:* | £ |  |
| Net profit before tax | 40 000 |  |
| *Add* back depreciation | 2 000 |  |
|  | 42 000 |  |
| Decrease in debtors | 8 000 |  |
| New issue of shares | 6 000 | 56 000 |
|  |  | 81 000 |
| *Sources of decrease:* |  |  |
| Additional premises | 29 000 |  |
| Increase in stock | 10 000 |  |
| Decrease in trade creditors | 1 000 |  |
| *Tax paid | 29 000 |  |
| Dividends paid | 9 000 | 78 000 |
| *Balance of Cash at end of* 19–7 |  | £3 000 |

*Tax Account

| | £ | | £ |
|---|---|---|---|
| Cash (paid) | 29 000 | Balance b/f | 32 000 |
| Balance c/d | 23 000 | Tax prov. | 20 000 |
| | £52 000 | | £52 000 |
| | | Balance b/d | £23 000 |

**11** **T. GOODY** **Cash Budget**

|  | July £ | Aug. £ | Sept. £ | Oct. £ | Nov. £ | Dec. £ |
|---|---|---|---|---|---|---|
| Balance b/fwd. | 3 000 | 2 380 | 4 760 | 9 340 | 7 400 | 16 260 |
| Receipts (see schedule) | 9 600 | 11 200 | 12 800 | 14 400 | 15 200 | 10 400 |
|  | 12 600 | 13 580 | 17 560 | 23 740 | 22 600 | 26 660 |
| Payments (see schedule) | 10 220 | 8 820 | 8 220 | 16 340 | 6 340 | 5 260 |
| Balance c/fwd. | 2 380 | 4 760 | 9 340 | 7 400 | 16 260 | 21 400 |

*Receipts Schedule*
N.B. Month in brackets is the month in which the goods were sold.

|  | July | | August | | September |
|---|---|---|---|---|---|
|  | £ | | £ | | £ |
| Debtors (May) | 9 600 | (*June*) | 11 200 | (*July*) | 12 800 |
|  | October | | November | | December |
|  | £ | | £ | | £ |
| Debtors (August) | 14 400 | (*Sept.*) | 15 200 | (*Oct.*) | 10 400 |

*Payments Schedule*
N.B. Month in brackets is the month in which the units are produced.

|  |  | July | |  | August | |
|---|---|---|---|---|---|---|
|  |  | £ | £ |  | £ | £ |
| Raw materials | 300 (*April*) × 12 | | = 3 600 | 340 (*May*) × 12 | | = 4 080 |
| Direct labour | 400 (*July*) × 10 | | = 4 000 | 260 (*Aug.*) × 10 | | = 2 600 |
| Variable | 360 (*June*) × $\frac{1}{3}$ × 6 | | = 720 | 400 (*July*) × $\frac{1}{3}$ × 6 | | = 800 |
|  | 400 (*July*) × $\frac{2}{3}$ × 6 | | = 1 600 | 260 (*Aug.*) × $\frac{2}{3}$ × 6 | | = 1 040 |
| Fixed expenses | (*June*) | | 300 | (*July*) | | 300 |
|  |  | | ——— |  | | ——— |
|  |  | | 10 220 |  | | 8 820 |
|  |  | | ═══ |  | | ═══ |

|  |  | September | |  | October | |
|---|---|---|---|---|---|---|
|  |  | £ | £ |  | £ | £ |
| Raw materials | 360 (*June*) × 12 | | = 4 320 | 400 (*July*) × 12 | | = 4 800 |
| Direct labour | 220 (*Sept.*) × 10 | | = 2 200 | 200 (*Oct.*) × 10 | | = 2 000 |
| Variable | 260 (*Aug.*) × $\frac{1}{3}$ × 6 = | | 520 | 220 (*Sept.*) × $\frac{1}{3}$ × 6 = | | 440 |
|  | 220 (*Sept.*) × $\frac{2}{3}$ × 6 = | | 880 | 200 (*Oct.*) × $\frac{2}{3}$ × 6 = | | 800 |
| Fixed expenses | (*August*) | | 300 | (*September*) | | 300 |
|  |  | | ——— |  | | |
|  |  | | 8 220 |  | | |
|  |  | | ═══ |  | | |

Machine                                                          8 000
                                                                 ———
                                                                 16 340
                                                                 ═══

|  |  | November | |  | December | |
|---|---|---|---|---|---|---|
|  |  | £ | £ |  | £ | £ |
| Raw materials | 260 (*Aug.*) × 12 | | = 3 120 | 220 (*Sept.*) × 12 | | = 2 640 |
| Direct labour | 180 (*Nov.*) × 10 | | = 1 800 | 140 (*Dec.*) × 10 | | = 1 400 |
| Variable | 200 (*Oct.*) × $\frac{1}{3}$ × 6 = | | 400 | 180 (*Nov.*) × $\frac{1}{3}$ × 6 = | | 360 |
|  | 180 (*Nov.*) × $\frac{2}{3}$ × 6 = | | 720 | 140 (*Dec.*) × $\frac{2}{3}$ × 6 = | | 560 |
| Fixed expenses | (*October*) | | 300 | (*November*) | | 300 |
|  |  | | ——— |  | | ——— |
|  |  | | 6 340 |  | | 5 260 |
|  |  | | ═══ |  | | ═══ |

**12**            **Payments to Creditors**

| *Preliminary workings:* | June £ | July £ | August £ |
|---|---|---|---|
| Budgeted cost of sales | 1635 | 1405 | 1330 |
| *Add* desired closing stock | 1200 | 1100 | 1000 |
| | 2835 | 2505 | 2330 |
| *Less* opening stock | 1300 | 1200 | 1100 |
| Budgeted purchases | 1535 | 1305 | 1230 |
| *Add* opening creditors balances | 2110 | 2000 | 1950 |
| | 3645 | 3305 | 3180 |
| *Less* closing creditors balances | 2000 | 1950 | 1900 |
| *Budgeted payments to creditors* | 1645 | 1355 | 1280 |

**Receipts from Debtors**

| | June £ | July £ | August £ |
|---|---|---|---|
| Budgeted sales on credit | 2100 | 1800 | 1700 |
| *Add* opening debtors' balances | 2570 | 2600 | 2500 |
| | 4670 | 4400 | 4200 |
| *Less* closing debtors' balances | 2600 | 2500 | 2350 |
| *Budgeted receipts from debtors* | 2070 | 1900 | 1850 |

**Cash Budget**
**for 3 months ending 31st August 19–4**

| | | June £ | July £ | August £ |
|---|---|---|---|---|
| Opening balance | | 545 | 315 | 65 |
| *Add* receipts from debtors | | 2070 | 1900 | 1850 |
| Sale of investments | | | 700 | |
| Sale of plant | | | | 50 |
| | (*a*) | 2615 | 2915 | 1965 |
| *Less* payments to creditors | | 1645 | 1355 | 1280 |
| Expenses | | 255 | 210 | 195 |
| Capital expenditure | | | 800 | |
| Purchase of investments | | 400 | | 200 |
| Dividend payment | | | 485 | |
| | (*b*) | 2300 | 2850 | 1675 |
| Closing cash balance (*a*) − (*b*) | | 315 | 65 | 290 |

**Budgeted Sources and Application of Funds Statement for 3 Months Ending 31st August 19–4**

|  | £ | £ | £ |
|---|---|---|---|
| Opening cash Balance 1st June 19–4 |  |  | 545 |
| *Sources of increase:* |  |  |  |
| Net profit before tax for 3 months | 390 |  |  |
| *Add* back depreciation 3 × 60 000 | 180 | 570 |  |
| Proceeds of sale of investments |  | 700 |  |
| Decrease in debtors |  | 220 |  |
| Decrease in stocks |  | 300 |  |
| Sale of fixed assets |  | 50 | 1840 |
|  |  |  | 2385 |
| *Sources of decrease:* |  |  |  |
| Purchase of investments |  | 600 |  |
| Decrease in creditors |  | 210 |  |
| Capital expenditure |  | 800 |  |
| Dividend payment |  | 485 | 2095 |
| *Balance of cash at 31st August* 19–4 |  |  | 290 |

## Chapter 5

**1** Refer to pages 52–4. **2** Refer to page 53. **3** Refer to pages 54–7. **4** The statement is true in that, although certain costs can be directly identified with a specific product such as direct materials, direct labour and direct expenses, other costs which are indirect cannot be as readily identified with specific products. The works manager's salary, for example, has to be allocated on some arbitrary basis, since he himself carries out a variety of tasks, the costs of which in terms of his salary would be difficult to identify with specific products. The same reasoning would apply to internal transport where the transport carried a variety of different products at the same time. Since such indirect costs have to be allocated on the best basis available, such a base is inevitably arbitrary and under such conditions true cost ascertainment is not possible. But one could say that costs computed on such an arbitrary basis are a good estimate of cost.

**5**                         **Computation of Production Cost**

| Product | X | | Y |
|---|---|---|---|
|  | £ |  | £ |
| Direct materials 4 kg @ £1/kg | 4·00 | 10 kg @ £2/kg | 20·00 |
| Direct wages 2 hrs. @ £2·50/hr. | 5·00 | 2 hrs. @ £2·50/hr. | 5·00 |
| Prime cost | £9·00 |  | £25·00 |

| | | |
|---|---|---|
| *Product overhead: | £ | £ |
| 50% on direct materials | 2·00 | 10·00 |
| *Production cost* | £11·00 | £35·00 |

*Note:*

*Percentage of prime cost = $\dfrac{\text{Budgeted production overheads}}{\text{Budgeted direct materials cost}} \times 100$

$\dfrac{40\,000}{80\,000} \times 100 = 50\%$

This method of allocating overheads gives inaccurate costs. It will be observed from the above computation of production cost that although products X and Y have required the same time in production, product Y has been charged five times more overhead than product X, whereas in fact, had we used a more equitable basis for allocating overhead, namely a time base, both products would have been allocated with the same amount of overhead.

## Chapter 6

**1** Refer to page 65. **2** Refer to pages 66–7. **3** For a suitable chart showing the main and sub-variances refer to page 71. **4** The following is an illustrative statement which could be used for presentation to higher management:

### Profit and Loss Account for Month Ending——19–6

| | | Total |
|---|---|---|
| | | £ |
| Budgeted sales at standard prices | | 100 000 |
| *Less* budgeted cost of sales | | 40 000 |
| *Budgeted Profit* | | 60 000 |
| *Sales variances* | | |
| Price | 3 000 A | |
| Volume | 8 000 F | + 5 000 |
| | | 65 000 |
| *Material variances* | | |
| Price | 4 000 A | |
| Usage | 8 000 A | − 12 000 |
| | | 53 000 |
| *Wages variances* | | |
| Wage rate | 7 000 A | |
| Efficiency | 10 000 F | + 3 000 |
| | | 56 000 |
| *Overheads* | | |
| Variable overheads | 3 000 F | + 3 000 |
| | | 59 000 |

|  |  | Total |
| --- | --- | --- |
| *Fixed overhead* |  | £ |
| Expenditure variance | 2 000 A |  |
| *Volume variance | 5 000 F | + 3 000 |
| *Actual net profit* |  | £62 000 |

*Note:*
*The volume variance could be split down showing the capacity usage and efficiency variances separately.

**5** Once a standard has been set it should not be changed unless there has been a change in the conditions from which the original standard was formulated. In other words we do not change standards for the sake of change, but where there has been a change in the conditions such as modification of the design of the product, or a change in the method of doing a job then it is obvious that a new or revised standard should be evolved.

Management should always be on the look-out for improving standards by way of improved materials, improving production techniques, improved organisation, better plant layouts, new modes of distribution and so on. Therefore, if the firm is to be continually successful it is necessary for management to be continually assessing existing techniques and to be innovative in improving present standards, thereby increasing the efficiency of the firm as a whole.

**6**  (*i*)  Total direct material cost variance: $AC - SC$
Actual cost = actual qty used × actual price
Standard cost = standard qty × standard price
∴ *Direct material variance:*  $AC - SC$

$$600 \times £0.80 - 500 \times £1.20$$
$$£480 - £600 = \qquad £120 \text{ (F)}$$

| (*ii*)  (*a*) Price variance: | $AQ(AP - SP)$ |  |
| --- | --- | --- |
|  | $600(0.80 - 1.20)$ | £240 (F) |
| (*b*) Usage variance: | $SP(AQ - SQ)$ |  |
|  | $1.20(600 - 500)$ | £120 (A) |

*Check: total material variance* = price + usage  120 (F)

**7**  (*i*)  total wages variance:  $AC - SC$
$AC$ = actual wages paid.
$SC$ = Standard hours actually produced × standard rate per hour.
$AC = £5100.$
$SC = 2000 \times 0.75 \text{ hrs/unit} \times £3.20 = £4800$
∴ Total wages variance = $£5100 - 4800 = £300 \text{ (A)}$
(*ii*)  Wage rate variance:  $AH(AR - SR)$

$$1500\left(\frac{5100}{1500} - 3.2\right)$$

$$1500(3.4 - 3.2) \qquad\qquad 300 \text{ (A)}$$

(*iii*)  Efficiency variance:  Nil*
  2  (1500 − 1500)                                        Nil

Total wages variance = rate + efficiency                    300 A

*Note:*
*The standard hours are the hours it should have taken to produce that actual output *viz*:

Actual output (in units) × Standard hours/Unit
          2000 × 0·60                                    = 1500 hours

**8**  Variable overhead variance:  SC − AC

SC = Actual quantity produced × standard variable overhead rate

$$= 120\,000 \times \frac{£50\,000}{100\,000 \text{ units}}$$

$$= 120\,000 \times £0 \cdot 50 = £60\,000$$
AC $= £70\,000$
∴ Variable overhead variance: $60\,000 - 70\,000 = £10\,000$ A

**9**  Total fixed overhead variance:  SC − AC

The standard cost SC = actual output × standard overhead rate

$$3750 \times \frac{10\,000}{5\,000}$$

$3750 \times 2 = £7\,500$
Actual fixed overhead AC $= £12\,000$
∴ Fixed overhead variance $7500 - 12\,000 = £4500$ adverse

*Expenditure variance:*   BC − AC
          £10 000 − £12 000 = £2000 adverse

*Volume variance:*   SR (AQ − BQ)
          2 (3750 − 5000)     = £2500 adverse

*Check:* Fixed overhead variance = expenditure
                             + volume £4500 adverse

The volume variance can now be analysed into sub-variances, namely Capacity and Efficiency.

*Sub-variances*

| | | |
|---|---|---|
| Capacity variance: | SR (SQ − BQ) | |
| | 2 (4500 − 5000) | £1000 *adverse* |
| Efficiency variance: | SR(AQ − SQ) | |
| | 2 (3750 − 4500) | 1500 *adverse* |

*Check* Volume variance = capacity + efficiency          2500 *adverse*

It should be noted that the standard quantity SQ is the quantity that ought to have been produced in the actual time worked viz. actual days worked × standard rate of production:

$$18 \times 250 = 4500 \text{ units}$$

**10** (*i*) Total sales margin variance = AP − BP

where AP = Actual profit at standard purchase prices
BP = Budgeted profit

Now AP = Actual quantity × actual profit/kg
BP = Budgeted quantity × Budgeted profit.

∴ *Sales margin variance* = AP − BP

|  |  | £ |
|---|---|---|
| (AQ × AP) − (BQ × BP) |  |  |
| 'Glendale' = $120 \times £0.60 - 160 \times 0.50 =$ | | 8 A |
| 'Ireshire' = $40 \times £0.10 - 60 \times 0.30 =$ | | 14 A |
| | | £22 A |

(*a*) *Sales volume variance* = SP (AQ − BQ)
where SP = standard profit

| 'Glendale': $£0.50 (120 - 160)$ | 20 A |
|---|---|
| 'Ireshire': $£0.30 ( 40 - 60)$ | 6 A |
| | 26 A |

(*b*) *Selling price variance* = AQ $\left(\dfrac{\text{Actual profit} - \text{standard profit per kg}}{\text{per kg}}\right)$

| 'Glendale': $120 (0.60 - 0.50)$ | 12 F |
|---|---|
| 'Ireshire': $40 (0.10 - 0.30)$ | 8 A |
| | 4 F |

∴ Sales margin variance = volume + price
$$£22 (A) = £26 (A) + £4 (F)$$

(*ii*) Purchase price variance = AQ (AP − SP)
where AQ = Actual quantity
AP = Actual purchase price
SP = Standard purchase price

| 'Glendale': $120 (0.90 - 1.00)$ | $= £12$ (F) |
|---|---|
| 'Ireshire': $40 (0.80 - 0.70)$ | $= 4$ (A) |
| | 8 F |

(*iii*)
### DENBY CHEESE SHOP
### Profit and Loss Accounts for week Ending ——— 19–6

|  | *Cheese* | | 'Glendale' | 'Ireshire' | Total |
|---|---|---|---|---|---|
|  | kg | £ | kg | £ | £ |
| *Budgeted sales:* | (160 × £1·50 kg) | 240 | 60 × £1 kg | 60 | 300 |
| *Less* budgeted cost of sales: | | | £ | | |
|  | (160 × £1·00) | 160 | 60 = 0·70 | 42 | 202 |
| *Budgeted profit* | | 80 | | 18 | 98 |
| *Sales variances:* | | | | | |
| Price | | | 12 F | 8 A | + 4 F |
| Volume | | | 20 A | 6 A | − 26A |
|  | | | | | 76 |
| Purchase price variance | | | 12 F | 4 A | 8 F |
|  | | | *Actual profit* | | £84 |

(*iv*)  **Conventional Profit and Loss Account for Week Ending**
——— 19–6

Actual sales = AQ × actual selling price/kg

|  |  | £ | £ |
|---|---|---|---|
| 'Glendale' | 120 × £1·60/kg = | 192 | |
| 'Ireshire' | 40 × £0·80/kg = | 32 | 224 |
| *Less* costs: | AQ × actual costs/kg | | |
| 'Glendale' | 120 × £0·90/kg | 108 | |
| 'Ireshire' | 40 × £0·80/kg | 32 | 140 |
|  |  | *Actual profit* | £84 |

It will be noted that the budgeted profit has not been attained because of the failure to achieve the planned volume of sales, although the fall in volume has been partly offset by favourable selling price and purchase price variances.

## Chapter 7

**1** Refer to pages 83–5. **2** Refer to page 102. **3** Since one of the major functions of management is to control, it must have a feedback on the actual results attained and compare such results with the planned performance in order to take corrective action. An analogy of this control concept is the thermostat: if one has a central heating system one plans the room temperature and sets the heating system at a level which will attain the desired aim. The room temperature will be continually monitored and fed back to control – the thermostat. If the actual room temperature falls below the planned room temperature the deviation will be corrected and the heating system adjusted to comply with the plan.

Since management is concerned with deviations from the plan rather than actual figures, it is only the deviations from plan that need concern them. Budgetary control is an example of management by exception.  **4** Refer to page 87.

**5**  (*i*)  **Sales budget**   'OK' HOTEL LTD.

|  | Budgeted quantities | Budgeted selling price | Budgeted sales |
|---|---|---|---|
|  |  | £ | £ |
| Cigarettes | 2 000 | 1·40 | 2 800 |
| Beer | 1 800 | 60·00 | 108 000 |
| Wines: X | 400 | 2·80 | 1 120 |
| Y | 300 | 2·00 | 600 |
| Z | 200 | 2·10 | 420 |
|  | *Total Budgeted Sales* | | £112 940 |

(*ii*)  **Purchasing budget**

|  | Cigarettes | Beer | Wines and spirits | | |
|---|---|---|---|---|---|
|  |  |  | X | Y | Z |
| Planned sales (units) | 2 000 | 1 800 | 400 | 300 | 200 |
| *Add* planned closing stock | 60 | 20 | 30 | 20 | 10 |
|  | 2 060 | 1 820 | 430 | 320 | 210 |
| *Less* opening stock | 100 | 100 | 10 | 10 | 20 |
| Purchasing budget (in units) | 1 960 | 1 720 | 420 | 310 | 190 |
| Budgeted purchase price | £1·00 | £32 | £1·60 | £1·40 | £1·20 |
| Purchases budget (£'s) | 1 960 | £55 040 | 672 | 434 | 228 |
|  |  |  | 58 334 | | |

(*iii*)  **Closing stock budget**

|  | Cigarettes | Beer | Wines and spirits | | |
|---|---|---|---|---|---|
|  |  |  | X | Y | Z |
| Closing stock (units) | 60 | 20 | 30 | 20 | 10 |
| Purchase price/unit | £1·00 | £32 | £1·60 | £1·40 | £1·20 |
| Closing stock (£'s) | 60 | £640 | 48 | 28 | 12 |
|  |  |  | 788 | | |

## (iv)  Labour costs budget (bar)

|  |  | £ |
|---|---|---|
| Wages | $6 \times 130 \times 52 =$ | 40 560 |
| Meals | $6 \times 6 \times 52 =$ | 1 872 |
| Accommodation | $4 \times 10 \times 52 =$ | 2 080 |
|  |  | £44 512 |

## (v)  Overhead expenditure budget

|  |  | £ |
|---|---|---|
| Depreciation cutlery, glass etc.  $2\% \times £112\,940$ |  | 2 259 |
| Linen and uniforms  $52 \times £6$ | = | 312 |
| Laundry and dry cleaning  $52 \times £12$ | = | 624 |
| Commission  $5\% \times £112\,940$ | = | 5 647 |
| Indirect supplies  $10\% \times £112\,940$ | = | 11 294 |
|  |  | £20 136 |

## (vi)

### Budgeted Bar Trading Account
### For Year Ending 31st December 19–7

|  | £ | Budget £ | Actual | Variances |
|---|---|---|---|---|
| Sales |  | 112 940 |  |  |
| Opening stock | 3 164 |  |  |  |
| *Add* purchases | 58 334 |  |  |  |
|  | 61 498 |  |  |  |
| *Less* closing stock | 788 | 60 710 |  |  |
|  |  | 52 230 |  |  |
| *Less* labour costs | 44 512 |  |  |  |
| overheads | 20 136 | 64 648 |  |  |
| *Budgeted gross* loss |  | £12 418 |  |  |

## 6  (a)                Preliminary Workings

| Product | A £ | C £ | E £ |
|---|---|---|---|
| Sales | 4 200 000 | 3 800 000 | 10 080 000 |
| Standard profit: % of selling price | 20%: 840 000 | 25%: 950 000 | $16\frac{2}{3}\%$: 1 680 000 |
| Cost of sales (a) | 3 360 000 | 2 850 000 | 8 400 000 |
| Unit cost (given) (b) | £24 | £15 | £20 |
| Units budgeted  a to be sold  b | 140 000 | 190 000 | 420 000 |

## Production budget (in units)

|  | A |  | C |  | E |
|---|---|---|---|---|---|
| Budgeted sales (in units) | 140 000 |  | 190 000 |  | 420 000 |
| *Add* planned closing stock $\frac{£600\,000}{24} =$ | 25 000 | $\frac{£570\,000}{15} =$ | 38 000 | $\frac{£1\,000\,000}{20} =$ | 50 000 |
|  | 165 000 |  | 228 000 |  | 470 000 |
| *Less* opening stock $\frac{£720\,000}{24} =$ | 30 000 | $\frac{£540\,000}{15} =$ | 36 000 | $\frac{£1\,800\,000}{20} =$ | 90 000 |
| Net production after loss | 135 000 |  | 192 000 |  | 380 000 |
| *Add* normal loss $\frac{10}{90} \times 135\,000$ | 15 000 | $\frac{1}{4} \times$ 192 000 | 48 000 | $\frac{1}{19} \times$ 380 000 | 20 000 |
| Gross production required | 150 000 |  | 240 000 |  | 400 000 |

*(b)*                    **Direct Wages Budget**

**Dept F**

*Product A*

| Labour grade: | | Hours per unit | Rate per hour £ | Unit Cost £ | Units | Total Cost £ | £ |
|---|---|---|---|---|---|---|---|
|  | 1 | 2·00 | 0·9 | 1·8 | 150 000 | 270 000 |  |
|  | 2 | 1·50 | 0·8 | 1·2 | 150 000 | 180 000 |  |
|  |  |  |  |  |  |  | 450 000 |

*Product C*

| Labour grade: | | | | | | | |
|---|---|---|---|---|---|---|---|
|  | 1 | 3·00 | 0·9 | 2·7 | 240 000 | 648 000 |  |
|  | 2 | 2·00 | 0·8 | 1·6 | 240 000 | 384 000 | 1 032 000 |

*Product E*

| Labour grade: | | | | | | | |
|---|---|---|---|---|---|---|---|
|  | 1 | 1·00 | 0·9 | 0·9 | 400 000 | 360 000 |  |
|  | 2 | 1·50 | 0·8 | 1·2 | 400 000 | 480 000 | 840 000 |

| | | | | | | |
|---|---|---|---|---|---|---|
| | | Total Grade | 1 | 1 278 000 | |
| | | Total Grade | 2 | 1 044 000 | £2 322 000 |

**Dept G**

*Product A*

| Labour grade: | | | | | | | |
|---|---|---|---|---|---|---|---|
|  | 1 | 3·00 | 1·00 | 3·0 | 150 000 | 450 000 |  |
|  | 2 | 2·00 | 0·90 | 1·8 | 150 000 | 270 000 | 720 000 |

*Product C*

| Labour grade: | | | | | | | |
|---|---|---|---|---|---|---|---|
|  | 1 | 1·00 | 1·00 | 1·00 | 240 000 | 240 000 |  |
|  | 2 | 1·50 | 0·90 | 1·35 | 240 000 | 324 000 | 564 000 |

| Labour grade: | | | *Product E* | | | | |
|---|---|---|---|---|---|---|---|
| | | | £ | £ | | £ | £ |
| | 1 | 1·00 | 1·00 | 1·00 | 400 000 | 400 000 | |
| | 2 | 2·50 | 0·90 | 2·25 | 400 000 | 900 000 | 1 300 000 |
| | | | | | | | |
| | | | Total Grade | 1 | | 1 090 000 | |
| | | | Total Grade | 2 | | 1 494 000 | 2 584 000 |
| | | | | | | | |

*Budgeted total wages cost Dept. F + Dept. G*                    £4 906 000

## 7   (a)  Raw Materials Stock Budget in £'s

| | Jan. | Feb. | Mar. | April | May | June |
|---|---|---|---|---|---|---|
| Opening stock | 1000 | 700 | 500 | 400 | 400 | 500 |
| *Add* purchases | 300 | 400 | 500 | 600 | 800 | 640 |
| | 1300 | 1100 | 1000 | 1000 | 1200 | 1140 |
| *Less* used in production | 600 | 600 | 600 | 600 | 700 | 700 |
| Budgeted closing stock | 700 | 500 | 400 | 400 | 500 | 440 |

## (b)  Production Budget (In Units)

| | Jan. | Feb. | Mar. | April | May | June |
|---|---|---|---|---|---|---|
| Opening stock finished units | 150 | 170 | 180 | 180 | 150 | 130 |
| *Add* budgeted production | 60 | 60 | 60 | 60 | 70 | 70 |
| | 210 | 230 | 240 | 240 | 220 | 200 |
| *Less* planned sales | 40 | 50 | 60 | 90 | 90 | 70 |
| Budgeted closing stock-finished units | 170 | 180 | 180 | 150 | 130 | 130 |

## (c)  Production Costs Budget in £'s
### (*Based on Marginal Cost Approach*)

| | Cost/Unit | Jan. | Feb. | Mar. | April | May | June |
|---|---|---|---|---|---|---|---|
| Materials | 10 | 600 | 600 | 600 | 600 | 700 | 700 |
| Labour | 8 | 480 | 480 | 480 | 480 | 560 | 560 |
| Variable overhead | 6 | 360 | 360 | 360 | 360 | 420 | 420 |
| | | 1440 | 1440 | 1440 | 1440 | 1680 | 1680 |

*Total marginal cost of goods completed = £9120*

(d)                    **Creditors Budget (For Raw Materials)**

|                           | Jan. | Feb. | Mar. | April | May  | June |
|---------------------------|------|------|------|-------|------|------|
|                           | £    | £    | £    | £     | £    | £    |
| Opening balance           | 600  | 660  | 700  | 900   | 1100 | 1400 |
| *Add* purchases           | 300  | 400  | 500  | 600   | 800  | 640  |
|                           | 900  | 1060 | 1200 | 1500  | 1900 | 2040 |
| *Less* payments           | 240  | 360  | 300  | 400   | 500  | 600  |
| Closing creditors' balances | 660 | 700 | 900 | 1100 | 1400 | 1440 |

(e)                    **Debtors' Budget**

|                          | Jan. | Feb. | Mar. | April | May   | June  |
|--------------------------|------|------|------|-------|-------|-------|
|                          | £    | £    | £    | £     | £     | £     |
| Opening balance          | 2700 | 3060 | 4140 | 5400  | 7200  | 8640  |
| *Add* planned sales      | 1440 | 1800 | 2160 | 3240  | 3240  | 2520  |
|                          | 4140 | 4860 | 6300 | 8640  | 10440 | 11160 |
| *Less* cash received     | 1080 | 720  | 900  | 1440  | 1800  | 2160  |
| Closing debtors' balances | 3060 | 4140 | 5400 | 7200 | 8640  | 9000  |

(f)                    **Cash Budget**

|                    | Jan. | Feb. | Mar.   | April  | May    | June |
|--------------------|------|------|--------|--------|--------|------|
|                    | £    | £    | £      | £      | £      | £    |
| Opening balance    | 1300 | 1100 | 420    | (4020) | (4020) | 2100 |
| *Add* receipts     | 1080 | 720  | 900    | 1440   | 7800   | 2160 |
|                    | 2380 | 1820 | 1320   | (2580) | 3780   | 4260 |
| *Less* payments    | 1280 | 1400 | 5340   | 1440   | 1680   | 1780 |
|                    | 1100 | 420  | (4020) | (4020) | 2100   | 2480 |

(g)                    **Receipts Schedule**

|                                                         | Jan. | Feb. | Mar. | April | May  | June |
|---------------------------------------------------------|------|------|------|-------|------|------|
|                                                         | £    | £    | £    | £     | £    | £    |
| Planned receipts from debtors (sold 3 months previously) | 1080 | 720 | 900 | 1440 | 1800 | 2160 |
| Proceeds from shares                                    | —    | —    | —    | —     | 6000 | —    |
| Total receipts                                          | 1080 | 720  | 900  | 1440  | 7800 | 2160 |

(*h*)                             **Payments Schedule**

|  | Jan. £ | Feb. £ | Mar. £ | April £ | May £ | June £ |
|---|---|---|---|---|---|---|
| Planned payments to creditors for materials bought 2 months previously | 240 | 360 | 300 | 400 | 500 | 600 |
| Fixed overheads | 200 | 200 | 200 | 200 | 200 | 200 |
| Machine |  |  | 400 |  |  |  |
| Direct wages (see production cost budget) | 480 | 480 | 480 | 480 | 560 | 560 |
| Variable overheads (see production cost budget) | 360 | 360 | 360 | 360 | 420 | 420 |
| *Total payments* | 1280 | 1400 | 1740 | 1440 | 1680 | 1780 |

(*i*)   **Budgeted Profit and Loss for 6 Months ending 30th June 19–7**

|  | £ | £ | £ |
|---|---|---|---|
| Sales |  |  | 14 400 |
| Opening stock finished goods |  | 1 800 |  |
| *Add* cost of goods completed |  | 9 120 |  |
|  |  | 10 920 |  |
| *Less* closing stock finished goods: |  |  |  |
| *Var. cost/unit* |  |  |  |
| 130 units × £24 |  | 3 120 |  |
| Cost of goods sold |  |  | 7 800 |
| Gross margin |  |  | 6 600 |
| *Less:* |  | £ |  |
| Fixed overheads 6 × 200 |  | 1 200 |  |
| Depreciation (see question): | £ |  |  |
| Machinery | 900 |  |  |
| Motor vehicles | 400 | 1 300 | 2 500 |
|  | *Budgeted net profit* |  | £4 100 |

(*j*)        **Projected Balance Sheet as at 30th June 19–7**

| Fixed assets | Cost £ | Accumulated Depreciation £ | Net Book Value £ |
|---|---|---|---|
| Machinery (8000 + new machine 4000) | 12 000 | 4 100 | 7 900 |
| Motor vehicles | 4 000 | 2 000 | 2 000 |
|  | 16 000 | 6 100 | 9 900 |

| Current assets | £ | £ | |
|---|---|---|---|
| Stock: | | | |
| Finished goods | 3 120 | | |
| Raw materials | 440 | 3 560 | |
| Debtors | ——— | 9 000 | |
| Bank and cash | | 2 480 | |
| | | ——— | |
| | | 15 040 | |
| *Less current liabilities:* | £ | | |
| Creditors (for materials) | 1 440 | | |
| Creditors (for fixed | | | |
| overheads) | 200 | 1 640 | 13 400 |
| | | ——— | ——— |
| | *Net capital employed* | | £23 300 |
| | | | ——— |

| *Represented by:* | £ |
|---|---|
| Issued share capital: | |
| 14 000 ordinary shares of £1 each fully paid | 14 000 |
| *Reserves:* | |
| Profit and Loss Account balance (5200 + 4100) | 9 300 |
| | ——— |
| | 23 300 |
| | ——— |

**8** (*a*) A flexible budget differs from a fixed budget in respect of the level of activity actually attained. A fixed budget is designed to remain unchanged irrespective of the level of activity, whereas the flexible budget is produced at different levels of activity.

The purpose of a flexible budget is to enable expenditure to be controlled more closely by relating actual expenditure to budgeted expenditure at an actual attained level of activity.

| (*b*) | | *Per Month* | | *Fixed* |
|---|---|---|---|---|
| | | *Flexible Budgets* | | *Budget* |
| *Activity Level* | | | | 3000 |
| (hours of work) | 2000 | 2800 | 3600 | |
| | ——— | ——— | ——— | ——— |
| | | | | (*Normal Activity*) |
| | £ | £ | £ | £ |
| Supervision | 250 | 370 | 490 | 430 |
| Heat and light | 45 | 55 | 60 | 55 |
| Rent and rates | 180 | 180 | 180 | 180 |
| Cleaning | 30 | 30 | 40 | 40 |
| Depreciation | 400 | 400 | 550 | 400 |
| Consumable supplies | 240 | 336 | 432 | 360 |
| Power | 300 | 420 | 528 | 450 |
| Repairs | 100 | 150 | 215 | 175 |
| Indirect wages | 400 | 560 | 720 | 600 |
| | ——— | ——— | ——— | ——— |
| | 1945 | 2501 | 3215 | 2690 |
| | ——— | ——— | ——— | ——— |

Standard overhead rates are *not* changed as activity levels vary.

(c)
$$\text{Departmental hourly rate} = \frac{\text{Fixed budget}}{\text{Fixed budget hours}}$$

$$= \frac{2690}{3000} = \text{\pounds}0{\cdot}897 \text{ per hour}$$

## Chapter 8

**1** Refer to page 111.  **2** Refer to page 115.  **3** Refer to page 116.

**4**  (*i*) Let C = Total cost per unit
  S = Selling price per unit
  P = Profit
 Then (*i*) C + P = S.

Now we know that total cost C can be divided into fixed cost F and variable cost V.

$\therefore$ substituting F and V for C in (*i*) we get
  (*ii*) F + V + P = S
$\therefore$ (*iii*) S − V = F + P
  where S − V = contribution towards fixed costs plus profit.

(*ii*) The break-even point from formula (*iii*) above must be just when sales = costs i.e. profit P will just equal zero; hence we have S − V = F + O

$\therefore$ break-even point $= \dfrac{F}{S-V}$ where:

 F = Fixed costs
 S = Selling price per unit
 V = Variable cost per unit.

**5** A firm might be willing to sell at below cost when there is short-term depression in the market or in cases where a product in a multi-product firm contributes to the sale of other products the company makes.

 In the first case, where there is a depression in the market, it may be advisable to continue to produce a product where the selling price is below total cost, providing that the selling price is greater than the variable costs, for in so producing there will be some contribution towards the fixed costs which will remain whether we produce or not. However, this is only a short run strategy and could not be continued over the long term since the firm which did not cover its total costs would eventually have to go out of business.

 Where the firm is working below full capacity and some products are making a profit while others are making a loss, providing the latter products' selling prices cover at least the variable costs, it would be advisable to continue producing these since they will make some contribution towards the

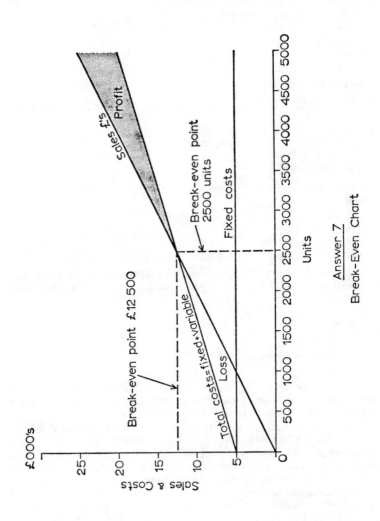

Answer 7
Break-Even Chart

firm's costs. If it were decided in the circumstances stated to cease production of these unprofitable lines then the total profit of the firm would be less than if it continued to make them.

Even though the firm may be working at full capacity in certain cases it might prove necessary to produce some products at a loss if it is proven that such products contribute to the sale of the profitable ones. This is akin to the 'loss leader' which supermarkets offer in order to attract customers to the more profitable lines. **6** Refer to page 117. **7** Refer to chart see page 226. **8** Refer to pages 120–1. The margin of safety in question 7 is as follows:

Total production capacity – break-even point
5000 – 2500 = 2500 units.

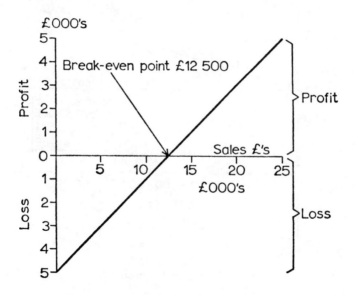

### Answer 9
#### Profit-Volume Chart

**9** See chart above. The significance of such a chart is that it is possible to read off the profit or loss at any given volume of sales. The slope of the line indicates the profit-volume ratio. This latter ratio is given by the formula $\dfrac{S-V}{S}$ where S = sales and V = variable costs.

From the above formula the greater the PV ratio, the greater will be the slope of the line indicated in the chart. It should be management's objective to increase this slope wherever possible by either increasing the selling price if possible or reducing the variable costs, thus attaining a higher profit–volume ratio. **10** Refer to page 122. **11** (*i*) See chart below.

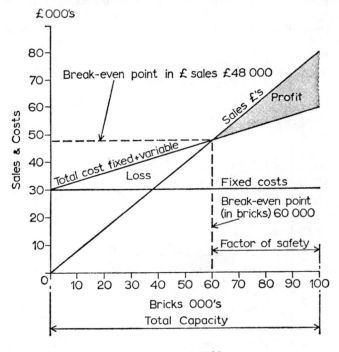

Answer 11 (i)

Break-Even Chart   Jolson Company

(*ii*)   From the break-even chart we can determine that

(*a*) the break-even point is 60 000 bricks or in terms of
£ sales £48 000.
(*b*) Factor of safety is 40 000 bricks.

(*iii*)   Break-even point = $\dfrac{\text{Fixed costs}}{\text{Contribution per brick}}$ = $\dfrac{F}{S-V}$

$F = £30\,000$
$S = £0 \cdot 80$
$V = £0 \cdot 30$

$\therefore$ Break-even point = $\dfrac{F}{S-V} = \dfrac{30\,000}{0 \cdot 80 - 0 \cdot 30} = 60\,000$ bricks

Selling price/brick:

In terms of £ sales = $60\,000 \times 0.80 = £48\,000$.

Factor of safety:

= Total production capacity − break-even point
$100\,000$ (bricks) − $60\,000$ bricks
= $40\,000$

The factor of safety is sometimes expressed as a percentage of total capacity; the formula will then be:

$$\text{Factor of safety} = \left( \frac{\substack{\text{Total production} \\ \text{capacity}} - \substack{\text{Break-even} \\ \text{point}}}{\text{Total production capacity}} \right) 100$$

$$\left( \frac{100\,000 - 60\,000}{100\,000} \right) 100 = 40\%$$

**12** (*i*) See chart below.

(*ii*) Profit–volume ratio = Contribution per £ of sales

$$= \left( \frac{S - V}{S} \right) 100$$

$S = £0.80$
$V = £0.30$

∴ PV ratio $= \left( \dfrac{0.80 - 0.30}{0.80} \right) 100 = 62.5\%$

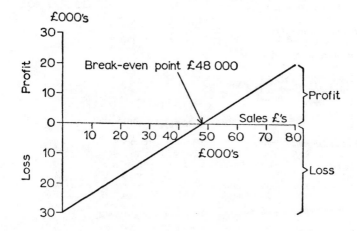

Answer 12 (i)

Profit-Volume Chart  Jolson Company

(*iii*)   (*a*)   New break-even point $= \dfrac{F}{S-V}$

$$= \dfrac{30\,000}{0.75 - 0.35}$$

$$= 75\,000 \text{ bricks}$$

or $75\,000 \times £0.75 = £56\,250$ *sales*

(*b*)   New factor of safety: total production capacity – break-even point

$$100\,000 - 75\,000 = 25\,000 \text{ bricks}$$

(*c*)   New PV ratio $\dfrac{S-V}{S} = \left( \dfrac{0.75 - 0.35}{0.75} \right) 100$

$$= \dfrac{0.40}{0.75} \times 100 = 53.3\,\%$$

**13**  (*i*)  Since there is a production constraint it is necessary before formulating the production plan to ascertain which products make the best contribution per key factor, that is to say, the contribution per hour.

| Product | A | B | C | D |
|---|---|---|---|---|
| | £ | £ | £ | £ |
| Selling price | 100 | 80 | 150 | 152 |
| Variable costs | 40 | 50 | 70 | 80 |
| *Contribution per unit* | 60 | 30 | 80 | 72 |
| Process time *in hours* | 5 | 5 | 8 | 9 |
| *Contribution per hour* | £12 | £6 | £10 | £8 |

*In order of ranking*
1st choice   Product A
2nd choice  Product C
3rd choice  Product D
4th choice  Product B

(*ii*)                         **Schedule**

| Product | Demand unit | Process time in hours | Total Hours Utilised | Produce (units) | Contribution per unit | Total Contribution |
|---|---|---|---|---|---|---|
| | | | | | £ | £ |
| A | 2 000 | 5 | 10 000 | 2 000 | 60 | 120 000 |
| C | 5 000 | 8 | 40 000 | 5 000 | 80 | 400 000 |
| | | | 50 000 | | | |
| D | 8 000 | 9 | 36 000 | 4 000 | 72 | 288 000 |
| B | 1 000 | 5 | — | NIL | 30 | — |

| Total available production capacity | 86 000 | *Total contribution* | ⸍808 000 |
|---|---|---|---|
| | | *Less fixed costs* | 400 000 |
| | | *Maximum profit* | £408 000 |

**14**   Let $x$ = number of units of 'Basic' quality to be produced
Let $y$ = number of units of 'De-luxe' quality to be produced

*Process* (1)     $2x + 3y = 6000$ hours

*Process* (2)     $4x + y = 8000$ hours

*Objective function* (iii)
   Maximise contribution $C = 5x + 6y$

*See graph:*

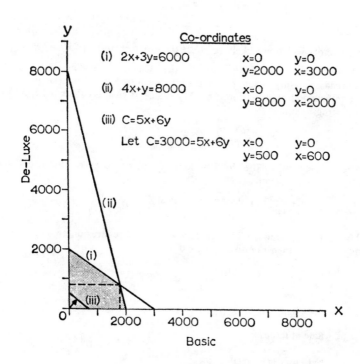

Answer 14

The optimal solution is to make 1800 of 'Basic', and 800 of 'De-luxe'. Substituting for $x$ and $y$ in equation (*iii*) we get

$$\text{Maximum contribution } C = 5 \times 1800 + 800 \times 6$$
$$= 9000 + 4800$$
$$= \pounds 13\,800$$

# Chapter 9

**1** Refer to page 138.   **2** Refer to page 138.   **3** Refer to page 139.
**4** The formula for calculating the average period in which debtors pay their accounts is as follows:

$$\frac{\text{Debtors}}{\text{Sales} \div 365}$$

**5** Factors which are likely to affect the gross profit ratio are:

(*i*) Changes in selling prices. (*ii*) Changes in material prices (purchases). (*iii*) Changes in manufacturing costs where the firm is a manufacturing organisation.   **6** The dividend yield is calculated from the following formula:

$$\frac{\text{par value of share} \times \text{dividend } \%}{\text{market value}}$$

Alternatively where the dividend is given in pence as is now usual, the dividend yield formula is:

$$\frac{\text{dividend in decimal } \pounds\text{'s}}{\text{market value}} \times 100$$

Thus, if the dividend is $\pounds 0 \cdot 10$ per share and the shares are quoted on the stock market at $\pounds 2$ then the dividend yield is:

$$\frac{\pounds 0 \cdot 10}{\pounds 2} \times 100 = 5 \%$$

**7** Refer to page 147.   **8** (*i*)

|  |  | 19–7 | 19–6 |
|---|---|---|---|
| (*a*) | Rate of turnover | 4·67 | 8·4 |
| (*b*) | Net profit/net capital employed | 28·5 % | 56·7 % |

(c) Credit period given

$$\frac{\text{debtors} \times 365}{\text{sales}}$$

$$= \frac{22\,00 \times 365}{110\,000} \qquad \frac{30\,000 \times 365}{182\,500}$$

$$= \quad 73 \text{ days} \qquad = \quad 60 \text{ days}$$

(d) Working capital ratio

$$\frac{45\,000}{40\,000} \qquad \frac{65\,000}{50\,000}$$

$$= \quad 1 \cdot 125 \qquad 1 \cdot 3$$

(e) Liquidity ratio

$$\frac{25\,000}{40\,000} \qquad \frac{55\,000}{50\,000}$$

$$0 \cdot 625 \qquad 1 \cdot 1$$

(f) Net worth ordinary share

$$\frac{70\,000}{36\,000} \qquad \frac{53\,000}{30\,000}$$

$$£1 \cdot 94 \qquad £1 \cdot 77$$

(ii) The chief points are:

(a) Poor liquidity.
(b) High dividend pay out maintained despite poor liquidity and profit decline.
(c) No investments outside the firm to replace plant.
(d) Stock turnover has considerably declined. Greater co-ordination required between purchases and sales functions.
(e) Need for tighter debtors control.

*Recommendations*

(a) Endeavour to increase profitability by increasing volume of sales and cost reduction programme.
(b) Improve liquidity by:
  (i) Greater control over stocks and greater co-ordination between purchases and sales thereby increasing rate of turnover of stocks;
  (ii) Reduce dividends;
  (iii) Lease back assets if feasible and desirable;
  (iv) Tighter debtor control.
(c) Increase the earnings per share by infusing some debt capital in the capital structure, provided future earnings are likely to cover the fixed interest charges.

## Chapter 11

**1** Refer to pages 166–7.  **2**  Refer to pages 167–76.

**3** (a)

|  | Alpha | Sigma | Omega |
|---|---|---|---|
| Pay back period (in years) | $3\frac{3}{4}$ | $3\frac{3}{4}$ | $3\frac{3}{8}$ |

(b) Average rate of return on
   original investment

$$= \frac{\text{Average yearly income net of depreciation}}{\text{Original capital outlay}} \times 100$$

*Alpha* $\left(\dfrac{6100-4000}{20\,000}\right)100 = \dfrac{2100 \times 100}{20\,000} = \underline{10 \cdot 5\,\%}$

*Sigma* $\left(\dfrac{5000-4000}{20\,000}\right)100 = \dfrac{1000 \times 100}{20\,000} = 5\,\%$

*Omega* $\left(\dfrac{4700-4000}{20\,000}\right)100 = \dfrac{700 \times 100}{20\,000} = \underline{3 \cdot 5\,\%}$

(c) *Net Present Value (Discounted at 10 %)*

|   | **Alpha** | | | | **Sigma** | | |
|---|---|---|---|---|---|---|---|
|   | *Cash flow* | *Discount factor* | *Present value* | | *Cash flow* | *Disount factor* | *Present value* |
|   | £ | | £ | | £ | | £ |
| 0 | −20000 | 1 | −20 000 | | −20 000 | 1 | −20 000 |
| 1 | 3 000 | 0·909 | 2 727 | | 5 000 | 0·909 | 4 545 |
| 2 | 4 000 | 0·826 | 3 304 | | 6 000 | 0·826 | 4 956 |
| 3 | 7 000 | 0·751 | 5 257 | | 6 000 | 0·751 | 4 506 |
| 4 | 8 000 | 0·683 | 5 464 | | 4 000 | 0·683 | 2 732 |
| 5 | 8 500 | 0·621 | 5 278 | | 4 000 | 0·621 | 2 484 |
|   | | | £22 030 | | | | £19 223 |
| − original investment | | | 20 000 | | | | −20 000 |
| Excess net present value | | | +2 030 | | Deficiency | | −777 |
| Profitability index | | | 1·1015 | | | | 0·961 |

|   | **Omega** | | |
|---|---|---|---|
|   | *Cash flow* | *Discount factor* | *Present value* |
|   | £ | | £ |
|   | −20 000 | 1 | −20 000 |
|   | 6 000 | 0·909 | 5 454 |
|   | 6 000 | 0·826 | 4 956 |
|   | 6 500 | 0·751 | 4 881 |
|   | 4 000 | 0·683 | 2 732 |
|   | 1 000 | 0·621 | 621 |
|   | | | £18 644 |
|   | | | −20 000 |
|   | | Deficiency | −1 356 |
|   | | | 0·932 |

(*d*) Since Alpha has the highest net present value it is now desired to compute the internal rate of return. Since we already have the NPV for Alpha at discount rate of 10% as a guide, we now, by trial and error, choose a suitable discount rate which will discount Alpha's cash flows ± 1% either side of the initial outlay. What we are really trying to do is to find a discount which discounts the cash inflows to a total present value equal to the initial outlay. Let us try 14%:

**Alpha**

|        | Cash flow | Discount factor | Present value |
|--------|-----------|-----------------|---------------|
|        | £         |                 | £             |
| Year 0 | −20 000   | 1               | −20 000       |
| 1      | 3 000     | 0·877           | 2 631         |
| 2      | 4 000     | 0·769           | 3 076         |
| 3      | 7 000     | 0·675           | 4 725         |
| 4      | 8 000     | 0·592           | 4 736         |
| 5      | 8 500     | 0·519           | 4 411         |
|        |           | Total present value | £19 579   |

Since at 14% we are very close to the initial outlay figure of 20 000 we can go one step further by choosing 13%, which should give us a present value figure a little over the £20 000 initial outlay.

Discount rate 13%:

|        | Cash flow | Discount factor | Present value |
|--------|-----------|-----------------|---------------|
|        | £         |                 | £             |
| Year 0 | −20 000   | 1               | −20 000       |
| 1      | 3 000     | 0·885           | 2 655         |
| 2      | 4 000     | 0·783           | 3 132         |
| 3      | 7 000     | 0·693           | 4 851         |
| 4      | 8 000     | 0·613           | 4 904         |
| 5      | 8 500     | 0·543           | 4 615         |
|        |           | Total present value | £20 157   |

By interpolation time yield $= 13\% + \left(\dfrac{20\,157 - 20\,000}{20\,157 - 19\,579}\right)(15 - 14)$

$= 13·3\%$

Hence the management will choose Alpha, since it scores higher on all the various methods used; Sigma and Omega are not viable propositions since they do not even cover the cost of capital of 10%, both giving negative net present values.

**4** (*a*)  *Pay back period*

|  | A | B | C |
|---|---|---|---|
| In years | $2\frac{3}{5}$ | 2 | $2\frac{3}{4}$ |

(*b*)  *Average rate of return on original investment*

|  | A | B | C |
|---|---|---|---|
|  | £ | £ | £ |
| Forecast net income for 4 years | 1600 |  |  |
| „      „      „      „ „    „ | | 1400 | |
| „      „      „      „  5 years | | | 1800 |
|  | 1600 | 1400 | 1800 |
| *Less* 100% depreciation on investment | 1000 | 1000 | 1000 |
| Net income after depreciation | 600 | 400 | 800 |
| ∴ Average yearly income | £150 | £100 | £160 |
| Average yearly income as a percentage of original investment | $\frac{150}{1000} \times 100$ | $\frac{100}{1000} \times 100$ | $\frac{160}{100} \times 100$ |
| = | 15% | 10% | 16% |

(*c*)  *Net present value using* 8% *discount rate*

|  | A | | | | B | |
|---|---|---|---|---|---|---|
|  | Cash flow | Discount rate | Present value | Cash flow | Discount rate | Present value |
|  | £ | | £ | £ | | £ |
| 0 | −1 000 | 1 | −1 000 | −1 000 | 1 | −1 000 |
| 1 | 200 | 0·926 | 185·2 | 500 | 0·926 | 463·0 |
| 2 | 500 | 0·857 | 428·5 | 500 | 0·857 | 428·5 |
| 3 | 500 | 0·794 | 397·0 | 300 | 0·794 | 238·2 |
| 4 | 400 | 0·735 | 294·0 | 100 | 0·733 | 73·5 |
| 5 | | | | | | |
| Total present value | | | 1304·7 | | | 1203·2 |
| *Less* outlay | | | 1000·0 | | | 1000·0 |
| *Net* present value | | | +304·7 | | | +203·2 |
| Profitability index | | | 1·31 | | | 1·20 |

|  | Cash flow | C Discount rate | Present value |
|---|---|---|---|
|  | £ | | £ |
|  | −1000 | 1 | −1000 |
| | | | |
|  | 300 | 0·926 | 277·8 |
|  | 400 | 0·857 | 342·8 |
|  | 400 | 0·794 | 317·6 |
|  | 400 | 0·735 | 294·0 |
|  | 300 | 0·681 | 204·3 |
| | | | |
|  | | | 1436·5 |
|  | | | 1000·0 |
| | | | |
|  | | | +436·5 |
| | | | |
|  | | | 1·44 |

Thus on all methods C is the project which should be chosen.

**5(a)**                         **Machine X**

|  | Cash flow | Discount factor at 10% | Present value | Disount factor at 15% | Present value |
|---|---|---|---|---|---|
|  | £ | | £ | | £ |
| Year 0 | −25 000 | 1 | −25 000 | 1 | −25 000 |
| End of | | | | | |
| Year 1 | 4 000 | 0·9091 | 3 636 | 0·8696 | 3 478 |
| 2 | 8 000 | 0·8264 | 6 611 | 0·7561 | 6 049 |
| 3 | 10 000 | 0·7513 | 7 513 | 0·6576 | 6 575 |
| 4 | 5 000 | 0·6830 | 3 415 | 0·5718 | 2 859 |
| 5 | 4 000 | 0·6209 | 2 484 | 0·4972 | 1 989 |
| | | | | | |
| | | | 23 659 | | 20 950 |
| *Trade-in value* | | | | | |
| End of | | | | | |
| Year 5 | 3 000 | 0·6209 | 1 863 | 0·4972 | 1 492 |
| | | | | | |
| Present value | | | 25 522 | | 22 442 |
| *Less* capital expenditure | | | 25 000 | | 25 000 |
| | | | | | |
| Net present value | | | +522 | | −2 558 |

**Machine Y**

|  | Cash flow | Discount factor at 10% | Present value | Disount factor at 15% | Present value |
|---|---|---|---|---|---|
|  | £ | | £ | | £ |
| Year 0 | −30 000 | 1 | −30 000 | 1 | −30 000 |
| End of | | | | | |
| Year 1 | 6 000 | 0·9091 | 5 455 | 0·8696 | 5 218 |
| 2 | 12 000 | 0·8264 | 9 917 | 0·7561 | 9 073 |

|  | Cash flow | Discount factor at 10% | Present value | Disount factor at 15% | Present value |
|---|---|---|---|---|---|
|  | £ |  | £ |  | £ |
| 3 | 10 000 | 0·7513 | 7 513 | 0·6575 | 6 575 |
| 4 | 6 000 | 0·6830 | 4 098 | 0·5718 | 3 431 |
| 5 | 4 000 | 0·6209 | 2 483 | 0·4972 | 1 989 |
|  |  |  | 29 466 |  | 26 286 |
| *Trade-in value* End of year 5 | 5 000 | 0·6209 | 3 105 | 0·4972 | 2 486 |
| Present value |  |  | 32 571 |  | 28 772 |
| *Less* capital expenditure |  |  | 30 000 |  | 30 000 |
| Net present value |  |  | +2 571 |  | −1 228 |

(b)  *True rates of interest by interpolation*

Machine X   $10\% + \dfrac{25\,522 - 25\,000}{25\,522 - 22\,442}$  $(15 - 10)$

$\qquad\qquad 10\% + \dfrac{522}{3080} \times 5 = \underline{\underline{10·85\%}}$

Machine Y   $10\% + \dfrac{32\,571 - 30\,000}{32\,571 - 28\,772}$  $(15 - 10)$

$\qquad\qquad 10\% + \dfrac{2571}{3799} \times 5 = \underline{\underline{13·38\%}}$

The internal rate of return for machine Y is greater than that for machine X .·. Machine Y is the machine to be acquired.

(c)  (i)  *Purchase for Cash*

|  | Actual | Discount factor at 12% | Present value |
|---|---|---|---|
|  | £ |  | £ |
| Purchase price | 30 000 | 1 | 30 000 |
| *Less* estimated trade-in value at end of year 5 | 5 000 | 0·5674 | 2 837 |
| Net cost | 25 000 |  | 27 163 |

(*ii*)   *Purchase by instalments*

|  | £ | Discount factor at 12% | £ |
|---|---|---|---|
| Deposit | 6 000 | 1 | 6 000 |
| Instalment at end of year 1 | 6 720 | 0·8929 | 6 000 |
| 2 | 6 720 | 0·7972 | 5 357 |
| 3 | 6 720 | 0·7118 | 4 783 |
| 4 | 6 720 | 0·6355 | 4 271 |
| 5 | 6 720 | 0·5674 | 3 813 |
|  | 39 600 |  | 30 224 |
| *Less* estimated trade-in value at end of year 5 | 5 000 | 0·5674 | 2 837 |
| *Net cost* | 34 600 |  | 27 387 |

(*iii*)   *Leasing*

|  | £ | Discount factor at 12% | £ |
|---|---|---|---|
| Rental payable at end of Year 1 | 7 500 | 0·8929 | 6 697 |
| 2 | 7 500 | 0·7972 | 5 979 |
| 3 | 7 500 | 0·7118 | 5 338 |
| 4 | 7 500 | 0·6355 | 4 766 |
| 5 | 7 500 | 0·5674 | 4 256 |
| Net cost | 37 500 |  | 27 036 |

On the above calculations machine Y should be leased rather than purchased for immediate cash or by instalments.

# Glossary of Terms

This glossary is compiled as a quick reference guide to terms which are used in the book. Simplicity rather than precision has been the criterion adopted.

**Absorption costing**  A method of product costing in which fixed and variable costs are allocated to cost units.

**Accounting equation**  Assets = Liabilities + Owners' Equity.

**Accumulated depreciation**  The portion of an asset which has been used up in previous accounting periods and shown as a reduction from the historical cost figure to give a value of the unused portion of the asset.

**Administrative expense**  An operating expense associated with the administrative function, e.g. general management, secretarial and accounting expenses.

**Allocated cost**  An indirect expense which is assigned to a unit of product, an activity or a department.

**Asset**  Any item which is measurable in monetary terms and represents value to the firm being available for current or future use.

**Asset turnover ratio**  A measure of asset utilisation calculated by dividing average assets utilised during a period by the net sales for a comparative period.

**Attainable standard**  A standard capable of attainment under existing operating conditions.

**Authorised shares**  The number and nominal value of the shares of a limited company which it is authorised to issue by its Memorandum of Association.

**Book value**  This is the amount of any balance sheet item as stated in the company's books. It is specifically applied to fixed assets that have been depreciated e.g. Cost – Accumulated Depreciation = Book Value.

**Break-even chart**  A graph depicting the relationship between revenue, variable expenses and fixed expenses, at varying volumes of output.

**Budget**  A financial plan covering all aspects of the organisation for a specific future period that is intended to express corporate objectives in financial terms. The plan may also be used to control current operations.

**Budgeted cost**  Any cost which is included in a budget.

**Conservatism**  A tendency in financial reporting to anticipate no gains and to provide for all losses. It may lead to an understatement of asset values and an overstatement of liabilities.

**Contribution**  The amount by which sales revenue exceeds variable expenses and which is available to cover non-variable costs, i.e. fixed costs.

**Controllable cost** An expense capable of being controlled by management within the time period under consideration.

**Cost** Expenditure incurred on or attributed to a specified activity or item.

**Cost of goods sold** The cost to the seller of goods sold measured by the total purchase cost or total manufacturing cost.

**Current asset** An asset which will normally be in the form of cash or capable of being turned into cash during the next operating period.

**Current liability** A debt which will become due within the next operating period.

**Current ratio** A measure of liquidity obtained by dividing current assets by current liabilities.

**Depreciation** The amount written off the value of a fixed asset during the current period of operation.

**Direct cost** A cost which can be directly identified with a product or service.

**Earnings** The excess of revenues over expenses during a specified period.

**Earnings per share** Earnings divided by the number of ordinary shares issued.

**Equity** The total of owners' interests in a company, including issued shares, share premium – revaluation of assets and retained earnings.

**Expense** A cost incurred in the process of earning revenues.

**FIFO** First in, first out. A method of calculating the cost of end-of-year stocks and the cost of goods sold, whereby the first item in stock is regarded as being the first item to be used in the production process.

**Fixed budget** A budget based on a predicted level of output and not adjusted for the differences between predicted and actual output.

**Flexible budget** A budget which is constructed on the basis of differing expected levels of output.

**Going concern assumption** The assumption that a business will continue to exist in its present form.

**Goodwill** The difference between the amount paid for a company and the value of the net assets to the purchasing company.

**Gross sales** The total revenue received from the sale of goods or services without deduction for returns, allowances or discounts.

**Ideal standard** A standard based on the best possible operating standards.

**Indirect cost** A cost that cannot be identified with a product, service or department and must be allocated on some equitable basis.

**Inflation** A general rise in prices resulting in a fall in the value of the purchasing unit.

**Issued shares** The number of authorised shares of a company which have been issued to shareholders.

**LIFO** A method of calculating the cost of end-of-year stocks and the cost of goods sold, whereby the last item in stock is regarded as being the first item to be used in the production process and the stock valued accordingly.

**Liability**   A commitment to make a future payment arising from a past transaction.

**Long-term liability**   A debt that will not become due for payment within one year.

**Management by exception**   The practice whereby management only investigate significant variations in actual performance from the predetermined standard.

**Marginal cost**   The variable cost of one unit of product or service; the amount which would be saved if that unit were not produced or provided.

**Monetary asset**   Any asset which is not usually income-producing, such as cash, or debtors.

**Net assets**   The excess of a firm's assets over its liabilities.

**No par value shares**   Shares that do not have a nominal value.

**Obsolescence**   The decline in the value of an asset caused by technological factors or by the decline in demand for the product of the asset.

**Operating cycle**   The average length of time required to invest in stock, materials and labour and convert it into finished goods and services for which cash is ultimately received.

**Owner's equity**   The amount invested by owners of a firm in the form of issued share capital and earnings retained in the business. It represents the excess of total assets over total liabilities.

**Par value shares**   Shares with an authorised nominal value.

**Pay back period**   The time required to recover the initial outlay of a capital investment.

**Period cost**   A cost that is not directly related to current production, but is treated as an expense of the period to which it relates, e.g. rates.

**Present value**   The current value of a sum of money to be received in the future, calculated by discounting the future source by an acceptable rate of discount.

**Price-earnings ratio**   The market price of the shares divided by earnings per share.

**Price-level change**   Fluctuations in the purchasing power of the unit of measurement, e.g. the pound or dollar. It is usually measured by the Retail Price Index or the GNP Price Deflator.

**Price variance**   The portion of the total variance from standard cost which is due to a difference between actual and standard prices.

**Product cost**   A cost related to a product.

**Profit**   An increase in assets or a decrease in liabilities as a result of an excess of income over expenditure, arising from transactions carried out other than with shareholders.

**Profitability index**   A ratio calculated by dividing the net present value of a proposed capital investment by the capital outlay.

**Quantity variance**   The portion of the total variance from standard cost which is due to the difference between the actual and the standard quantities of raw material/components used.

**Quick ratio**   A measure of the short-run liquidity position of a firm, calculated by dividing current assets minus stock by current liabilities.

**Rate of return on investment**   A measure of performance calculated by dividing net assets by the earnings for a relevant period.

**Revenue**   An increase in a firm's net assets resulting from the sale of a product or service, or the receipt of dividends, interest, rent, etc.

**Selling expense**   An expense associated with the sales function of the firm, e.g. salesman salaries, commission and advertising.

**Semi-variable cost**   A cost which contains a variable element, i.e. the amount varies with production, and a non-variable element which does not change over the short run.

**Short-term investment**   An investment made from temporary excess balances, e.g. cash which may be turned back into cash quickly and easily.

**Standard**   A predetermined measure relating to activity or effort under specified operating conditions.

**Statement of cash flows**   A statement showing the sources and uses of cash over a certain period.

**Statement of funds flows**   A statement showing the sources and uses of funds over a certain period. This will include movements in long-term assets and liabilities as well as cash.

**Straight line depreciation**   A method of depreciation which allocates the same amount each year against an asset. It is calculated by dividing the net value of an asset when purchased by its expected life.

**Sunk cost**   A cost associated with present assets which was incurred in the past and is therefore irrelevant when contemplating the sale or current use of that asset.

**Variable cost**   A cost which changes in direct proportion to a change in the activity.

**Variance**   A difference between actual performance and standard performance.

**Working capital**   The difference between current assets and current liabilities.

# Bibliography

The following selected bibliography is classified under three broad headings but many of the books listed will cover more than the particular category under which they appear.

## Financial accountancy and financial management

*Accounting in Business*, R. J. Bull, Butterworths.
*Accounting and Finance: A Firm Foundation*, A. V. Pizzey, Holt-Saunders.
*Foundation in Accounting*, R. Lewis, I. Gillespie, Prentice Hall.
*Business Accounting*, F. Wood, Longman.
*Financial Accounting Techniques*, A. V. Pizzey, A. R. Dennings, Holt-Saunders.
*Financial Accounting Theory*, M. Harvey, F. Keer, Prentice Hall.
*Modern Financial Reporting*, G. A. Lee, Nelson.
*Company Financial Reporting*, T. A. Lee, Nelson.
*Accounting Standards*, J. Blake, Longman.
*Income and Value Measurement*, T. A. Lee, Nelson.
*Accounting Theory and Practice*, Glautier and Underdown, Pitman.
*Financial Management*, R. B. Brockington, DP Publications.
*Accounting: A Modern Approach*, Wallis, McGraw Hill.
*Financial Management Handbook*, Gower Press.
*Introduction to Accountancy and Finance*, Briston.
*Capital Budgeting and Company Finance*, Merrett and Sykes, Longman.

## Cost accountancy

*Principles of Cost Accountancy*, C. Buyers, G. Holmes, Cassell.
*Cost and Management Accounting Made Simple*, J. Baggott, Heinemann.
*Bigg's Cost Accounts*, J. Wald, Macdonald and Evans.
*Cost Accounting: A Managerial Emphasis*, C. T. Horngren, Prentice Hall.
*Weldon's Cost Accounting and Costing Methods*, Owler and Brown, Macdonald and Evans.
*Costing*, A. V. Pizzey, CAET.
*Standard Costing*, J. Batty, Macdonald and Evans.
*Principles of Cost Accounting*, C. J. Walker, Macdonald and Evans.
*Cost Accounting*, G. Riddle, Northwick Publishers.
*Costing Matters for Managers*, E. G. Wood, Business Books.

## Management accountancy

*An Insight into Management Accounting*, J. Sizer, Penguin.
*Fundamentals of Management Accounting*, Anthony and Welsh, Irwin.
*Accounting for Management Decisions*, Arnold and Hope, Prentice Hall.
*Management Accounting*, Amey and Egginton, Longman.
*Managerial Accounting and Finance*, Brown and Howard, Macdonald and Evans.
*Cost Control Handbook*, R.M.S. Wilson, Gower.
*Financial and Cost Accounting for Management*, Taylor and Shearing, Macdonald and Evans.
*Cost and Management Accountancy*, J. Battye, Heinemann.
*How to Make and Control a Budget Plan*, B. H. Walley, Business Books.
*Management of Working Capital*, J. C. V. Smith, West Publishing.
*Working Capital, Its Management and Control*, Howard, Macdonald and Evans.
*Interfirm Comparison*, H. Ingham and L. Taylor Harrington, Heinemann Ltd.

# Index

Acceptance credits, 29
Accounting concepts
    consistency, 16
    entity, 17
    going concern, 16
    matching, 16
    measurement in money terms, 17
    prudence, 16
    stable monetary unit, 18
Accounting for price level changes
    current cost accounting, 199
    current purchasing power, 196
    Sandilands Report, 198
    value to the business concept, 199
Accounting ratios
    capital employed to fixed assets,
        140
    dividend cover, 146
    dividend yield, 145
    expense, 145
    gearing, 140
    gross profit, 143
    limitations, 136
    liquidity, 138
    net current assets to fixed assets,
        139
    net profit, 143
    price earning, 146
    proprietors, 139
    purchases to creditors, 142
    sales to debtors, 141
    sales to fixed assets, 142
    stock turnover, 143
Angle of incidence, 121

Balance sheet, 9
Bank loans, 25
Bank overdrafts, 28

Break-even analysis
    charts, 118
    limitations, 122
Budgeting
    advantages of, 83
    budget committee, 85
    budget manual, 84
    budget procedure, 84
    budgetary control, 104
    capital budget, 93
    cash budget, 46
    definition, 82
    long-range budget, 85
    manpower budget, 91
    manufacturing overhead budget,
        92
    master budget, 87
    materials budget, 91
    plant utilisation budget, 91
    principal budget factor, 87
    production budget, 90
    rolling budget, 105
Budgets
    relationships, 86
    types of, 87
Business Expansion Scheme, 22

Capital
    employed, 163
    long-term, 23
    medium-term, 25
    short-term, 28
Capital investment appraisal
    discounted cash flow, 169
    effect of taxation, 177
    methods of evaluation, 167
    net present value, 173
    pay back method, 169

Capital investment appraisal (*contd.*)
    rate of return on average invest-
        ment, 168
    total income method, 167
    uncertainty, 179
    yield method, 172
Cash budget, 46
Contribution concept, 114
Costing
    direct expenses, 53
    direct labour, 53
    direct material, 53
    indirect expenses, 53
    indirect labour, 53
    indirect material, 53
    overhead expenses, 53
    reliability, 59
Cost centres, 65
Cost/profit/volume analysis, 117
Costing methods:
    job or contract, 61
    operating, 62
    process, 63
Credit sales, 26

Debentures, 23
Decision
    information, 6
    trees, 182
Depreciation, 37
Discounted cash flow
    internal rate of return, 172
    net present value, 173
    yield, 172

Elements of cost, 52
Equipment leasing, 26
European Coal and Steel Com-
    munity, 27
European Investment Bank, 27

Financial
    accountancy, 3
    institutions, 28
    planning, 5
Fixed expenses, 102, 112

Flexible budgetary control, 102
Funds flow analysis, 35

Gearing, 31
Gross profit, 43

Hire purchase, 26
Historical costing, 52

Income statement, 37
Index numbers, 193
Industrial holding companies, 28
Inflation, 190
Information manager, 2
Inter-firm comparisons, 150

Labour variances, 72
Limited liability, 21
Limiting factor, 87
Linear programming, 125
Liquidity ratios, 138
Loan capital long term, 23
Loan Guarantee Scheme, 25

Management accountant, 5
Management accounting, 1
Management by exception, 104
Margin of safety, 119
Marginal costing
    advantages and disadvantages,
        116
    equation, 114
    value of, 114
Market research, 89
Master budget, 87
Material variances, 68
Medium-term capital, 25
Mortgages, 25

Overhead
    administration, 57
    allocation, 54
    production, 54
    selling and distribution, 56
    under and over recovery, 56
    variances, 73
Overtrading, 138

Permanent capital, 21
Present value tables, 186–7
Prime cost, 52
Product mix choices, 124
Profit/volume chart, 121

Ratios, 136
Retained earnings, 29
Return on capital employed, 146, 163

Sales
    forecasting, 89
        statistical techniques, 90
    and lease back, 25
    variances, 78
Semi-variable expenses, 112
Shares
    buy back, 23
    ordinary, 21
    preference, 22
    valuation, 137
Short-term capital, 28
Sole trader, 20
Solvency, 38

Sources and application of funds, 37
Standard costing
    advantages, 65
    attainable standards, 66
    loose standards, 66
    strict standards, 66
    variances, 67
Statement of cash receipts and disbursements, 45

Trading and Profit and Loss Account, 11

Uncertainty, 178
Uniform costing, 149

Variable expenses, 102, 112
Variances
    labour, 72
    material, 68
    overhead, 73
    sales, 78
Venture capital, 27
    analysis, 42